PARENT-SCHOOL COLLABORATION

SUNY Series, The Social Context of Education
Christine E. Sleeter, editor

PARENT-SCHOOL COLLABORATION

*Feminist Organizational Structures
and School Leadership*

Mary E. Henry

STATE UNIVERSITY OF NEW YORK PRESS

Published by
State University of New York Press, Albany

For information, address State University of New York Press,
State University Plaza, Albany, N.Y. 12246

Production by Christine Lynch
Marketing by Fran Keneston

Library of Congress Cataloging-in-Publication Data

Henry, Mary E.
    Parent-school collaboration : feminist organizational structures
and school leadership / Mary E. Henry.
        p.   cm. — (SUNY series, the social context of education)
    Includes bibliographical references and indexes.
        ISBN 0-7914-2855-9 (alk. paper). — ISBN 0-7914-2856-7 (pbk. :
alk. paper)
        1. Home and school—United States. 2. Feminism and education-
-United States. 3. School management and organization—United
States. I. Title. II. Series: SUNY series, social context of
education.
    LC225.3.H468 1996
    370.19′312—dc20   95-8928
                                                                    CIP

10 9 8 7 6 5 4 3 2 1

To my dear mother and father,
Kath and Walter Gardiner

CONTENTS

FOREWORD

Last year a friend asked me to accompany her to a parent-teacher conference about her son's schoolwork. An African American woman, she had recently graduated from the university. We had become acquainted in several contexts, one of which was an African American history course I audited during a sabbatical. There I met her primary-grade son. She brought him to class one night; he seemed fascinated by college, and sat transfixed in the front row all evening. He had been an early reader; his mother reads voraciously, and had nurtured him on books all his life.

Her concern regarding this conference was that she was not being listened to. Her son, bored with school, had started to act out, which brought increasingly cold and negative responses from the teacher. This is a very common experience for African American students, particularly males. As a mother, she was frantic, and tried repeatedly to tell the teacher what does and does not work in motivating and teaching him. At one point I had armed her with information about culture and learning style, which confirmed to her that she was not crazy and gave her a technical vocabulary to attempt using with school authorities. But by the time she asked me to accompany her to a conference, she was at her wits' end because she was still being talked at rather than listened to.

Despite my presence, this was not a conference. Rather, it was a one-way exercise in self-defense on the part of the teacher. My friend was ready to acknowledge her son's shortcomings, but wanted to address them through his strengths and interests, which she knew well. She wanted a dialog in which she was heard, but instead got a barrage of complaints. She wanted collaborative problem solving, but received instead the teacher's frustration and blame. The irony was that the teacher was really frustrated—she did not know how to handle my friend's son. But rather than viewing the boy's parent as a resource, she viewed the parent as the source of the boy's problems—as a hindrance to learning, not as a collaborator.

ix

I strongly suspect that this white teacher's perception was grounded in racism and classism—my friend is dark-complexioned, single, and, until she gets her feet on the ground economically, poor. (The previous year she hadn't had a phone; I half-joked that she was spending all her money on books!) My friend subsequently transferred her son to a different school, where she continued to receive the same treatment, although to a lesser degree.

This incident highlights a tremendously important area of need in education today: the need for schools to establish constructive partnerships with parents, and particularly parents who are of color, from low-income backgrounds, from language-minority backgrounds, and/or from non-traditionally structured families. The statistics on demographic changes in U.S. schools should be well-known by now, highlighting the growing cultural gap between teachers and parents and the need for changes in educational policy and practice. The fact that demographic profiles of teachers and children in U.S. schools are increasingly at variance does not mean that teachers cannot be expected to learn to relate to the children and their families. It does, however, mean that we cannot simply expect this to happen "naturally." When nothing is done proactively to develop constructive parent-school working relationships, disasters such as the one described above are too often the result. Some parents are ignored entirely, and others are blamed for their children's problems when they are actually trying to help.

Contrary to stereotypes, low-income parents and inner city parents *do* care very deeply about their children's education (Chavkin, 1989; Ritter, Mont-Reynaud and Dornbusch, 1993) and *do* want constructive contact with teachers (Harris, 1987). My friend was far from alone in her strong desire for her child to learn and in her repeated attempts to engage in dialog with school people.

When structured in a way that builds on the perspectives and resources of parents, home-school partnerships substantially improve children's academic learning (McLaughlin and Shields, 1987). However, too often programs that attempt to involve parents are conducted on the school's terms rather than on the parents' terms (Calabrese, 1990; McLaughlin and Shields, 1987). When this happens, the children who are helped least are those who are always least likely to be helped: children from low-income homes, children of color, or language-minority children.

Parent-School Collaboration: Feminist Organizational Structures and School Leadership, by Mary Henry, examines why traditional parent-involvement programs such as PTA and Open House are not enough, and how we might rethink parent-school collaboration. This book analyzes institutional barriers to collaboration in order to get beyond simplistic explanations for why so many attempts at parent involvement don't work. Based on ethnographic research, the book presents many specific examples of organizational structures that blunt home-school communication, and includes interviews with parents, teachers, and administrators that express the feelings and viewpoints of the people involved. Issues of power and dominance, of class interests and social reproduction, are set alongside a framework for possibility and change. Henry argues for a feminist approach to leadership which involves an ethic of care that takes diversity into account proactively. She directs us to focus on what children need now, and how we as parents and educators can support children's needs for learning and growth. She challenges us to transform competitive school bureaucracies into caring communities, arguing convincingly that our children are too important not to do so.

Christine E. Sleeter
University of Wisconsin-Parkside

ACKNOWLEDGMENTS

Family, friends, colleagues and students have all contributed in countless ways to this study. I am indebted to Maxine Greene, Teachers College, Columbia for her profound teaching and modelling of an ethic of care while I was a graduate student at the University of Virginia. Also, Bronwyn Davies, James Cook University, Australia, was my first teacher and mentor in the university. Thank you, Bronwyn, for your profound friendship and guidance. Your scholarship has had a lasting effect on me and my students. I am grateful also to Donald B. Reed, Washington State University, and Eric Bredo, University of Virginia, for their scholarly concerns and useful discussions. Carol Merz, Dean of the School of Education, University of Puget Sound, organized a symposium at AERA, with Doug Mitchell, UC-Riverside, as discussant, that helped me to clarify some of my ideas. Ray McDermott, Stanford University, inspired me, as always. Thank you, Ray, for the opportunity to work on the Stanford Research Team in Milwaukee public schools during the final stages of write-up. I learned much, and came back ready to complete the seemingly endless task of completing the study. I also want to thank and acknowledge a debt to the late Mary Catherine Ellwein, University of Virginia, for helping me through graduate school. She was a truly great person, teacher and researcher.

Washington State University has been very supportive of my scholarship. Particular thanks for their fine mentorship, go to Walt Gmelch, chair of the Department of Educational Leadership and Counseling Psychology; Bernard (Bernie) Oliver, dean of the College of Education; and Sherry Vaughan, associate dean. Partial financial support for the study came from Washington State University's Research Grant-in-Aid program which provided research assistance from Ray Klapwyk and Jack Marchant, whose work in providing peer coaching, helping with analysis, and thoughtfully critiquing the manuscript was invaluable. Various graduate students have also studied parent involvement in the public schools and their contributions to class and to my own thinking and writing are gratefully acknowledged. Those students include: Yawarat Tusgate, Ray Klapwyk, Alan Lee, Russel May, and Anne Remaley. Margaret Grogan, now at the University of Virginia, who was working on her dissertation while I worked on this study, has been a wonderful colleague, and her husband, Michael, and daughter Klara, special friends. The following people read the manuscript in its entirety and commented thoughtfully on it: Margaret Grogan, Ray Klapwyk, Jack Marchant, Gordon Gates, Gisela Ernst, Sherry Vaughan, and Anne Woodward-Nakata. I owe them much. I also want to thank Jeanett Castallenos, Connie Currie, Jacqui Erickson, Tim Esche, Kevin Facemyer, Fumie Hashimoto, Robin Kirkland, Eileen Reilich, Mona Roach, Susan Smith, Linda Thomas-Buchanan, and so many other graduate students (too many to mention by name) for their intellectual presence in my life. In addition, Catherine Emihovich, SUNY Buffalo, showed an interest in my work and sent relevant articles and references. Anonymous reviewers for SUNY Press critiqued the book and offered advice for making the manuscript stronger. The cover design is the work of Natalie Gates, whose artistry is much appreciated.

I am grateful to my colleagues, Jack Burns, Sue Durrant, Walt Gmelch, Bob Harder, Etta Hollins, Don Orlich, Forrest Parkay, Michael Pavel, Don Reed, Mike Trevisan, and Jo Washburn, and also the office staff—Lynn Buckley, Patti Komp, Cindy Scott, Kristin Dannenberg and Corrie Hay—for their colleagueship and helpfulness. Barbara Symons beautifully transcribed hundreds of hours of interviews. Christine Sleeter, Series Editor at SUNY press, and Priscilla Ross, Acquisitions Editor, believe that we need to examine relationships between schools and community; they believed in me, and did everything possible to bring this manuscript to a timely completion. Christine Lynch, the production editor, and an unknown copy editor, attended carefully to technical details in the writing.

Of course, the study could never have been written without the full support of the many wonderful parents, teachers, and administrators whose voices are heard in this book. I salute them all for their faith in better schools and their valiant efforts to make a brighter world for children. Even where I disagree with some of them, it is done in the spirit of, "here is another approach, another way of looking at and understanding parent-school relationships," which almost everyone in the study argued is a problem. The study is transformative, in that I am critiquing the present system, and trying to contribute toward new possibilities.

My family in Australia, all the many Gardiners, have given a great deal of emotional and other support through letters, visits, and telephone calls. Thank you Mum and Dad for giving me the opportunities and education that I have. To Walter, Kath, David, Robyn Jeanette, Kurt, Mark, Tara, Tim, Anne, Thomas, Jonathon, Ben, Robyn Jane, Erin, Miriam and Jacob Gardiner I send heartfelt thanks. I love you all. The close friendship of David Mueller means more than I can say; and I am also grateful for the friendship of Cynthia Dillard, Gisela Ernst, Gail Furman, Lucy Hochstein and her daughters Julie and Lucy Ann, Pat Krysinski, Karen and Quin Michaelis, Darcy Miller, Eileen Oliver, Don Reed, Jennifer Taylor, Sherry Vaughan and Mimi Wolverton. And, though they cannot read, my cat Mitzi, and her buddy Darkmoon, have spent many, many hours with this manuscript—scattering the pages, flipping pens and pencils, curling up on newly printed copy. What would I do without them.

1

The Social Context of Parent-School Relations

> Without cooperative, collaborative rela-
> tionships, school problems are not going
> to be easy to address. (Comer 1980, 16)

Robertson School District—February, 16, 1994, 7:30 p.m.
Approximately thirty-five people sit in clusters of two or three in
the tiered seats of a large auditorium with a seating capacity of
five hundred. Superintendent Carroll, the five school board members, and the administrative assistant (who is recording the meeting
on a Powerbook), are seated at the front of the auditorium. People
wait expectantly for the meeting to begin: the First Annual
Robertson School District Stakeholders Meeting.[1] (The concept of
"stakeholders"—that the patrons of a school district have an important role to play in school decision making—has a long history, and
has had a recent revival due to state and federal educational reforms
emphasizing decentralization and grassroots participation by parents and community.)

A notice had been sent to all patrons of the school district
announcing a meeting seeking community input into decision making. I received my notice only one day before the meeting, and I
heard that an angry parent had called the superintendent to complain of the short notice. The parent reportedly said, "I don't want
you to be like the state senator who came to Robertson seeking
community input and we received the notice of that meeting the
day *after* it was held." Superintendent Carroll's response was that
the meeting had been announced at all PTA and Athletic Club
meetings and that an announcement had also been printed in the
school district newspaper. I turn and ask one of the principals
seated near me about the poor attendance. She says, "You can look

at it two ways. Either the parents are really happy with what we are doing and they're trusting us to take care of education, or they are apathetic and can't be bothered to take the time to attend another meeting."

Superintendent Carroll stands and welcomes everyone to the meeting, explaining that "We are fashioning ourselves after a large corporation," seeking the views of "you, the various stakeholders in the educational enterprise." The chair of the board also explains, "We want your ideas for school improvement. Please don't expect us to be able to answer your questions. We just want to hear and record everything that's said, to get your input."

The superintendent spends forty minutes outlining the achievements of the Robertson School District. The achievements highlighted include: instituting a sexual harassment policy; "site-based management"; "working with (total quality management) TQM and how to infuse that into our system"; the passing of bonds and levies; school facility improvements; "test scores going up"; "more and better communication with our community"; long-range facility planning; technological improvements; the development of a strategic plan for a "core curriculum of key academic areas"; the hiring of three additional psychologist/counselors; "improved efficiencies"; and "a new more broad-based goal-setting system." (The superintendent adds, "Tonight's meeting is part of that.") Numerous committees are also highlighted in the superintendent's address: the Diversity Committee, the Multicultural Committee, committees to improve the science and math curricula, and a committee to examine different organizational patterns in kindergarten.

No questions are asked. The meeting is turned over to the business manager who spends twenty minutes explaining the financial spreadsheets: "The second column from the right details actual expenditures," and so on. One person interrupts the report, seeking clarification. The business manager replies in institutional style, reading from his notes.

Superintendent Carroll then announces, "We already have twenty-one suggestions from parents, patrons, and the community. We solicited the input from PTAs, the Athletic Club, administrators, citizens, and parent groups. The suggestions have been compiled and will be translated into action. We had fifty-one unedited pages which we have compiled into the edited list you have. It was a very enriching experience for us to hear from our patrons. One of the themes is better attitudes in how students are treated and how classified staff are treated—better internal cooperation. It will be our job and the board's to sit down and evaluate all the ideas. We will take into account four criteria: the centrality of the suggestion; the quality of the suggestion; the need; and the cost. Our purpose and goal is to have our stakeholders give us their ideas and input so that we can make better educational decisions. I will now turn the meeting over to the chair of the school board."

The chair of the board announces, "Please come forward to the microphone with your comments and questions. State your name and why you're here. Limit your comments to three minutes. And don't expect answers from us. We're here to listen."

The superintendent begins listing the comments on the overhead projector as parents come forward with their suggestions. Suggestions include, "recognize the good teachers and get rid of the poor ones," and "implement a foreign language immersion program." One parent—the father of three children in the school district—is particularly nervous, as with trembling voice he explains, "My wife encouraged me to say this. The middle school library is closed to students other than prearranged, booked class time. It's closed before and after school and most lunches. My son also tells me that the library is used to punish students at the middle school. Couldn't they use another room and not the library? What kind of a message about learning is that?" The middle school principal glances at the parent as he sits down not far from her, but she does not reply to the criticism. Another parent steps forward to the microphone: "We are opposed to the all-day kindergarten. And we're worried we won't have any options." Superintendent Carroll replies, "We have a committee looking at that. They will report to the board and then the community will have a chance to express an opinion."

The meeting continues with parental comments being recorded on the overhead projector and some brief responses given by the superintendent:

Parent: You mentioned some proposed changes for site-based management? What will be different? (Apologetically.) Or isn't this the forum to ask that?

Superintendent: The state passed a reform bill a year ago and schools have to adopt, I forget the word, there's a word . . . (Pause.)

Principal:	(seated nearby) Shared decision making.
Superintendent:	Yes, that's it, shared decision making, where any instructional decision would involve parents, citizens, students, certificated and classified staff, and administrators. We are making the move to site-based councils to comply with state law.
Parent:	That sounds very interesting.
Carlson (school board member):	The most important thing is to hear from all of you. If you see things on the list we need to know how the public feels. As parents we all have kids in the schools, but we need to hear your priorities.
Phillips (school board member):	This is the first time we've seen this list too and the first time we've done this process. One thing you need to remember though is that we all have strong feelings, but there are other sides to most issues and we need to weigh them and listen to them, and money is one of the considerations.
Briney (school board member):	If you have an idea that is particularly important to you, don't just bring it to the attention of the board member who's representing you, but to all the board members. You shouldn't trust me with your favorite ideas. (Laughs.) If you want something done, share it with all the board members.
Farmer/parent:	I am very much in the minority here. Farming family children are less than 2 percent of the school district population, but you are serving us all well. I want to commend the school district on the type of education our kids get. What our kids get in fourth grade my sister's kids, who live in another state, get in sixth grade. I congratulate you. We appreciate what you are doing.
Chair of school board:	Thank you. It's so nice to hear a positive comment. Are there any other questions?
	(Silence.)

Superintendent: Thank you all for attending and for your input. We really appreciate this opportunity to hear from you, our patrons.

The meeting is closed at 9:10 P.M. (Fieldnotes)

INTRODUCTION

Educators complain about a lack of parent involvement in public schools, and they have sought greater engagement and even collaboration. But if this were easily achieved, schools would have long since forged successful home-school collaboration, which is the exception, not the rule. In the example above, even with good school administrators and conscientious teachers, relations between parents and educators are far from optimal. They may be cordial, but they are hardly dynamic or representative of shared decision making. Parents have not helped design the meeting, the agenda of school officials is the focus, and parents feel as if they are criticizing the school when they make a suggestion. To move in a direction of more successful collaboration, we need to know more about the perspectives of parents, teachers, and administrators, and about the constraints and dilemmas facing them.

This book is about school reform—not in the sense of tinkering with parts of the system—but deep systemic reform of the very organizational structures and leadership of schools. In this century, public schools have been engaged in increasing bureaucracy, with ever more specialized roles and a more hierarchical chain of command. In the 1990s, however, we need to be engaged in a new transformation—into organic, interactive organizations characterized by democratic, participatory governance. Parents are a key component of this movement. No longer are they to be kept out of schools and controlled by professional educators. The school becomes *their* school, and partnerships with other groups traditionally seen as "outsiders" becomes possible. The thinking of professional educators has to change in order for this to happen. One educator, in explaining his vision for participatory education argued, "We have to involve the parents. They don't understand what we are doing." This statement is indicative of the lines that have been drawn—a "we-they" division— that must be redefined so that the "we" includes the "they."

This is an ethnographic account, informed by feminist perspectives. Ethnographic studies such as this one are needed in a variety of settings if we are to base policy and practices on a working knowledge of what is done, thought, and desired in schools. Parent collaboration with schools under the new governmental reforms creates new work and a new culture in the public schools as a result of increased public input. We need to know the fears and anxieties on all sides—as well as the exciting possibilities—if we are to successfully implement meaningful reforms for enhanced parent-school relations. The findings of this book are drawn from an intensive study of parent-school relationships in Robertson School District in the northwest United States over a period of two complete school years—1992–93 and 1993–94. The final analysis and write-up was completed in 1995. Intensive interviews and observations were carried out by the author, with some help from two research assistants. In addition to the fieldwork data and analysis, other studies will be cited for supporting evidence.

Questions were raised around the following issues in the process of studying parent-school collaboration:

Parents' Needs

Equality becomes an issue if the scales are tipped in favor of enhanced outcomes for those students whose parents are involved in schooling when not all parents are able to participate equally. Do teachers judge children more in terms of their family background and somehow attend more to the children of the very active parents? What if a child has no advocate when school is restructured around parent-school collaboration? When schools institute site-based, school-based, or school improvement councils, how representative are these councils of the wider parent body? Can school-based councils simply become a mini-school board dominated by the civic elite? What are the possibilities for broad-based and diverse participation by all members of the school and community? Will the current practice of gendered parent involvement be perpetuated, with women shouldering the lion's share of family educational responsibility for schoolwork and homework?

Children's Needs

There may be good reasons for separating children from their families for the purposes of education. What is the benefit of parent-school collaboration if a child's parents are more interfering than helpful? For some children the added stress of having parents in and around schools may outweigh the advantages, particularly at certain points in a child's life. How can parent-school collaboration benefit students at all levels of schooling?

Organizational Structures and School Leadership

Opening the school to the community offers new possibilities for parents to contribute more to their children's education than ever before, but it comes at a price, which may include reduced autonomy and reduced independent decision making for teachers and administrators. How will the quality of parent-teacher relationships be maintained if parents criticize or micromanage the teacher's performance at every turn? How is it possible to create collaborative organizational structures? What is the role of administrators in the new schools of shared decision making? These are just a few of the issues raised and discussed in this book.

THE TRADITIONAL MODEL OF PARENT INVOLVEMENT

Parental presence is now routine in many schools and classrooms, as is parental representation on governing bodies. But presence and representation do not mean parents and educators necessarily work well together or equally share decision making. Parents have traditionally adopted the role of supporters or representatives, rather than full and equal partners. Many schools still consider parents as "intruders into their territory" and are not fully receptive to parental suggestions and participations" (Manaan and Blackwell 1992, 220). Traditional parent involvement in schools occurs through parent participation in a number of school activities that are managed by the school—on school territory and on the school's terms—without a transfer of significant power (Lareau 1989, 1989a; Woods 1988). Parents and community members are often involved in schools in the following ways:

Parent Teacher Associations (PTAs) or
Parent Teacher Student Associations (PTSAs)

Parents may attend PTA meetings and/or hold office in these organizations as a way to be involved in the public schools. PTAs have traditionally worked in supportive roles for school personnel—helping with fund-raising, teacher-recognition banquets, events, concerts, science fairs and open house evenings—but without decision making power on educational issues such as curriculum, finance, or personnel. In the words of Superintendent Carroll of Robertson School District, "The PTAs never have been a thorn in our side." At the national level, PTAs attempt to influence policy.

Parent and Community Groups

Independent parent and community groups have been formed in most states across the nation, *for example*, Advocates for Children of New York, the Philadelphia Parents Union, and the Massachusetts Advocacy Center in Boston (Moore 1992, 134). These groups take on an advocacy role, pressing for educational change and lobbying for school improvement around specific issues. In the state in which this study was conducted, a number of retired superintendents and other educators, along with community people, advocate for education through such a statewide organization.

Parent-Teacher Conferences

Parent-teacher conferences or student-led conferences, a traditional form of school-home interaction, are typically held two times a year for fifteen to twenty minutes with parents of young children (Lareau 1989, 175; Van Galen 1987, 82). Conferences with parents of older students are held less frequently—perhaps once a year—to supplement reports sent home by the school. At Robertson High School conferences are offered once a year, although generally most parents whose children are doing well choose not to attend. These conferences involve parents (and sometimes stepparents or guardians) meeting with the teacher. The parent-teacher conference can become a symbolic interchange or routinized ritual, more valued for its public relations contribution than anything else. Van Galen (1987, 83) found that from the teachers' position "being complimented" by a parent was a key ingredient of a "good conference." Particularly for low-income or minority parents, parent-teacher conferences can be intimidating. Conferences are more meaningful with students participating and with translators provided for speakers of other languages.

Open House

Open House can also be a ritual of carefully orchestrated people and events that does not really resemble everyday life in schools. Open House typically consists of a display of classroom and school achievements.

Parents are managed from the minute they set foot in schools until they leave. "Some information is exchanged, but often the events are not individualized, and they are relatively content-free" (Lareau 1989, 180).

Newsletters

Newsletters and other informational brochures sent home to parents are frequently welcomed as a source of staying in touch with school, but once again frequently a transmission model operates, whereby the school manages the flow of information to parents—sometimes with the aid of a few carefully selected parent volunteers.

School Volunteering

The emphasis is on parents as assistants or helpers performing nonspecialized, routine functions, such as listening to children read or sharing their occupational expertise with children. These noninstructional tasks are low-status, and usually do not involve collaboration with the teacher in the education of the child. As one principal put it, "Whenever we need volunteers our parents are there helping us out." Parents can use this opportunity of volunteering in the classroom (*e.g.,* helping with reading lessons) to increase their knowledge of their children so that education can be customized and not generic (Lareau 1989, 139). Volunteering can also enhance communication with the school.

Homework

At home, parents often supplement classroom instruction by providing a study area, supervising a time for home-study work, and expressing expectations for completion of assignments. Dauber and Epstein (1993, 65) report that in inner city elementary and middle schools, parents' education, family size, and marital status are not significantly associated with the time that parents spend with their children on homework. Nevertheless, at all levels of schooling, parents' desire, ability, and resources for assisting with homework vary. And homework, like parent-teacher conferences, can be fraught with difficulties on both the home and school fronts.

Student Work

Weekly or monthy folders of student work and student publications is often a way of letting parents know how a student is doing in school.

Parent- or Community-opinion Surveys

Schools or school districts may survey their constituents on particular issues (*e.g.*, support for a proposed alternate-day, all-day kindergarten) or to gain feedback on their own performances in the community. For Robertson School District, recently proposed legislation requires school self-study or evaluation—a "report card" which includes parent and community views of each school—to be conducted and made available to the public annually.

Paraprofessional Employment

Parents frequently work in schools as paid aides. Here parents' participation in the educational setting is supervised and controlled by the teacher and the school.

Parent-Initiated Requests

Parents may come to the school with a request or issue of advocacy for their child, such as requesting particular teachers or placement in special programs. Competition can be fierce and political strategies may be employed. Those parents who are more likely to adopt an aggressive advocacy role are: parents whose children have special educational needs; well-to-do parents with underachieving children; or parents of those children typically perceived as exceptional, such as gifted or talented students. Goldman and McDermott (1987, 290) note the unequal and competitive aspect of parental requests. Parents compete over scarce resources—for access to programs and special services for their children. Placement in classes is frequently informed by such parental pressures, as well as by test scores, teacher opinions, availability of programs, and special services. Intervention by parents is often considered necessary to help kids get ahead in the competitive culture of the school.

The Board of Education/Board of Directors
(commonly referred to as the school board)

The school board is composed of civic-minded community members who may or may not be parents. In traditional practice, the school board, made up of lay people, has control over the school superintendent who manages the school district. However, the school board may also be managed, controlled, or manipulated in some instances by the superintendent. The school board is in a unique position and may not be representative of many of the parents in the district. Many parents may feel that they have little power in the overall running of a school district.

NEW APPROACHES TO PARENT INVOLVEMENT

The practices outlined above, particularly the concept of local school boards, are part of an American tradition and of a historical context that has defined parents and professional educators as somewhat separate in their roles and responsibilities. A more recent development in parent involvement is the establishment of a parent advisory council as a governing body for each school site (as part of site-based management reform). Another development is the appointment of parent representatives to select committees, such as hiring committees.

Parent Advisory Councils (PACs), Site-Based Councils, School Improvement Councils (SICs), and Local School Councils (LSCs)

Many districts have established parent-advisory or decision-making councils for each school site, with various names for such organizations. Chicago is a city with an established system of school-site councils, with parent involvement in decision making since the signing in 1988 of the Chicago School Reform Act (P.A. 85–1418) (see Hess 1991; Hess and Easton 1992, 158; Moore 1992, 147). Researchers, policymakers, and others have both praised (*e.g.*, Hess and Easton 1992, 175) and criticized (*e.g.*, Walberg and Niemiec 1994, 715) the site-council reform. Many other states are implementing similar reforms, including the northwest state where this study was conducted. The superintendent, possibly following directives from the state legislature, may direct the principals to establish a parent advisory council or a site-council as an advisory or decision-making body for the school. The principal then solicits parents to serve on the council, composed of teachers, staff, students, and parents. Parents with time and other resources often volunteer, or are approached by the principal with a request for service; in this study they were most often upper-middle class parents who felt comfortable with schools and administrators. Parents may be selected for their fit with institutional values. Thus, even parent-advisory or site-based councils can be part of traditional parent-school relationships.

An alternative pattern is for parent representatives to be elected by parents of currently enrolled students, and for teacher representatives to be elected by teachers (see Etheridge and Collins 1992, 91; Seeley 1989, 47–48). In Chicago, site-councils have reportedly garnered broad-based participation (Hess and Easton 1992). Superintendents of a traditional ilk are sometimes resentful of edicts passed down from above, such as site-based management, and may seek ways to retain traditional practices: "The legislature is trying to micro-manage what goes on in schools" (Interview, superintendent). (More on this in chapter 4.)

Parent Representatives on Committees

In recent years, parents have also been included in making major decisions for districts and schools as representatives on committees responsible for such tasks as hiring, finance, and curriculum. Typically, such committees comprise two parents or community representatives, two classified staff, two students, two administrators, and two teachers. However, two parents on a hiring committee does not represent collaboration with public schools. The move to have parents represented on these committees, while commendable, is not the same as the organizational structures of broad-based collaboration and the mutual respect and trust between parents and educators advocated in this book.

HISTORICAL BACKGROUND OF HOME-SCHOOL RELATIONS

The state's responsibility in educating the child emerged in the United States in the 1800s. Public education provided by the state was seen as a means to enhance the public good—civility, training for citizenship, and the socialization (Americanization) of immigrants. Before the nineteenth century "the major ends of education . . . were pursued under the watchful eye of the individual, the family, and the church—not the state" (Hendrick 1992, 50). The shift from private responsibility to public responsibility, with the state superintending and even coercing the education of children, was seen as necessary for the development of the nation. The goal was to build a common political community through public education.

By 1865 common schooling was established. The first schools embodied community. The "little red schoolhouse" with its steeplelike bell tower resembling a church was closely interconnected with the social, political, and religious life of the community (Tyack and Hansot 1982). Teachers knew students in many contexts, and parents knew teachers in many contexts. The key attribute of a superintendent at the turn of the century was a match in values and religion with the community. (Then, as now, the superintendent was typically male.) School governance in nineteenth-century rural America was conducted by lay people—"educators in overalls,"—farmers acting as part-time school board members (Fuller 1982, 83–84). In the cities, separate "wards" for each community ensured that decision making was pertinent to the needs of each school. Local parents and citizens were thus heavily invested in their schools. However, despite a strongly interconnected home and school life, education at the time of the little red schoolhouse was not without its problems: "The little red schoolhouse . . . was likely to be full of children only when farm activities slackened. And it was likely to be a place of little joy, with daily rote memorization, line-by-line recitations, much drilling, and frequent physical punishment" (Kaestle 1983 in Crowson 1992, 24).

Over the next century, educators worked hard to professionalize teaching and improve schooling. With the move to professionalization and paid full-time school administrators came a separation between the roles and responsibilities of professional educators and lay people. The development of schooling meant increasing standardization of size, organization, and curriculum. Reforms were instituted to *disconnect* schools from their communities, making board members nonpaid and reducing the size of school boards so that professionals were clearly in charge. The lay boards turned to the professional superintendent for advice (Katz 1975).

As state-provided education became established across the United States, parents tended to send children to school and to stay away from schools themselves, apart from a minority of active parents. With paid administration, parents became largely disenfranchised from important decision making. Signs like these became commonplace in schools: "All visitors please report to the office." This was more than a matter of security: the control and management of visitors and parents—as well as the task of public relations—became the work of administrators. Katz (1971, 219) notes, "By the 1870s, American urban education had become bureaucratic: schools were hierarchical, differentiated, rule-bound organizations run by specialists." Bureaucracy in public education was the product of several discreet innovations, including the introduction of professional administrators and efforts to regularize, standardize, and centralize local educational arrangements.

The social and moral puposefulness of nineteenth-century schools and their connectedness with the community contrasts sharply with the twentieth-century professionalization of schools. Modern schools, for all their higher standards for physical plant, teacher-student ratio, and methods of instruction, are lacking in the integrative school-community concept that characterized earlier schools. The tight knit between school and community can still be found in some rural areas, where the school is the center of much of the life of the community (Peshkin 1978), but in most school districts, the increasing professionalization of teaching has meant a distancing of schools from their communities. The size of schools is another factor in the distance or closeness of school-community relations (Driscoll 1990, 1). Historically, small schools were consolidated into large schools in order to raise educational standards. Today, 85 percent of students are taught in 20 percent of the school districts (Ballantine 1989, 116). With consolidation came a separation of the community from the school.

Thus, it is ironic that the educational improvements and increasing professionalization of public education over the last century has served in many cases to exclude citizenry from the public schools. In Barr and Dreeben's (1983) detailed analysis, *How Schools Work*, for instance, parents are placed outside the organizational framework of schools— nowhere are parents to be seen. In the conclusion of their study of the history of the superintendency in the United States, Tyack and Hansot (1982) note the lack of citizen involvement in public education today and call for a renewed commitment to public education as a common good.

Change is occurring. The National Commission on Excellence in Education (1983) encouraged parents to participate in schools, but there were no strategies, processes, or organizational structures suggested to implement parent participation. National reform proposed in the Carnegie Task Force (1986; 1989) and Holmes Group reports (1986) was more specific, and has been played out across the nation in the establishment of local school councils to empower teachers and parents. Schools and communities are to become "partners" in educating young people (Carnegie 1989, 36). By 1990 the idea of parental involvement in education was the accepted practice of many state school systems, especially for early childhood education (David 1993, 157). Many researchers, in particular Joyce Epstein (1985, 1986, 1987, 1988, 1990, 1991; Dauber and Epstein 1993) began advocating strongly for parent involvement in schools. The U.S. secretary of education, Richard Riley, in his first annual address on February 15, 1994, announced a new "family involvement campaign" to encourage greater family, school, business, and community partnerships. The renewed interest in community-school linkages is evident not only in school reforms, but also in the wider public. As Comer notes, some of the impetus has come from parents themselves: "Desperate and determined parents have decided that their hopes for a better future ride directly on the success or failure of schools; these parents have taken power to control the schools into their own hands. There is a special emotional intensity where the future of children is at stake" (1980, 15). And yet in many schools, minimal parent involvement and a bureaucratic top-down management system remain the norm.

WHY COLLABORATE?

The walling out of the community occurred as a response to the professionalization of teaching. If schools were to do their job of educating without interference from the public, it was considered necessary for administrators to buffer teachers from unnecessary intrusions and demands from parents (Crowson 1992, 35). In recent years, conventional thinking has shifted to the view that schools do not exist in isolation from the larger society and that schooling can be revitalized with help from the community. "Interference" might better be seen as collaboration. Schools cannot do their work in isolation from parents, community agencies, industry, business, and universities. Today, a definition of what it means to be an excellent teacher or administrator includes responsiveness to parents and community.

Parent-school collaboration is sought on a number of grounds:

1. There is a sense of urgency to try something new, a sense that things currently don't work as they should and that *a new approach is needed*;
2. Teachers can learn from parents' intimate knowledge of their children. No one knows the child better than the parent, and parents are

likely to take a child's perspective and to advocate for children's rights
in making educational decisions;

3. Parents have a *right* to be involved in their children's education;

4. Collaborating with parents may be a way to avoid unexpected intrusions and to reduce antagonism between parents and educators. Relationships between teachers, administrators, parents, staff, and students have been shown to improve (Comer 1980, 189). Bringing parents, teachers and administrators together in shared decision making is a way to reduce "adversarial relations" and to contribute to better decision making (Streshly and Frase 1992, 100);

5. Parents can provide much needed resources to the public schools, such as free labor and expertise (Winters 1993). Parents can thus trade resources for access to the schools; for instance, financial and political support is likely to be forthcoming if parents become school advocates (Comer 1980, 126);

6. The involvement of parents can improve school accountability and make schools more responsive to community needs. Parents are not constrained by the politics of the school system; being "outsiders" they are free of some of the constraints on educators. Parents can bring new insights to the educational arena since they are not bound or limited by existing practices or by being a part of the system. Educators, for example, may not want to evaluate a colleague negatively even though this should be done for the good of the children (Moore 1992, 150);

7. Perhaps most importantly, a reason to enhance parent participation in public schools is that *student outcomes are thought to be positively affected by increased parent involvement* (Epstein 1988; Epstein 1990; Fullan 1991, 227; Henderson 1987, 1; Moore 1992, 131; Winters 1993; Ziegler 1987). Parent involvement in schooling in itself is believed to positively affect children's "achievements, attitudes, and aspirations, even after student ability and family socioeconomic status are taken into account" (Epstein 1987, 120). Walberg (1984) reviewed twenty-nine controlled studies and found that parent involvement in school was twice as predictive of academic success as socioeconomic status.[2]

In short, the potential benefits of parents and students being involved in the conversation about what education should be are considerable. It makes good sense for schools to partner with parents for several reasons: to gain access to the knowledge that parents have of their children; to make better decisions; to enhance learning opportunities; and to build support for schools. Educators may need to work with families, *not* by demanding ever more of parents, but by focusing on children and their needs and by figuring out how parents can be an integral part of the educational conversation.

FEMINIST ORGANIZATIONAL STRUCTURES
AND SCHOOL LEADERSHIP

Having reached a point where parent-school-community connections are considered desirable—and even necessary—we need to focus our attention on how this is going to be made possible. To move toward collaboration, this book examines the barriers on both sides so that we can better understand how parents, teachers, and administrators think, as well as how schools currently work. The book also explores feminist organizational structures and methods of school leadership that allow for collaborative parent-school relations, processes and activities. This view is in contradistinction to the bureaucratic organizational structures that traditionally dominate our public schools. It is my contention that bureacracy has slowly become a part of the public schools over the past 150 years, and that the time is right for a shift to post-bureaucratic structures that are organic, interactive, participative, and informed by feminist thought. Such change is likely to be incremental and long-term, just as bureaucracy was, but nevertheless revolutionary.

I began this study of parent-school relationships by drawing on traditional theories of community, and was led through fieldwork to feminism as the framework for explaining my data. I will thus begin this discussion with an overview of concepts of community. The traditional view of community—analyzed by Tonnies (1957)—distinguished between *gemeinschaft* and *gesellschaft* forms of community. A *gesellschaft* interpretation of education rests on the assumption that schools are like corporations. According to this view, stakeholders have a right to know what is going on, but professionals take care of the actual operation of the school. Community thus focuses on the specialized contributions of individuals toward the common good. Public schools are more typically seen as *gesellschaft* institutions: bureaucratic, somewhat distanced from the social context, with clients (parents/lay people) and providers (teachers/professionals) separate in their roles and responsibilities (*e.g.,* Meier 1991, 266).

A *gemeinschaft* interpretation of education focuses instead on the common feelings, traditions, and goodwill that bond people together in a community. Dewey argued, for instance, that the school needed to be a "little community" (1938). School was to be an extension of daily life, so that what one learned in the course of life could be elaborated and extended in the context of school. School was to be relevant and useful—not a separate activity devoid of meaning for everyday life (Spring 1986, 172–173). Dewey (1938) emphasized not only linkages between school and community, and the importance of community-building, but also the nature of *relationships* in education: between teachers and students, between teachers and other teachers, between teachers and principals, between principals and parents, between parents and teachers, and so on. To Dewey, the network of relationships in a school is critical to teaching and learning. A school that is distancing and fragmented in its social relationships is unlikely to be an educative one.

Traditional theory on community thus helps characterize different forms of community, which may be occurring simultaneously in organizations. The reforms of today are also shown to be *gemeinschaft* in nature—attempting to personalize education and to form connections between school and society. But the technology for accomplishing the reforms is *gesellschaft* in nature, with specialized roles and a bureaucratic structure (*e.g.*, parent involvement through such formalized, school-initiated-and-controlled bodies as task forces on specific issues, committees, local school councils, and parent advisory councils).

The analysis of community outlined thus far helps identify the paradox of *gemeinschaft* aims instituted through *gesellschaft* means, but it is not adequate to explain what goes on in schools, or to offer new directions. Here the book is informed by feminist ideas, providing a direction for school leaders and those concerned with school improvement—a way to conceptualize and implement systemic organizational changes and a new approach to school leadership. We cannot simply revert to pre-bureaucratic communal forms of organization, for society has changed. This is where feminist thinking, with its emphasis on politics (multiple voices) and participative and relational knowledges has much to offer in defining a direction for schools.

Feminism is characterized by multiple theoretical orientations, each with its own assumptions (*e.g.*, Marxist-socialist, radical, liberal, poststructuralist). Following Capper (1993), I have drawn on various feminist ideas where they inform my analysis—"feminism" signifying *a way of looking at the world as a feminist* across traditions and disciplines. This is not to say that women and men live in "separate worlds." Rather, women and men share the same world, but given their different relationships to the dominant cultural model of the world, they have different standpoints and perspectives on society and its institutions (Moore 1988). Feminists theorize about these different relationships.

The feminist approach that I have developed in this study places people before mechanical rules or bureaucratic responses. Feminism stems from a concern not just with humankind, but with *all* living things and their interdependence in the universe, with a view to redefining male-female and other relations away from a notion of dominance and subordination and toward the ideal of equality and interconnectedness. Central to the discussion of a feminist view of organizational structures and school leadership are the notions of: (a) an ethic of care and connectedness; (b) collaboration and community-building; and (c) a focus on the core technology of teaching and learning. "Technology" refers here to the means or methods of accomplishing the goals of education. I am arguing that we need a new technology in education to meet the needs of the twenty-first century and of our pluralistic society, and that a feminist approach is helpful. The point of view dominating the Western social world—mechanistic, Eurocentric, hierarchical, bureaucratic—is linked to critical problems in relations among men, women, and children, to our relationship with the natural world in the context of contemporary ecological crises, and to problems within our social institutions, including schooling. A mechanistic frame of mind is part of a competitive, individualistic view, rather than part of a collaborative, socially concerned way of thinking, feeling, and acting. A feminist approach also highlights the educational and social problems that arise from the present advantaging of white males by the school system, as well as the marginalizing of ethnic, racial, and gender concerns.

The dictionary definition of collaboration given at the beginning of this chapter notes that to collaborate means to work together, especially in a joint endeavor. To view parent-school relations as collaborative is a very different way of viewing them than is currently constructed in bureaucratic organizational structures, with only a portion of parents (typically the civic elite) represented in schools, and with parents and community separated from administrators and teachers in their roles and responsibilities. In the contemporary model, superintendents style themselves as CEOs—directors or managers of corporations—and administrators view their work as separate from teaching and learning. A feminist approach casts these relations between parents, teachers, and administrators quite differently: as interdependent. All human beings are seen as enriched by a feminist way of seeing and relating to the world. Instead of autonomy, separation, distance, and a mechanistic view of the world, feminism values nurturing, empathy, and a caring perspective (Desjardins 1995; Gilligan 1982; Keller 1985, 79). I want to make clear that I am not advocating a reproduction of the gendered society we presently have where women "have been told all their lives that they must obey and care for others" (Rockhill 1987, 165). Instead, an ethic of care for all—men, women, and children—is a way to reframe competitive and hierarchical social relations in the educational system toward more inclusive and interconnected relations that will benefit the learning potential of students.

Traditional school organization follows an industrial model—hierarchical and bureaucratic—with lines of command clearly designated as in the organization of the military. In the feminist organizational structures that I am proposing, decisions get made, information is disseminated, and plans are created by the problem solving of people closest to the problems. People and information-sharing become the focus, rather than procedures and segmented roles. Feminism is able to provide a useful framework for *redefining school organization and leadership*, one that recognizes the interdependence of all living things in our natural environment and encourages collaboration, teamwork, and a concern for the inclusion of diverse needs.

OVERVIEW OF THE BOOK

Parent-School Collaboration: Feminist Organizational Structures and School Leadership provides a conceptual basis for viewing the school as an ecology of people and events that goes beyond the school walls. Parents and families are shown to be an important part of teachers' and administrators' professional work. The book argues that everything that goes on in school is inextricably linked to the home—from patterns of thought and behavior to attitudes toward school. The book also provides strategies for parents, teachers, and administrators to enhance collaborative dialogue and action. Moreover, the view of parent-school partnerships is an inclusive one. Biological parenting is not the only kind of parenting that matters. Schools have traditionally kept out many people who are not seen as having a legitimate claim to the educational agenda. I am arguing that we need to be much more open to diverse perspectives and multiple input if we are to provide for the needs of all children. Where the term parent is used in this book I want it to be read as "parent"—more broadly defined to include community people, such as grandparents, aunts and uncles, many of whom have ideas and perspectives to offer schools.

The book has been written for in-service and pre-service administrators and teachers, as well as for parents. Since the book offers a number of specific strategies and a unified approach for parent-school collaboration, I hope it will prove useful for school districts in their school-improvement efforts. The book is designed to be read sequentially in the order of chapters given. This chapter provides an introduction to the social and historical context of school-parent relationships. I have argued that the culture of the public schools has come to embody a strong distinction between professional educators and lay parents, which means a distancing of parents from schools and from school decision making. A feminist framework is used to redefine parent-school relations as collaborative, and to imbue public school organizational structures and school leadership with an ethic of care, community-building, and a focus on teaching and learning. Chapter 2 moves to the specific context in which the study was conducted and gives details of the ethnographic and feminist approach used to study and analyze parent-school relations. This chapter will be of interest not only to those interested in establishing more responsive schools, but to those who are themselves doing field studies.

Chapter 3 examines the variety of ways that schools alienate and distance parents, perhaps even while instituting reforms, and the part that parents play in that process. Schools have traditionally developed an elaborate hierarchy and a chain of command that prevents decision making at the grassroots level.

The logic of school organization and of the construction of schools as competitive bureaucracies—the focus of chapter 4—must be under-

stood if we are to change current practices in long-lasting and meaningful ways. The fifth chapter takes up the issue of the different organizational structures of elementary, middle, and high schools, and the
social and cultural differences between schools and homes. Since
schools represent the state and parents represent the family, a gap can
arise between home and school cultures, and conflict can occur over
whose values are to be most important. In particular, the focus of this
chapter is on social class, since many of the difficulties experienced by
students—those labelled "at-risk," "dropouts," or "underachievers"—
stem from a lack of appreciation of the implications of social class for
schools.

In the sixth chapter, "An Ethic of Care—Celebrating Diversity," I
argue that in any public school, diverse parents' interests in their children's education are frequently not met, and that a moral ethic of care
can provide direction for meaningful change. At present, diversity
issues, even at the level of representation, have not been adequately
addressed. Participation in schools has to go beyond the civic elite to
include all types of parents—divorced, teenage, single, working, elderly,
alien, widows and widowers, low-income, disabled, gay, bilingual, culturally and ethnically diverse, professional, and so on. I examine the
reasons given by parents, teachers, and administrators for the way things
are in schools, and offer a basis for change around relationship-building
and an ethic of care.

Chapter 7 further explores the issue of collaboration and community-building, arguing that educators today, more than ever, must be
committed to working with parents from a variety of social classes and
ethnic and cultural backgrounds. Parents' reluctance to be involved in
school is shown to be connected with cultural or language barriers, and
with not feeling welcome. Teachers and administrators are provided
insights into a process of collaboration and community-building, so that
parents can be authentically connected with schools. Parents, in turn, are
shown how they may be distancing teachers, and how more collaborative relationships can be built around educational and social interests and
purposes. Chapter 8 continues the feminist approach by focusing educational leadership and school work in general where it rightly belongs,
on teaching and learning. If all decision making begins and ends with
the student and with what is good for instruction, it is clear that administrators need to be more fully involved in instruction, and that parents

and other community members are an integral part of the school community. Good schools use the energy of a personalized approach, and focus on the student in order to inspire more broad-based and collaborative projects. Chapter 9 draws together the findings of the study that parent-school collaboration is essential to the creation of responsive schools, and that this is not an impossible task.

In this book I am trying to show how simplistic notions of reform for parent-school collaboration can be informed by an understanding of the classist, racist, and gendered practices of schools and of the wider society. The bureaucracy of schools, with its explicit hierarchy and fragmentation, is a manifestation of a hierarchical social world where men's and women's work is still premised on the notion of dominance and subordination. Creating school contexts where caring, community, teaching, and learning are celebrated has always been the work of good educators, and in today's society this needs to be the hallmark of the new organizational structures and of a vibrant educational leadership.

NOTES

1. The parents, teachers, administrators, schools, and school district referred to in this book have been given pseudonyms to provide for confidentiality.
2. However, it may be too early to expect test score increases as a result of parent-school collaboration, particularly when the ways and means of these relationships are still in their early stages of development. Many schools are just now moving towards site-based management and figuring out what shared decision making and democratization means for all concerned: parents, teachers, students, staff, and administrators. Further, we should note that the reliance on test scores in the public schools as a key indicator of educational efficacy, even to measure the success of parent involvement, is evidence of a bureaucratic approach. Despite the recent rhetoric of "partnerships," it is testing, not collaboration, that has been the focus of business leaders' and politicians' efforts to improve education (Lytle 1990). One educator wryly queried, "If test scores went down after using increased parent involvement for one year, would we conclude that parent involvement is a bad idea and decide to "professionalize" teaching further?"

2

Doing Fieldwork

> Each fragment of the study . . . is like the shards of pottery, the fragments of other lives that archeologists dig out of the earth, and through which they imaginatively construct lives other than their own. In this sense I too am an archeologist, piecing together meaning from what the children [participants] say, from my own memories and the memories of others. And you as reader are the same . . . using your existing ways of knowing, your immersion within, your subjectification through the same discourses out of which these children [participants] fashion their lives (Davies 1993 15).

Through fieldwork, I set out to learn about and to give voice to a variety of perspectives—of parents, teachers, and administrators. I set out to relate to participants in the field and to make sense of the data by way of theory and by way of my own knowledge and experience. In this chapter I explain what it means to be ethnographic, and I explain the feminist approach and the framing of my questions. I also try to demystify the analytic process that led to my conclusions and to the thesis of this book. One of the questions every researcher asks her/himself is how reliable and valid are the findings? Will they transfer to other situations and inform people outside the setting in which the study took place? Ethnographers try to provide as much rich context and situated data as possible, so that readers can make up their own minds as to just how much of the study can be usefully applied to similar settings elsewhere. A criticism of anthropological fieldwork is that it is a thorough and detailed look at only one situation, and situations can vary so widely. My reply is that a close and detailed look at particular schools, or in this case a school district, can tell us more than data gathered and aggregated into an "average" look at schools or school districts. In the field study the reader can gain a much clearer grasp of what the actual dynamics and processes are, and can recognize situations and strategies that apply elsewhere. In contrast, no-one has ever been in the "average school" or taught the "average student" as created by a statistical profile. In the former we can recognize real life—real players with real interests and purposes. In the latter, all the life and variability has been averaged out, and what we are left with is a picture of an average student or school that approximates none in particular.

Given recent reform movements across the United States emphasizing site-based management, local school councils, and parent participation in schools, the aim of this book is to examine in close detail relationships between parents and educators. I want to contribute to our understanding of present day practices, and to the organizational structures and school leadership we will need for parent-school collaboration to really work. Using an anthropological approach and feminist theory I will argue that families and schools cannot be viewed as separate institutions; instead, family and school powerfully influence each other. The school influences the family through the way it educates the student, and through the demands it places on families to participate in education. The family influences the school as well, for children take their family backgrounds and experiences into the school setting, whether or not parents ever actually participate in school.

I also show the stresses in relations between parents and educators, and suggest that feminist thought offers a basis for systemic change. My argument is that the professionalization of teaching and administration has led to a distancing and separation of families from schools. As schools became more "professional," part of the administrator's job became the *management* of parents and community, rather than participating in *collaborative* relationship. Further, as we will see in later chapters, the white, middle class culture of the school encourages uneven participation amongst parents, and those who most match the school's interests and purposes are further advantaged by the system.

Finally, the "reforms" of local school councils can be simply more of the same: a preserver of the *status quo*, with the circle of voices represented in the school not significantly extended. More radical changes are called for. A redefinition of professionalism to include a knowledge of family and social contexts and how to work with communities is essential. The school has to be willing to change in order for this to happen. We can't demand ever more of parents while schools remain the same. Many new practices, ideas for organizational change, and vital questions that must be addressed will be explored in the chapters ahead.

THE SETTING AND THE STUDY

Robertson School District was selected for this study based on the following criteria: (a) it is a school district with a reputation for excellence, and there is evidence that it is incorporating reform for school-based management and participatory governance; (b) access was available to the researcher for a two-year field study. The work has involved over eighty in-depth interviews with parents, teachers, and administrators, more than forty observations in the five public schools, and the analysis of documents and materials pertaining to school-parent-community relations.

The following ethical procedures were observed to protect the interests of participants in the study: (a) informed consent; (b) confidentiality of people and places (and the use of pseudonyms); and (c) the right to withdraw at any time. Ethics in ethnographic work is critical because of the personal, intimate, and intrusive nature of the work. The possibility of change in the setting is always there, representing a threat to participants: "fieldwork represents an intrusion and intervention into a system of relationships" (Stacey 1988, 23). Another difficulty is the closeness with which the ethnographer works with participants, which can lead to confidences and access to "backstage" knowledge that would otherwise not be forthcoming. Equality and respect between the researcher and those being studied is something that has to be worked on constantly, with an overriding issue being the researcher's authenticity and integrity as a human being. Ethical tenets, especially that no harm should come to participants as a result of participating in the study, helped guide daily actions and decision making.

Robertson School District is best characterized as a district serving a university town. Residents of university towns typically have a high level of education: "more Ph.D.s per square inch than is healthy" (Interview, parent), and are able to participate in a variety of cultural activities. The city of Robertson is West of the foothills of the Rocky Mountains, with an average elevation of 2,500 feet above sea level. The university, Northwest University, with 18,400 students, was founded during the last century as a land-grant university. It dominates the township, and is the main "industry." A nearby university town with a cosmopolitan outlook adds to the region's social and cultural horizons, which would otherwise be predominantly white and largely conservative. Robertson School District comprises five public schools: three elementary schools—Horace Mann Elementary School, Fairfield Elementary School, and Riverview Elementary School (kindergarten through grade 5); Park Middle School (grades 6 through 8); and Robertson High School (grades 9 through 12)—with a total population of approximately 2,500 students and 145 teachers.

The people of Robertson are predominantly middle class whites, with some cultural, ethnic, linguistic, and religious diversity provided by the university students and faculty. The public schools have a reputation in the community for excellence and attention to extracurricular activities. This is often attributed to the university and its promotion of an atmosphere of "competition," "enterprise" and "scholarship." A high percentage of high school seniors consistently qualify for National Merit Scholarships each year, and Robertson School District is frequently rated among the top three of the state's schools, as measured by standardized test scores. While competition and high academic standards are central to the community, the social dynamics of the larger society are also present: racism, sexism, classism, and homophobia. While racism is difficult to document, in a recent poll in Northwest University, 40 percent of the minority student leaders and counselors characterized the campus racial environment as "negative." Nearly 45 percent reported encountering overt racism very frequently or frequently, although nearly 70 percent say the environment for people of color and ethnic minorities is "improving." Headlines in the Robertson daily newspaper attested that in one case, "Racism prompted a [Latino] family to leave Robertson" (January 18, 1994). The reported racism included allegations against a Robertson High School teacher who, in the mother's words, "searched for excuses to kick him [her son] out of class."

Generally, however, from the Superintendent's position and from that of the school board members, the schools have strong reputations in the community as "good schools" with good leadership and strong connections between school and community. Nevertheless, philosophy (and hence practice) in these schools remains influenced by the general conservatism of the area (tempered by some liberal and radical impulses from the university). It is influenced as well by public school traditions and organizational structures which, as the study shows, are at odds with current reform efforts. It should also be noted that a sense of urgency surrounds local efforts to move to school-based management and to parent and community partnerships with the schools, because many current research grants offered by the Department of Public Instruction are contingent upon parent involvement and the implementation of successful local school councils.

In beginning the study I read widely in the literature on parent involvement, and became interested in finding answers to the following questions: How are parents involved in the public schools? Why are parents involved in these particular ways and not in others? How might parents be more meaningfully included in the process of educating children? Over the course of the study my focus shifted to the process of implementing school reform for parent-school partnerships, and I began asking: What are the tensions surrounding parent-school relations? What will it take for parent-school collaboration to really work?

Interviews formed a substantial body of data. Interviewees were selected using a "snowball technique." The first person that I interviewed was Superintendent Carroll of Robertson School District, as a "gatekeeping" interview to gain access to the schools. At that first interview I explained my purposes and the study's design, submitted a written research proposal and the approval of my sponsoring university. Consent forms were also submitted that would be taken to the school board and signed by the principals of Robertson School District and by the superintendent, Dr. Carroll. The superintendent also provided me with a list of twenty "key parents" who would be critical, in his mind, for my study. Once I had secured formal approval for the study, I contacted each person on the superintendent's list by telephone, explained what I was doing, and arranged a time and place for the interview. The initial set of parents soon grew to include those outside the purview of the superintendent—those who were dissatisfied with their schools (such as people who were now home-schooling) as well as strong school supporters.

Interviews with parents were conducted in their own homes, in my home, at their places of work (the university, a florist shop, businesses), or in restaurants. I would request to tape the interview and, with one exception, was granted permission. I also took notes, although I tried to keep interviews as nonthreatening as possible. All interviews were transcribed in the manner in which I have come to work best, with the transcripts in a left-hand column, leaving a wide margin for my own work with the data, and for making theoretical notes, posing questions, and making connections.

Interviews with administrators were usually conducted in their offices during the school day. Interviews with teachers were often held during teachers' free periods either in the faculty lounge or in their classrooms before or after school. Interviewees were selected for the range of viewpoints that they brought to the study. For instance, if I heard that a parent was unhappy with a new school policy or practice, or that a parent was advocating for the school around a particular issue, I sought them out and requested interviews. I went to each interview with a yellow writing pad, pens, tape recorder, and tapes, along with some general questions that could be amended to allow for probing and for elaboration of specific issues that might arise during the course of the interview (see Appendix). I always found it helpful to ask for examples and stories to illustrate the general point being made, so that people didn't become conjectural or analytical, but rather provided specific behavioral and other evidence.

Over the course of the study I attended and engaged in parent and community meetings and events: school board meetings; school improvement council meetings; site-council meetings; the First Annual Robertson School District Stakeholders Meeting; the Second Annual Robertson School District Stakeholders Meeting; and parent and teacher meetings. And I observed teachers interacting with parents, para-professionals, and parent volunteers. At Fairfield Elementary School I served on the site-council along with a retired elementary school principal, two parents, two teachers, a certificated person (the school secretary), and the principal. It was challenging to keep up with the research, which soon took on a life of its own, with parents recommending other parents that I should interview. At Robertson High School, the school improvement council consisted of eighteen people: the six department head/teachers, four parent representatives from the Athletics Club and the PTA, two community people, four students (two sophomores and two juniors), the principal, and the assistant principal—with myself as observer. As a member of the school improvement council at Fairfield Elementary School I was able to participate in decision making as a team player, whereas at Robertson High school I was able to observe more closely the decision making of other people. Both experiences proved valuable. School board meetings allowed for virtually no interaction with the school board during the meetings, although my presence at these meetings was appreciated, and led to further contacts and opportunities for study.

In addition, while I was at the schools I looked for evidence of and noted all reference to and contact with parents and community. Immediately after each period of participation or observing, I tried to set aside time to write up field notes, to reflect on the experience, and to write analytic notes and questions and concerns to be followed up.

Documents relevant to the study were also collected and analyzed, including school correspondence and newsletters to parents, school board minutes, copies of school policies, site-council minutes, school improvement council minutes and readings, learning-improvement plans, the Robertson School District's strategic planning document, improvement grants, newspaper articles on the schools, school demographic data, and so on.

WHEN IS AN ANALYSIS?

Using the tools of anthropological fieldwork and analysis I engaged in a to-and-fro process between data and theory, immersing myself in the lives of parents, teachers, and administrators, seeking their "local knowledge," reading extensively in the literature to gain insights into possible ways to explain my data, and revising and refining the ideas based on what I was finding in the field. The research and writing of feminists and other critics who have argued against bureaucracy and top-down, linear modes of management proved to be useful as I tried to make sense of my own field data. That body of work includes, among others: Burbules (1989); Capper (1990); Dantley (1990); Ferguson (1984); Foster (1986); Heckscher and Donnellon 1994; Shakeshaft and Newell (1984); West

(1987); and Wheatley (1994). The interplay of my daily experience—time for reflection and writing following time in the field; reading the literature; trying on a variety of explanatory frames; talking with participants to test those ideas—was an essential part of the research process. My role in the field was that of a researcher and educator who is interested in school renewal. I wanted to study the process of reform, with an aim to better understanding social dynamics in order to work toward more equitable and responsive schooling. Throughout the fieldwork I was also sometimes in a teaching role in that the questions asked, the issues I addressed, and the talks I gave contributed to an ongoing dialogue in the schools and community.

Interviews were tape-recorded and transcribed. Each interview filled approximately thirty to fifty pages of transcript, and altogether they made up over 3,300 pages of data. The process of analysis was one of making sense of the data in terms of the participants' perspectives (LeCompte and Goetz 1992; Strauss 1987). I was constantly comparing incidents from one school, source, or event with other incidents, searching for and considering negative cases for all the themes presented. I wrote memos, engaged in member checking (discussing my preliminary findings with participants) and triangulation (use of multiple methodologies such as interviews, observations, document analysis), and eventually reached a point of emergent themes and an explanatory framework. This was followed by oral and written presentations and debate in the public forum. Writing occurred throughout the research process, and I shared my preliminary and tentative findings with participants in the study, students in my classes, and educators at national meetings (Henry 1993a; 1994; 1995).

Thus, ideas were continually developed from the data and tested for their usefulness in helping to interpret data. The data was grouped and regrouped in analytic categories and more data was generated to help refine the analysis. The process (working between data and theory) continued throughout the study. Consistent with constant comparative analysis and theoretical sampling, informants were sought across the range of parents who view schools positively (describing themselves as "school supporters" and the like) and those who are alienated from schools (self-proclaimed "unhappy parents") (Glaser and Strauss, 1967; 1971). Triangulation (Lincoln and Guba, 1985, 305–7; Wolcott, 1988, 192) and member checking (Lincoln and Guba, 1985, 314–316) were also used to enhance trustworthiness. Finally, conceptual categories were established in light of the evidence, and a theory of feminist organizational structures and school leadership for parent-school collaboration was conceptualized.

But qualitative research is not a clear-cut process. When is an analysis done? As a researcher, I never feel as though my work is finished. Anthropologist Marily Strathern (1991, 119) argues that we "produce infinite complexity out of complexity." I am always aware, as Emihovich and James aptly put it, that "all representations (both tentative, oral forms and more precise written forms) are, by their very nature, partial" (1993, 10). They are "shards of glass" that can be looked at from many different angles in different lights (Davies 1993). Recognizing partiality does not render the account less relevant: "The fusion of a feminist and ethnographic consciousness can allow us to construct cultural accounts that, however partial and idiosyncratic, can achieve a contextuality, depth and nuance unattainable through more remote and detached research methods" (Stacey 1988, 27). I sought to hear the voices of parents and educators and to remain true to their intent. At the same time, I sought to contribute to our understanding of the issues of parent-school relationships by engaging in a close study of what people are thinking/doing/desiring in schools, and by using a feminist perspective to reframe current problems.

My writing had to tell stories, convey real life, and be accessible to teachers, administrators, and parents. I wanted them to be able to see the results of my labor in the field. Feedback from discussions of what I was finding had been ongoing, but the participants in the study also had a right to interact with the text and to offer their criticisms. This cannot occur if the language mystifies the participants concerning "the very conditions of their lives about which the researcher theoretically aims to develop critical understanding" (Roman 1992, 590–591). In seeking to illuminate the relationships between home and school, and the ways that parents are implicated in the culture of the school, I tried not to obscure the participants' access to my writing through the dense and obscure language that is seen so often in the academy.

If my work was to be read not only by the participants, but by the wider group of teachers, administrators, and parents for whom this book was written, it also had to be written with a recognition of the author's hand. In other words, I am in the book in the sense that the fieldwork was conducted from my vantage point and with my questions and concerns. I could not for a moment be disengaged as I pressed for further meanings and worked to assemble an account that would be useful to others. The view presented here is intended to invite further studies on home-school relations, and thoughtful reflection on what *is* and on what *could be.*

Analysis was helped through the use of a methodological log, a means of examining, as author, my assumptions and decisions in relation to the research project. A well-known educational anthropologist poses the following question: "Is it possible to write a book about human beings in their social capacities without that book also being about its author?" (Peshkin, 1986, 19). Peshkin thinks not, a view I share. One of the assumptions of qualitative research is that the phenomenon studied is affected by the researcher. In qualitative research on schools and schooling we try to introduce various participants' voices into current educational, social, and policy debates. We also try as researchers to recognize that ethnography is cultural construction—construction of self as well as of the other (Stacey 1988, 24). We consider how we have shaped the story that is told: "Anthropologists and their reactions are thus part of the data, rather than being mysterious hidden hands" (Strathern 1987, 288). Subjectivity is inevitable in all research, therefore researchers should systematically seek out their subjectivity while the research is actively in progress.

What is known as "reflexivity" thus begins with the assumption that the observer is both the instrument and also at times partly the object of observation (Whitehead and Conaway 1986). In other words, systematic thinking about one's own experience in the field is a source of knowledge and insight (see, for example, Geer 1969; Peshkin 1988; Plath 1980, 19–37; Smith 1988). I wrote in a journal throughout the study to help identify any possible conflict in my analysis and to help identify my own preconceptions.

DEVELOPING A THEORY

Much of the postmodernist debate on ethnography criticizes traditional approaches to fieldwork on the grounds of "colonialism" (see Bhabha, 1992; Clifford, 1992; Haraway, 1992; Martin, 1992). In other words, the greater social power of the researcher is seen to overwhelm the subjects (McCarthy Brown, 1992, A56). In my own case, working with parents, teachers, and administrators in a university town, I did not have any "greater social power," for I was not "studying down" to a less powerful group as anthropologists are wont to do. Many of the administrators, teachers, and parents were of the same or of a higher social class than myself, and many were more established than I am as a single, white woman who is an immigrant from Australia. Other participants included lower-income parents, and those ethnically and culturally different from me. I wanted to meet people on their own terms and to respect their positions. I also thought about the issue of voice: Whose voice receives greater authority? What if the participants do not agree with the final analysis?

Even though the analysis was continually refined by checking with the participants, they may not all embrace the final stories that are presented since they come from so many different perspectives. However, while seeking to be ethical at all times, I did not shy away from asking difficult questions, or from presenting what I was finding, provided I made it clear that this was *my* interpretation. It is supported with the procedures of anthropological field research, including checks for trustworthiness, but ultimately the analysis is mine. I had to always be aware that there were many sides to each issue, and sought to hear and understand the competing views: I needed to be ever aware that I was not using the participants for my own interests and purposes, but rather working with them for better education, even when we represented different viewpoints.

The data was generated with the input of many, many participants, I engaged in peer debriefing with two research assistants, and I shared and checked the ideas with participants. Close interrelationships developed. I had to find a way to ethically bring the study to publication in order to share my findings with a wider audience, and do so without violating the trust that people had given me to present their views of their world. There were many conflicting views, and I had my own views. (I am still involved in the school district, a relationship that is likely to be ongoing).

The framework of feminism that I use to interpret the findings did not emerge magically over the course of the study. Instead, a struggle occurred throughout the fieldwork as to how to organize the data in a way that would make sense to the reader and shed new light on the people and processes involved. Ecological theory, particularly Bateson's work in *Steps to an Ecology of Mind*, was initially useful in showing how home and school life are mutually embedded. Children do not leave their identities and experiences from home at the school door, neither can school experiences be left at school. The interface of school and home was a point that I wanted to make based on what I was finding, and the ecological model, wherein an action done in any one part affects the entire loop, illustrates that relationship.

In this view, all behavior in an ecological system is viewed as interaction or communication, but not in terms of the individual. Communication is intelligible only in the context of a relation (Bateson 1972; Poster 1986, 110). Bateson uses the analogy of a lake to show how different parts of a system have a relationship to the whole:

> When you narrow down your epistemology and act on the premise "What interests me is me" . . . you chop off consideration of other loops of the loop structure. You decide that you want to get rid of the by-products of human life and that Lake Erie will be a good place to put them. You forget that the eco-mental system called Lake Erie is a part of your wider eco-mental system—and that if Lake Erie is driven insane, its insanity is incorporated in the larger system of your thought and experience. (Bateson 1972, 484)

In order to make sense of parent involvement in schools, schools can thus be seen as an ecology of interactional relationships between the child, parents, teachers, staff, and administrators. In the ecological theory of Gregory Bateson we see a concern for viewing people and events *in context*. In this view, school organization is conceived as an organic structure, rather than as a mechanical one (Kanter 1983, 396). Bateson's ecological theory has much in common with feminism and other holistic theoretical bases, such as Native American, African American, and whole-language views of the world (Palmer 1987, 20–25). The *relationships* of people in the organization are what defines the organization. It is the work done by those in the organization—their ties and relationships—that characterize a school district or individual schools within a district. Bateson (1972) shows how it is impossible to cut off parts of a loop structure without affecting other parts of the loop. Central to the idea of schools as organic structures is the assumption that organizations are invented social realities (Greenfield 1988). Humans spin webs of meaning—they create and help define the reality in which they live and work, negotiating with one another for a particular kind of reality which is constantly in change and flux: a process.

The second theoretical point that came from the study was that the reforms that were being instituted to involve parents and community in the public schools were being translated by the bureaucratic system of the schools and by prevailing cultural practices into the opposite of what they were intended to achieve. Personalization was being sought through depersonalized means. The reforms were supposed to connect schools and community, but this could not be done using bureaucratic organizational structures and traditional leadership. For instance: creating a site-based council with limited decision making powers and an elite representation of parents, along with continued mystification of school practices through language and a continued separation of roles and responsibilities, ensured that the *status quo* was maintained. Challenging and problematic viewpoints were kept out of the discussion by the use of the same bureaucratic procedures and structures that had been instituted a century ago to *disconnect* school and community. In short, *Gemeinschaft* ends (personalized school-community relationships) could not be achieved using *gesellschaft* (depersonalized, bureaucratic) means. Thus, traditional sociological theory on community helped identify the paradox of *gemeinschaft* ends sought through *gesellschaft* means. In examining further the way the reforms were being translated into action, such as the annual stakeholders meeting described in chapter one, I came to feminist thought.

As a feminist, I have to acknowledge that this was no detached, intellectual decision, but one that was personally meaningful. Just as I have experienced and interpreted the world in a certain way, so too would I select and edit the social world that I studied. Feminism's political stance and understanding of oppression helped explain the patterns of inclusion and exclusion that I saw in the schools, and the dominance of the competitive bureacracy of schools. With the superintendency the most powerful position in public education, with most of those positions held by men, and with the culture of administration created and defined largely by men (with a subordinate teaching force composed largely of women), the cultural values of hierarchy, competition, individualism, and specialization are continually reproduced in schools. While feminism is deeply divided in its political movement and in its theoretical base, feminism clearly provides a way to see and to understand structures of dominance and subordination, and to analyze hegemonic discourse. A feminist approach is concerned with bringing to mind the difference it makes to consider women's interests (Strathern 1987, 286). Just as women teachers are inscribed by the bureaucratic system as less powerful than people higher up in the hierarchy, so too do teachers and administrators frequently inscribe parents as "lay" people outside the educational conversation. (This division may be tempered only by the other powerful inscriber, social class. Upper-middle class parents' needs' are met and their voices are heard more often in the schools because they have greater access to the system's cultural meanings, and can manipulate the system to have their needs met.)

Thus, in studying parents and schools I found that in the settings of schools and homes, it was my sense of feminist justice that inspired the analysis. In particular, the work of Belenky (1986), Gilligan (1982), Noddings (1984), Shakeshaft (1993), Tannen (1990) and Wheatley (1994), among other feminists, helped shape my thinking and observations. Critical ideas include the following: the value of horizontal/inclusive/lateral leadership; the interconnectedness of everything; the importance of context and holism (synthesizing the whole rather than pulling things apart); and the urgent need for knowledges and relations of care, rather than simplistic solutions imposed from above. The process of establishing rapport and communication is central to the new leadership which can no longer rely on a military or factory model where everyone follows unilateral orders without thinking.

Feminism also adds to the theoretical discussion in its politicization of the analysis. Feminist thought shows us that all participants in the culture are not given equal opportunity, even when structurally that appears to be the case. Throughout this book, situations are described in which some parents and families are alienated and excluded from the school. And even those parents with access to the center of the organization are often defined as different—"lay"—and therefore marginal to "professional" decision making.

School programs and policies, such as curriculum, testing, and evaluation, are currently inaccessible to many parents other than the "special" parents in the center: those on the school board, on site-based councils, and PTA leaders. At the crux of the situation are two concerns: (a) shifting from a bureaucratic organizational model to a more holistic one; and (b) educating parents and teachers and administrators on how to work together within a new collaborative, structural arrangement.

Analysis also depends on reflections on the field experience and on personal feelings. The autobiography of the researcher can be important in the search for meaning. The narrative may be as much woven with sympathy, tacit knowledge, intuition, and feeling as it is with logic and observational details. Certain personal subjectivities may come to the fore, such as social class, sexuality, age, sexual preference, statuses, values, ethics, ethnicity, and gender. Having been in and around schools for over twenty years in both Australia and the United States (including east and west coast U.S., public and private schools), I was able to see some parallels and differences in school organization and leadership styles, and to see how the predominantly competitive, individualistic, and bureaucratic cultures of the public schools could be informed by feminist thought. My intuitive sense of injustice and oppression along gender lines, from my own experience, led to a useful interplay of data with theory. I reflect on how feminism has impacted my own life:

> As a child I saw my mother, who did not work in paid employment outside the home, have difficulty raising four children. I saw my mother in a situation of economic and emotional dependence; she had no other way of dealing with the world than through my father. My mother's apparent difficulties were set in contrast to my father's seemingly endless powers and access to the public world. Later, when I wanted to have children, the memory of my mothers' struggles would always resurface, and I would have second thoughts. I rationalized that I could contribute to the world in other ways, through my work as a teacher. My friends tease me that since we always study something from the heart, that it's because I am not a parent that I am doing this study. I tell them it's because it's a pressing educational issue that needs addressing, a problem to solve. My choice of feminism as a way to explain the world, and my focus on parents and family are obvious ones, given my life experiences.

I also have an empathy for those struggling in the world, the underachieving children and parents "on the edges" of school life. I believe we can learn a great deal from the experiences of those who are marginalized in schools about why this occurs. Journal writing was a space in which to reflect on life experiences, and begin to make connections with what I was seeing in the schools:

> Fresh out of college, I remember so well how excited I was to go work in Moree in Northern New South Wales teaching Aboriginal children. This experience taught me much about inclusion and exclusion, dominance and subordination. The Aboriginal culture was portrayed in the dominant white discourse as idle, neglectful, and unattractive. Only upon experience with the people did I begin to see differently. The so-called characteristic of "idleness" is in part the ability to fit in with the rhythm of nature, rather than dominating and controlling it. Many ways of being that are part of traditional Aboriginal culture include an easy acceptance of things and not altering the natural landscape, as opposed to productivity. Another example is the Aboriginal tradition of leaving a job to go on a spiritual or other journey without warning, which is seen as irresponsible. With my experiences I came to have a great amount of respect for Aboriginal people and to see how we can learn from their wisdom. Our exploitation of natural resources and the diminishing of non-renewable resources is just one lesson about the value of different ways of seeing.

In Robertson I also saw boundaries and patterns of inclusion and exclusion, and reflect on my own perceptions.

> Some of these children do not like school and are faced with a daily question of whether they will get to finish high school, even though Robertson School District is a well-to-do district. Too many people seem to want to just get them out of the school as soon as possible—either into an alternative school/setting, or likely into unemployment. When I was a teenager, I too went through a difficult period and very nearly dropped out of school. The well-adjusted primary school student found herself an alienated and marginalized adolescent. Both school and home became places of perceived oppression to me. However, my family insisted that we all continue through school and college, even though that was not always easy for my parents, who had four children to educate. Much later in graduate school in Australia, once again I considered dropping out of school, after an enormous investment of time, energy, and money, because I felt that I did not quite fit in. The

question of boundaries and exclusion seems to be critical. Why do we set boundaries of success and failure that excludes and alienates so many people? How do we create inclusive schools, that do not label some students, parents and families as "good," and others not? Is true collaboration with families possible? How will it help students?

Just as I, as researcher, struggled to find answers to these and many ongoing questions, to make meaning out of the research puzzle, so too are the other participants in the study trying to make meaning out of their own lives. The stories told here are a journey of self-discovery, putting together different facets of experience through analysis, reflection, and writing. The book is not one person's story, but a collage that evokes a particular educational and social experience for the considered reflection of the larger educational community.

To further understand parent-school relations we now turn to some of the ways that the bureaucracy of schools controls and limits parents' participation in school, even while instituting more participatory reforms (chapters 3, 4, 5, and 6). In later chapters (6, 7, 8, and 9) I will reframe existing practices using a feminist perspective to show new possibilities for parent-school collaboration. School reform has been said to be a "predictable failure" because we have engaged in piecemeal reform and "accepted the (intractable) system as it is" (Sarason 1990, 14). I will argue instead that the solutions are available to us in feminist ideas on schools and leadership, that we can create systemic and conceptual change from within, and that the feminist perspective provides a necessary direction and purposefulness.

3

Consorting with the Enemy

> Very few people would disagree that there
> needs to be real collaboration between the
> school and teachers and parents, but when
> we get down to the nitty-gritty of it, then
> teachers feel kind of threatened by just the
> demands of their job and expectations that
> they feel that parents have of them and
> that they have of themselves (Interview,
> middle school principal, 1995)

Willard Waller, in the classic *Sociology of Teaching* (1932), argued that teachers and parents, given their different goals and interests, are "natural enemies"; Lightfoot (1978) used the term "worlds apart"; and at a recent educational conference, a keynote speaker quipped that parents and educators as "collaborators" is an oxymoron, a contradiction that just doesn't reflect reality. Hence the title of this chapter—"Consorting with the Enemy"—for the professional-lay distinction and its inherent tensions remain to this day. The shift to parent-school collaboration has not been and will not be easy. Historically embedded ideas and practices cannot easily be overturned, particularly if there is not systemic change.

The themes discussed in this chapter emerged over the course of the study in Robertson School District. To begin, a key principle affecting parents, teachers, and administrators is the notion of "professionalism" as distinct from "lay" and community input. We need to understand this notion of professionalism, and the organizational structures of schools, if we are to redefine them in a way that allows for collaboration between school and community.

On the difficulties faced by educators in moving toward a more democratic and inclusive model of schooling, a principal says this:

> I found the first meeting of the school improvement council very difficult. I was trying to tell them basically just what a site-council is and why we need to have them. I guess it's frustrating for me because of the time it takes to explain things and why we do things. And time is our most valuable commodity. (Interview, principal)

Shifting parent involvement from a passive relationship to a more active one is seen by many teachers and administrators as time-consuming, difficult to achieve, or threatening. Educators may not easily give up their historically-embedded control over parents' "lay" participation in schools, which was established early this century with the move to scientific management and the professionalization of teaching (Tyack and Hansot 1982). Superintendents or principals may continue to view parental and civic involvement in traditional terms, as a means to an end—a way to garner financial backing. And in traditional practices, the superintendent recommends and the board approves (see Cuban 1976). But today, the connection between parent-school relationships and financial backing extends far beyond approval and the passing of bonds and levies.

In the current reforms, state and federal legislation and monies are often tied to the provision that schools have policies and practices of site-based or school-based management, shared decision making, and strong parent-community collaboration—which forces the issue. In Robertson School District this meant that administrators and teachers scrambled to institute closer ties with families through site-based councils in order to gain state grant monies. Yet, to really work, the partnership must not simply be instrumental, and must overcome historically embedded practices that have separated parents from professionals.

THE BELIEF THAT TEACHERS SHOULD TEACH
AND PARENTS SHOULD PARENT

Ironically, distancing of parents from schools can occur as a result of the demands of the new reforms that emphasize participatory decision making and parent-school collaboration. Parents are now being asked to switch roles from that of more or less passive recipients of public schooling to an active, participatory role. An administrator argues: "Parent collaboration with schools is not a controversial issue. This is what we need to be doing. No-one is going to argue with that." Some parents have always been active in their public schools, but of late educators are demanding that *all* parents exercise their "responsibilities" toward schools (Crowson 1992, 11).

At the same time, educators are questioning the ability of parents to parent well. Many educators argue that there has been a decline in "parenting" in today's society, which means more work for schools with fewer resources:

> We are so vulnerable to criticism because we are trying to do so many things with an intangible variable like a human being, and the parents are not parenting. There is just less parenting today. Even those you assume would be good parents such as those up on the hill (university students and faculty) don't necessarily do a good job. Some of these kids are treated so badly by their parents. Kevin, the other day was repeatedly insulted by his mother in public. He said to me "It doesn't hurt. I'm used to it." Well no kid should get used to abuse. Many of these kids are suffering from bad parenting or lack of parenting. (Interview, teacher)

> There's just so many things we're trying to get in because the parents are just not parenting anymore. The abuse issue, and now we're covering sex ed and personal safety and all those things. It's just a multitude of stuff you have to put together, whereas the curriculum used to be simplified. There were basics we had to teach. Well, good luck getting those in anymore! (Interview, teacher)

Educators feel that they are performing a wide range of responsibilities that were once undertaken by parents and others. Schools are now providing breakfasts, some health and dental care, psychological aid, driver education, conflict resolution training, and so on. It is necessary for schools to do this work, but tensions have arisen around the issue of educators as social workers. Teachers argue:

> I want to teach, not be a parent. If parents would only do their job of parenting, life would be so much better for all of us. For many kids there isn't dinnertime. The idea of having a family discus-

sion at dinnertime is foreign. Kids are expected to get their own
dinner, to forage and graze. And they will perpetuate this with
their own children. (Interview, teacher)

Some parents also blame schools for increasingly neglecting their primary purpose—to teach. The state and federal governments add to the
tension between parents and educators by mandating that schools take
on responsibilities such as monitoring sexual abuse, *while measuring
schools by their test scores* and issuing report after report that seems to
blame educators for the declining state of public education.

Parents may be wary of school demands for their inclusion. To
some it feels as though the *blame* for the perceived failure of the educational system is being switched to parents. And the notion of shifting
the blame to parents is evident in some of the reforms, (see National
Commission on Excellence in Education 1983; Chubb and Moe 1990).
Parents may also feel as though they are being talked down to by educators. Now parents are being instructed through parenting classes, parent guidelines, and handbooks on how best to raise their children. Some
parents complain about schools trying to take on parenting responsibilities:

> I'm the kind of parent that they all want to re-educate. I represent a
> large group of parents. We send our kids to school to learn aca-
> demics, not values, and not to teach them things we should teach
> them as parents at home. (Interview, parent)

> Just because there are problems in society, doesn't mean we have
> to fix them in schools. The role of schools is to teach. (Interview,
> parent)

Other parents do not have the fear about "values" instruction, or a narrow self-interested view, but simply feel that they don't have time to do
all that the school wants them to do. As researchers point out, more
and more is being asked of parents: the duties and responsibilities of
mothers today include that of intellectual growth—a far cry from the historical tradition of mothers providing love and emotional support (Arnot
1984; Lareau 1989, 84). These new duties are sometimes resented by
parents who may nostalgically wish that they could enjoy parenting
and leave the education to the schools:

The one aspect that I don't want to be involved in is as a teacher. Part of the expectation from the school that I deliberately avoided last year was to teach her. Because the teacher would occassionally say to Diane [daughter], "Practice this with Mom at home," or they'd send a little note, saying "Please go over this at home," or "Please do this at home." I have a strong reaction to that. Probably because I'm a teacher and I don't want to confuse the relationship with my child. I want to have a mother's relationship to my child and not a teaching relationship. What I don't want for my daughter to feel is that the teacher said, "Your mother's going to do this, or your father's going to do this, at home with you." So then the kid has to come home and be subjected to the parent doing this at-home thing. I resisted that. And I discussed it a little bit with the teacher. I said that I didn't really think it was such a good idea for me to do that. And we moved on. I think the teacher is the person that is responsible for what goes on in the classroom and for the actual instruction. (Interview, parent, who is also a teacher)

Parents may have the concern that the parent-child relationship can end up resembling that of the child with the school. If the school gets to define what happens educationally in the home, then stesses can arise around homework and resentments toward the school can be exacerbated (see also Ulich 1989, 7). The recent reform movement is toward parents becoming more involved in educational activities, both in school and at home: as volunteers, as decision makers on site-based councils and other bodies, as fundraisers, and so on. And many of these reforms are being instituted *from the school end of things*, without considering the different roles and expectations that this places on parents at home (David 1993, 157).

In addition, some parents express concern that if parents are heavily involved in schools this may take time and resources away from instructional purposes. This is not to argue against site-based management or participatory decision making, but to point out that embedded in what has been called a "noncontroversial" issue, are some deeply controversial issues, and that we cannot simply mandate changes in parent roles while the school remains the same. Parents do not always feel that parent involvement is more than a one-way street. The schools have not yet demonstrated that they are also willing to change the organizational structures of the school to accommodate the needs created by an inclusive agenda for parent-school collaboration.

PROFESSIONAL AUTONOMY AND INTEGRITY

Educators have struggled to develop a technology that is distinctively theirs. They have fought to achieve empowerment and recognition that they are truly professionals with a distinctive technology that enables them to make sound decisions on administration, student growth, learning, and development. However, the more educators are accorded the status of professionals, the less they are able to confer with parents on an equal footing. Having gained some status and recognition as professionals, educators are sometimes reluctant to change their roles and give back power to parents and lay people in the community. In the words of the superintendent: "I went to school for ten years to get the education that I have and the knowledge and expertise, and now I'm evaluated by a bunch of lay persons," i.e., the school board. A principal also states, "I just don't know what my role is any more." And a teacher argues, "As a professional I don't mind putting together and justifying what I'm doing, but I don't want my teaching to be micro-engineered by a group of parents."

The fear of educators is that the very commitments and beliefs that the educator holds dear may not be understood or valued by lay persons, who are nevertheless in a position to undermine or alter the course of the educator's aims, curriculum, preferred teaching methods, and even tenure. Thus, an administrator argues:

> I have seen some teachers suffer from a witch-hunt at the hands of parents. They can get a mindset that says a particular teacher is no good and then they repeatedly pound and pound and the administrator is forced into a tight corner. I have seen it happen. Even some very good teachers may get this treatment. (Interview, administrator)

As another example of parental pressure on educators—if an upper-middle class parent, such as an architect, comes into the school wanting a particular outcome, such as having his/her student placed in particular classes, the educator can feel pressured to bend to the parent's wishes, even if they conflict with professional judgement. As one principal put it:

> That's fine. I agree that parents should have a say, but not to the point where it interferes with my professional judgement. Let's take the class placement issue. A parent may only hear the child's

desire to be in a particular class with his or her friends, or they may have heard a rumor that a particular teacher is excellent or to be avoided at all costs. As a professional I may have many more things to consider. Parents may want what may, or may not, be best for their child—or for all children for that matter. I may want to separate out students who act out in class. Or I may want classes balanced in size, academic achievement levels, gender, ethnicity, or what not. These are professional decisions that I must make without interference.

In other words, educators have fought to gain a professional identity and are wary of reform movements that seem to threaten their professional integrity. In 1906, Nicholas Murray Butler argued that it is as foolish to talk of the "democratization of schools" as it is to talk of the "democratization of the treatment of appendicitis" (Tyack 1981, 19). Doctors in an operating room do not ask lay people for their input; neither, it is argued, should professional educators be collaborating with parents and citizens. A professional is not a professional if a lay person can make the decisions equally well.[1] Crowson argues that "while teachers and school administrators admit that in the professionalization of their field they are far from the standard represented by physicians—key questions of instructional method, pupil grouping, choice and sequencing of learning materials, and the evaluation of student progress are still considered the special province of the trained educator" (1992, 14). Teachers possess some technical knowledge, ethical norms of conduct, and specialized practices in relation to their clients, and professionalism has been defined as professional autonomy for educators by virtue of which they have control over the educational process and decision making. Shared decision making and collaboration with parents may represent to many educators a threat to established practices of professionalism.

In the superintendent's office, gatekeeping to keep the public managed from a distance, but not collaborated with, may also occur:

> If someone calls the superintendent's office then we think of three things. Is it a complaint from a parent? Does the person want a job? Or do they want to talk privately with the superintendent, in which case everyone is very concerned. (Interview, administrator)

> I get the impression that it's their school and we are the guests there. (Interview, parent)

Lines of distance and isolation are reflected in building-level organization, where teachers often teach in isolation with little input from their colleagues, other government or social service agencies, parents, or the community.

In one school, teachers felt strongly about "professional" autonomy; they did not want parents on the school site council and voted accordingly. But it did not take long for parents to find out that they were unwanted, nor for the superintendent to exercise leadership in pointing out that state law now required parent and community participation (Simpson 1994). The school is now in the process of repairing relationships.

Two reform movements are clearly going on at the same time: parents want a greater say in education, and teachers want empowerment and greater decision-making powers. And until teachers' unions in the various states embrace sharing power between educators and parents and community, the latter group will continue to be "advisory" to the professionals. Teachers' unions support the empowerment of teachers, but what about the empowerment of parents? In Robertson School District, sharing power between reading specialists (chapter 1 certificated personnel/teachers) and paraprofessionals (classified as personnel/parents) has become a potentially litigious battle. The shift in power is seen by reading specialists as threatening: "the teachers don't like it" (Interview, principal). Teachers' union representatives point out that giving decision-making power to site-councils, parents, and parent bodies violates the work contract and the collective bargaining agreement between the education authority (the teachers' union) and the employer (the state). The law as it currently stands gives the school board full decision-making powers as representatives of the state, yet site-councils with an ambiguous and undetermined charter are also attempting to impact the educational agenda. Until such time as state legislation passes into law and is negotiated with teachers' unions, many school districts empowering parent decision making are considered to be in violation of their contracts (see Patterson 1993).

CONFLICT OVER GOALS AND INTERESTS

Conflict between parents and educators also arises over educational goals and interests. Lightfoot (1978) notes that schools and families are "worlds apart," while Van Galen (1987) explains the conflict as arising from teachers' professional insecurity and a need to "control" the educational agenda. One of the key arguments used by educators in Robertson School District to explain the difficulties that they have working in collaborative partnerships with parents is that parents often have their own child's interests in mind—a personalized, particularistic approach which is seen as "self-interested"—whereas educators are trying to contribute to society in a broader sense—"the big picture"—so that all children matter. Thus, they express a more rule-governed view:

> Because the professional gets this big picture in their minds when they're dealing with each individual child, the informed decisions that the professional educator makes are different from those that the parent might like to see made. (Interview, teacher)

> We have an accelerated learner committee with parents—it's really for gifted kids, but we wouldn't want to call it that. And those parents who are more active, visible, and vocal have a vested interest. They have emotions and egos wrapped up in it. Their child is the only one who matters. They only see their own interest, it might be pushing German in the curriculum. But I teach 150 kids a day. It's impossible for them to not be judgmental about things when their kid is involved. (Interview, teacher)

> You get very willing parents to come in and sit on committees and help with decision making, but it's rare that you find a parent who has the "big picture." If a parent has a sixth grader, then he or she may not know what goes on at seventh or eighth grade, or if they have an eighth grader, they may not know or remember what went on at sixth grade. They have a rather narrow vision of what goes on here. (Interview, teacher)

One parent who is also a teacher noted that her decisions made as a parent and those made as a teacher frequently conflict:

> As a parent I would say no to gay rights education in schools, but as an educator I would say, "Yes, we should be teaching that in schools." It's hard to explain, and I know I'm being inconsistent here, but it's a matter of rights and principles that are hard to deny, and on the other hand protecting my own children and wanting to take care of personal matters with them myself. (Interview, parent)

Educators have a mission of taking children out of their unique cultural contexts and socializing them toward common American (middle class) public values such as the work ethic, a value for learning, and good character—even if the particular community views these qualities differently. The structured environment of the school is intended to take children out of the home and socialize them toward different norms and expectations. A struggle can ensue over goals or outcomes:

> Parents have their own home values, whether its fundamentalist, liberal, Republican, whatever, and they come to the school on these councils and committees with their own agendas. It's not easy to reach collaborative decision making with so many diverse views. In some ways it's like playing Russian roulette. You never know what is going to happen. Some of these parents have little tapes in their heads of when they were in school, and so they have an ax to grind that we may not agree with. (Interview, assistant principal and parent)

Tensions thus arise around the issue of particular/personalized (parent) versus universal, rule-governed (school) responses. The teachers may be seeking assurance that parents are supportive and appreciative of his/her overall "big picture" educational goals and efforts. In the present study, formalized evenings and events sometimes took on a ritualistic "performance" character, serving a function of recognizing teachers and parents and their separate roles, without dispelling either group's distrust of the other, or moving into real problem solving.

THE TRADITION OF TEACHERS WORKING
IN ISOLATION WITH CHILDREN

Teachers have a long history of working in isolation with children and may not want parents to intrude on their educational turf. In traditional practices teachers aren't bothered by their principals, provided they keep their students quiet and seemingly at work in the classroom, and provided there aren't too many complaints from parents:

> I wouldn't want to see parents in my classroom. They can interfere. But they should know what their kids are doing and be supportive. (Interview, teacher)

My focus is on students. If a parent gets in the way then that will make me very angry. (Interview, teacher)

In Robertson, all parents think they're experts, especially the professors, and this threatens the teachers' autonomy. And part of being a teacher traditionally has been that behind closed doors there's a certain sacredness about teaching with the students. (Interview, teacher)

I avoid it like the plague (having parent volunteers), because I'd much rather spend a half an hour working with one student on English than a half hour on trying to schedule parents to come in and making phone calls. (Interview, teacher)

School is a place to give children a second chance, an intervention to guard against children turning out just like their parents, and schools are given considerable freedom to shape children's lives (see also Lightfoot 1978, 121).

Parents often seem to collude in the notion of teacher autonomy: "You just hope and pray that when they go in behind those closed doors with that teacher that they're very competent and very moral because you're entrusting your children to those teachers" (Interview, parent).

Teachers frequently argue that any tasks that take the teacher away from the primary work of teaching is not important work. The belief is that the closer the teacher is to the children, the greater the sense of commitment and rewards. Moves to have teachers work more closely with parents are viewed with suspicion by some teachers and by a sense that this is "something other than teaching" (Johnson 1989, 110). Adding on responsibilities to the work of the classroom teacher is thus viewed with distrust by some teachers, administrators, and parents. Parents may also be concerned that if teachers are spending more time with parents, this may be taking time and attention away from instruction: "If there are parents in the classroom, I want to say what about my child's learning opportunities? I want to say, 'Get those parents out of there!'" (Interview, parent)

A common argument is that school resources will be channeled into managing home-school relations—teachers "must take time away from teaching to coordinate, train, and make effective use of parents in the classroom" (Lareau 1989, 163). As one principal argued: "Every time I have to deal with a parent, that takes me ultimately away from dealing with instructional issues" (Interview, high school principal). And teachers can become frustrated with needing to explain to parents their educational purposes:

> This parent [volunteer] was asking, "why?" all the time, as if she didn't trust my professional judgment. I didn't want to have to train her in addition to everything else. It would take time away from my work with kids. (Interview, teacher)

> If everybody's going to have a voice in running the school, then you're not going to be able to get anything done because you're going to be constantly called to task by those outside the system. (Interview, administrator)

Administrators can resent the time that is spent managing adults and not teaching kids:

> Parents get in the way. We start managing adults rather than kids. It's very time-consuming. Our job is to teach children—not to teach adults—and to protect the children. If we have a parent who's out of line and we ask them to leave, and we tell them why and they choose not to, we call the police. Now that's very rare, but I've had to do it. Our responsibility is to provide a safe, nurturing environment for children, and so we have to make sure we're doing everything we can to do that. (Interview, principal)

In addition, teachers sometimes have very good reasons for wanting to limit parent involvement if that involvement means intense scrutiny of the child, who may be better off with independence from parental pressures. Parental pressure on children to achieve at a high level can be detrimental to some children, who respond more to a nurturing, indirect approach. Ironically, the very motive for some parents' involvement in school—to have closer knowledge of the child's work in school, may work against the child. Pressure from within families and conflicts over education may result in children having less autonomy and less control over their own intrinsic motivation to succeed in school. Intensity and pressure is not the best approach for many children, and educators may feel they need to control or limit the zealous involvement of certain parents in their children's schooling. This, despite the common plea of teachers that many parents are not involved in school at all.

A negative implication, however, of teachers working in isolation with children is that they may disregard parents and fail to see that parents, and particularly mothers who may not be employed in such high-status or well-paid positions as fathers, have anything worthwhile to offer the school. An administrative intern wrote in her log of professional activities under the category "School, Home, and Community," "Working with those idiots is impossible." Those idiots she is referring to are parents. The journal is a tool for reflecting on administrative work with no holds barred in terms of what one can say. The purpose is to speak honestly and then begin to analyze it to see what the problems are. She clearly was not used to working with parents as a classroom teacher, but her work as an administrative intern was placing her in much greater contact with parents, and she did not have a respectful attitude toward parents. She had defined parents as the "other," as less qualified to make decisions, and as troublemakers.

A CONSERVATIVE ADMINISTRATIVE CULTURE

Schools are remarkably resistant to change. Administrators in particular have created a conservative culture. Despite all the reforms public schools have changed very little. Although administrators may welcome parent involvement in some areas of school life, the mission, finance, budget, personnel, and curricular issues may be jealously guarded and administrative control held onto. A fear expressed by administrators is that if one lets go, one will still be held accountable for acts that are no longer controlled. Moreover, it may be feared that too much inclusion will lead to chaos:

> The big threat for teachers, not just teachers, for me too, for all of us, is level of involvement in policy-making. Real basic school decision making. Loss of control over the policies and operations of the school is threatening. We have parents on all of our hiring teams and I'm real comfortable with that. And to me it's sort of a process of moving toward more inclusion. (Interview, principal)

Traditional administrative norms stress the need for good school-community relations, particularly for financial backing, but this is not the same as collaboration. Parents have traditionally been managed by schools and their support garnered. In public schools, the financial and other support of schools by parents is indirect, but nevertheless critical. Tax revenues, the passing of bonds and levies for the construction of new schools (often requiring a 60 percent majority), a favorable board majority, and the hiring of superintendents essentially depend on the support of parents and community members. Parents and community have thus always been courted (and managed) by the schools.

One would expect the new reforms of shared decision making and site-based councils to have prompted a shift in administration from a management approach to a more collaborative stance. However, in the present study, parents and community people were still often managed by schools. As an example, parents on site-councils were often hand-picked by administrators for their "fit" with the dominant norms; new perspectives and critical input was thus minimized. At a site-council meeting, a principal explained her view of the importance of maintaining teacher control and integrity:

> What we have decided to do is allow the faculty to keep the decision making power on what we want to do conceptually, and then have the site-council work on all the details. Teachers don't have time to do all the details. Otherwise you can have the situation where teachers are being told what to do and teachers don't like that. (Principal's statement to the site-council)

> The faculty agrees that on major issues they need to be in agreement and the site-council will "hammer" out the details. However, anyone is welcome to be involved in the "hammer" process. (site-council minutes)

> Essentially what happened is that the teachers developed the grants and the council said, "OK, that looks fine." (Interview, principal)

The principal is torn between empowering the faculty and empowering the parents, and it is the faculty that she must work with on a day-to-day basis and to whom she is most directly responsible in the organization of the school.

A problem is that a concern with the management of public relations and with school-community politics can result not only in a lack of new perspectives, but in a perception that the image-making itself takes time and resources away from the real business of educating. Teachers can become resentful of the extra time and energy that they are asked to contribute in moving to collaboration on site-councils and on other parent and community bodies. The cynical belief can take hold that appearances dominate, and that parents take precedence over educators: "The administration attends to the politics and do things look right and are parents happy. We feel this has taken precedence over educational concerns. The administrators don't have to make teachers happy, just parents. Teachers feel second place." (Interview, teacher)

Parents argue in turn that they are sought, in the rhetoric, as partners with the public schools, yet many parents are unable to participate in the plans that are proposed, and their voices are not really heard in shaping new directions for education. Those people who are invited to participate, or who volunteer for local school councils or parent advisory councils, are the ones who already have the time and resources to be involved in school. Those parents who stay away are the same ones who traditionally stayed away from school for a variety of reasons: alienation, work commitments, lack of confidence. Many parents simply cannot afford the loss of wages, or possibly even loss of employment, to do the kind of volunteering and participation that some schools expect or desire. Changes for enhanced parent involvement frequently overlook the diversity of family situations and considerations of class, race, and gender.

SCHOOL BOARDS AS LEGITIMATORS OF SCHOOL DECISIONS

Another practice that separates professionals from lay people is the traditional working relationship of the school board with the administration. The school board may be in the business of representing the administration and its policies to the people, rather than representing the people to the administration. Kerr argues that: "School boards chiefly perform the function of legitimating the policies of the school system to the community, rather than representing the various segments of the community to the school administration, especially with regard to the educational program" (1964, 35).

Even though Kerr's study was done thirty years ago, in Robertson School District, and possibly in other parts of the country, the school board legitimizes the policies of the school system. The school board socializes incoming board members to the norms established by the superintendent—for example, the rule of letting the superintendent know business and voting positions ahead of board meetings: "I want no surprises" (superintendent). As can be seen in the following account, the principal's work is facilitated when the school board members are supportive of professionals' decisions:

> The school board has a definite impact on the quality of my life both personally and professionally. Some of my most memorable, stressful moments have been with the school board. Parents will call the school board and complain about this or that, and now the school board members won't even listen to them because they've been socialized by the superintendent. They'll say, "Have you been to the principal? Have you been to the superintendent?" And they'll make sure the parents go through the proper channels. But when these board members first came on, that was their power thing. They loved to have people call and they'd talk for hours with these people about problems that they'd try to fix, but they didn't have the background. (Interview, principal)

The school board is expected to select a highly competent "professional" educator as superintendent, and then act as a watchdog over his/her decisions instead of dealing directly with problems that parents might have, or telling the superintendent how to get things done, or engaging in shared decision making. A recent manual called "Effective School Board Governance," written for board members attests:

> Relationships with top management are critical to the success of the implementation and effectuation of board or system policy. Unless boards build into their operations and responsibilities the monitoring and nurturance of top management leadership, their efforts to support quality in the system may be thwarted. However, boards often confuse monitoring of executive functioning with prescribing "how" [emphasis added] to get things done or which things to do first. This provides a stultifying and confusing process of governance. Such *interference* in school operations causes counterproductive activity . . . The board's job is to govern not manage. As one veteran school board member, a highly successful businessman with over forty years of service, once said, "You don't need a dog if you're going to do your own barking." (Poston 1994, iii)

The question may then be raised as to why school board members would allow educators such free reign in decision making. The social class and motivation of school board members may help explain their actions. Only a minority of school board candidates may be backed by particular groups in a community, and common motives for seeking a board position include gaining political experience and performing civic duty. In Robertson School District, four of the five members of the school board have children in the district, and the fifth member's children graduated only recently from Robertson High School. They argued that their motives were civic responsibility and an extension of involvement in the schools as parents. Yet they have been brought over toward seeing themselves as representing the administration to the people, rather than the reverse.

The socialization, involving board members socializing incoming members to the norms established by the superintendent, is enhanced by practices such as board-member training at state professional organizations like the Northwest State School Directors' Association. School board members attend the training, along with their superintendents, in order to develop a team perspective. As one principal notes: "Two times a year they go to the professional meetings and I don't care what it costs the school district, it's worth it. They go off to these things with the superintendent and they really do learn a lot."

Additionally, school board members are typically civic-minded people in the community, but they may fail to represent the diverse voices of their constituents. As noted they may be trained and encouraged to think like the superintendent and not challenge the *status quo*. The superintendent, in turn, attends very closely to the school board, aware of its power to hire and fire the superintendent: "I worry about the school board. They're the most, the five most relevant people I worry about. They're my bosses and that's who evaluates me and keeps me around." (Interview, superintendent)

However, parents are typically much more diverse than the school board. Parents belong to different social classes and ethnic groups, and different family configurations, and they may not always receive the attention of the superintendent. Parents' varied interests also tend to divide their voices. When issues arise parents frequently go to the teacher who is most directly concerned, or to the building principal, or to the PTA. Concerns may never reach the school board for consideration. As the following excerpt from my field notes shows, the level of interchange of the general public at school board meetings may be minimal:

The superintendent and the school board members are seated in a formal directors' meeting format with a podium facing the board and the general public behind the podium. Speakers address the board from the podium with their backs to the general public. Apart from the item on the agenda entitled "Visitors" there are no opportunities for participatory dialogue. No visitors raise issues, and the meeting continues uninterrupted.

Questions have been raised in recent years about how truly representative the school board is of the people's views, despite their elected position. Finn (1992) suggests that with reforms for site-based management and parent participation, the focus should be on more immediate local control, not on the "municipal school system." He claims that "middle management," *i.e.,* the school board, is redundant and should be abolished. Finn calls the local school board and its superintendent the "preserver of entrenched interests and encrusted practices" (p. 25). Danzenberger and Usdan (1992) argue instead that school boards need to strengthen their "grassroots" linkages between parents, community, government, and social services to be more accountable to the people (p. 122).

School administrators have tended to operate as bureaucrats in their decision making. Important decisions are made behind closed doors, in executive sessions with the superintendent and the school board, not in the public forum. A long history of "closed decision procedures" in public schooling has ensured that professional educators have not come under the close scrutiny of the general public (Mann 1976, 58). The "lay" school board may thus be co-opted by the "professional" superintendent. The most personalized contact may be between the school board president and the superintendent, with the board president talking with the superintendent frequently (sometimes up to seven times a week) and being consulted about what to let other board members know. The board president then acts as a focal point for the media, representing school issues and decision making in a positive light. Typically, parents and community people receive only limited information on what goes on in schools.

QUESTIONS OF LOYALTY AND RESPONSIBILITY

Since schools are hierarchical, bureaucratic, specialized organizations, questions of loyalty and responsibility are raised when new partnerships between schools and families are proposed. The question may be asked: Who should the principal or the superintendent support in the face of conflicting interests—the parents or the teachers? While a superintendent's or a principal's response may vary according to the nature of the problem, parents and teachers can see each other as divisive, and a struggle can occur around who is loyal to whom. The issue is one of control and the power to set the educational agenda.

Traditional professionalism can also work against parent and community involvement through such practices as administrators protecting teachers from the public. Principals are under pressure from teachers to provide support for teacher empowerment, which usually means protecting teachers' judgement and autonomy, buffering teachers from parents, and backing teachers one hundred percent in disputes with parents. Administrators have seen their work as "putting out fires" in conflicts between teachers and parents (see also Grant and Sleeter 1986, 72). As we saw in the earlier example, teachers can feel "second place" if parents begin to be heard more by administrators. Unfortunately, framing the issue as a competitive game—as an *either* teachers *or* parents situation—is counterproductive. If teachers become dissatisfied with a school's pro-parent and pro-community stance they will likely resist the changes or transfer to a school where there are fewer demands—a school where traditional "professionalism" is guaranteed (Connell *et al.* 1982). If the administrator is pro-parent, a struggle can ensue between the administration and resistant teachers:

> There are some teachers who are less willing to work with parents. Some teachers are a little more autocratic in their classroom or the direct instruction has to come from them as opposed to diversifying. And so you have to channel those teachers in the right direction. (Interview, principal)

The same questions of loyalty and protection are often asked of the superintendent who is hired by the school board to represent their views, but who works as a team player with principals and is sometimes accused of siding with the administrative team.

CONCLUSION

Relationships between parents and educators are affected by social and cultural practices that divide educators into a "professional" camp and parents into a "lay" one. Collaborative partnerships between parents and educators are set in a context of viewing the "other" as different and sometimes even at odds. This chapter showed a number of present-day divisive policies and practices that have effectively diminished school-family collaboration. These traditions, practices and relationships contain implicit underlying tensions that separate parents and community people from educators.

The professional context of the school has been defined as one informed by the following assumptions: (a) the belief that "teachers should teach and parents should parent"; (b) an emphasis on professional autonomy and integrity for educators; (c) conflict over goals and interests (the "big picture" of educators versus the "self-interested" motives of parents); (d) the tradition of teachers working in isolation with children; (e) a conservative administrative culture—with well-established norms, practices, and ways of doing business that define school administrators' work with the community as "managing" community relations; (f) school boards as legitimators of school decisions; and (g) questions of loyalty and responsibility, whereby administrators feel they have to support either teachers *or* parents in the face of conflict.

Underpinning these parent-school relations is the hierarchical and bureaucratic organization of public schools, which serves to *reproduce* the hierarchical and unequal relationships in the larger society, and also to *produce* social class, gender, and race ideologies in day-to-day life in schools (Apple 1985). In other words, given the increasingly wide gap between rich and poor in U.S. society,[2] it follows that schools, as part of society, would also reflect inequity. Such inequalities include differential treatment of school children through financial, pedagogical, curricular, and other processes (*e.g.*, different tracks, labelling of students, "inner city" *versus* "suburban" schools, and so on). Thus, teachers and administrators' differential power and privilege in traditional school organization reflects social, political, and economic inequities.

The shift to increase community control of the schools can be seen as a move to break down some of these inequities, and to enhance and reframe democratic rights and participation. Instead of top-down administrative decision making, a broader base of constituents is included in shared educational decision making. These reforms to empower parents present educators with new and previously unknown challenges. The professional school as an entity needs broader and more inclusive boundaries that can be informed by feminist thought. Feminists have long struggled for a social and natural world less defined by boundaries, dominance, and subordination, a world where all people—men, women, and children—participate and contribute, and where systematic patterns of exclusion are replaced by multiple voices and multiple concerns. Part of a teacher's and administrator's education has to be learning how to change the organizational structures, to reframe school-home relations as collaborative, to relate to and communicate with parents in all their diversity, as well as with children. This is not to say that the professional rejects professionalism as a value, but rather that professionalism is redefined. To be a professional educator would include the ability to relate to and team with a variety of people and organizations—such as parents, citizens, and social agencies. The next chapter further explains a view of the current hierarchical and bureaucratic organization of schooling, which is brought into question for its mismatch with the current reforms and with schooling for the twenty-first century.

NOTES

1. On the contrary, I would argue that doctors, for all their hierarchical power relationships with clients, nevertheless consult with parents on matters concerning the child, even in the case of life-or-death decisions. Educators do not always consult with parents, yet the consequences of their decisions for the child are just as powerful as medical decisions in terms of life opportunities given or denied. Educators clearly have specialized knowledge and expertise that can be enhanced by consultation and collaboration with parents.
2. Barlett and Steel (1992) report that between 1980 and 1989 the average wage earned by people earning less than $20,000 a year rose by 1.4 percent compared to an average salary increase of 49.5 percent for those earning one million dollars.

4

Schools as Competitive Bureaucracies

> Schools followed the lead of the turn-of-the-century municipal reform to become more hierarchical as well as professional. . . . Heavy emphasis on efficiency and, essentially, a misreading of Taylor's scientific management turned schools into *competitive bureaucracies*, rather than collaborative service organizations, emphasizing *control over instruction*. (Ortiz and Marshall 1988, 123)
>
> The history of bureaucracy in education provokes uncomfortable questions. City schools must provide for a large, diverse clientele. Is bureaucracy the only form of organization through which this can be done? *Is bureaucracy inevitable*? Or is it inevitable only in the presence of certain priorities such as efficiency over participation and harmony over conflict? (Katz 1971, 221)

Public schools employ a specialized hierarchical, segmented organizational model that many of the recent reform efforts are designed to reverse. Traditional bureaucratic school organization and day-to-day functioning occurs along the following lines, similar to the traditional organization of large corporations. The superintendent typically acts as the CEO of a quasi-corporation. In the superintendent's words: "we are modelling ourselves after a large corporation." However, the state has ultimate power over the creation or dissolution of a school district, and legal responsibility for education (Patterson 1993). The Robertson School District organizational chart shows a series of boxes starting with one for the board of directors at the top, followed by the superintendent and the assistant superintendent, and branching down like a family tree—four at the next level, eight at the next level, and so on. Each unit is responsible for certain designated work, with someone heading each unit having control over the work. However, in the classroom, the teacher has control over the technical core of teaching, with people further up the hierarchy—the principal and superintendent—influencing from outside what goes on, for they are ultimately responsible.

The work of the people further up the hierarchy than the classroom is different from the central business of schools, viz., teaching and learning. The more one is promoted up the hierarchy, the more removed one becomes from the day-to-day teaching of students. Traditionally, principals have had very little control over what happens in the classrooms that he or she supervises. Yet the classroom, and teaching and learning, is the center of the educational endeavor. The irony is that the principal as instructional leader actually has limited opportunities to engage in the core work of the school, teaching. (See Wolcott's *The Man in the Principal's Office* [1973] for a classic study of the principalship and the dilemmas inherent in the position). Thus, the principal is in charge of supervising teachers, while only indirectly involved with teaching and learning. Principals may devise ways to appear to be in touch with classroom practice as they move further and further away from teaching. They teach classes, keep up on current practices in the literature, engage in coaching teachers, arrange for in-service opportunities, and so on. However, the fact remains that the administrator is defined in the bureaucratic system as someone who is expected to administer, not teach. "You get paid to do the administering," is a common refrain. And schools, in line with their management practices, have tended to be "egg crated" into separate classes, grade levels, tracks, and departments (Page 1990).

Traditional professionalism in education has thus led to a separation of roles and responsibilities, which adds to the fragmentation of interests, purposes, and loyalties. Ayers (1992, 15) argues that teachers become "cogs in a machine," unable to be creative or to take initiative.

Goodlad (1984) notes that schools are remarkably standardized, bound by bureaucratic limits. And Harrington and Cookson (1992, 177) argue that teachers must teach in "spite of the educational bureaucracy." Bureaucracy was supposed to facilitate efficiency when it was introduced by Ellwood Cubberly and the new administrative progressives at the turn of the century. The "lure of science" and rationality—scientific expertise coupled with notions of business—was intended to provide the structural organization for efficient and modern education (Tyack and Hansot 1982, 118–120). Scientific management, rationality, and bureaucracy became the model for educational administration which remains in place to this day (Foster 1986; Greenfield 1986).

However, bureaucracy has become a barrier to change and dynamic schooling. Administrators, for all the talk of "instructional leadership," are not fully involved in teaching, and teachers are not fully involved in administrative decisions (on resource allocation, finance, supervision, policy, and school-community relations) despite all the rhetoric and some practice in school-based management. As Linda Darling-Hammond (1988, 65) puts it, "practitioners operate autonomously." Having been educated in a system that emphasizes individualism and competitiveness, teachers and administrators carve out their separate areas of responsibility and continue to operate individually. Even with dedicated administrators who are working with the best intentions on behalf of students, "the bureaucracy as an educational enterprise appears to acquire a purpose all its own" (Prasch 1984, in Ogletree and Schmidt 1989). School professionals have had little training or experience in an organizational model that is not specialized, hierarchical, and segmented. As one teacher noted concerning collaboration: "We're supposed to be site-based but we don't know how to do that yet [work collaboratively with administrators and parents]. Teachers are not fully involved in decision making, let alone parents."

An administrator, in a planning meeting for a leadership academy sponsored by the university, argued, "If you make it applicable to teachers, then not so many administrators will come." Bureaucracy has led to a separation of interests and a culture of exclusion within the education profession. In what follows we will examine how parents are defined and excluded by the bureaucratic system.

DISTANCING OF HOME AND SCHOOL

Parents can feel threatened by the authority of the school and not see it as a responsive institution. Even in Robertson School District, where teachers and administrators believe they are being inclusive the school is somewhat distant from the home. Parents argue that teachers rarely know the students in contexts other than the school. Teachers thus have limited knowledge of many of the children they teach and of their home backgrounds:

> I don't think teachers feel any more that they have a customer response, you know, your son is doing really lousy and so I'm calling you up and maybe we can do something about it. I just feel a tremendous distance. There is no external entrance to the system except through the PTA and the Athletic Club. I don't want to use Gerry [the superintendent] as a whipping boy, but it's kind of like a "circle the wagons" kind of mentality. You know, if parents really get up in arms they might take over the system. I do believe in local public education, but our children are entrusted with these people and if they're not doing what I want, where do I go for recourse? There is no such thing. The thing that disturbs me more than anything is lack of attention to parents. Everybody is talking though, the key words are "parent, parent, parent"; and when you finally get down to it, you aren't involved in this at all. It's impossible. An example of what happens in the system: Dennis is a very bright kid, and he told us he was bored, and we said, "Why don't you talk to your teacher about doing something extra?" Well, they put him out in the hall to read whatever he wanted to. My kids are very bright and wanted something extra, and that's how they handled it. We were told nothing. It's an example of what happens in the system. All our kids are very bright. Clare is talented and musical, Myra is taking music and I'm sure Kathleen will; Larry and Dennis are computer fanatics. Larry also loves astronomy. But all the things that they want to do in school they never have been able to do in school. And while the words are there, and they're all very nice, our needs for our children are not being met and we have no recourse. (Interview, parent)

In effect, a situation can arise whereby schools and parents are operating in separate spheres of influence, and are not collaborating in a meaningful educational experience for children.

When volunteers—typically women—are used by the school, a common complaint is that they are taken for granted. Parents feel that the school demands too much of them (when they are already overburdened), and that they are not properly appreciated for the work they do:

> Last year the principal used to call me at the last minute and say I need four volunteers tomorrow. It kind of irritated me because it was almost a demand. It was almost, well, "Your time is not that valuable and I know there's a bunch of women out there who don't have anything to do." Well that's wrong. You have to show volunteers that their time is valuable and that you appreciate the time that they're giving. I think that supervisors of volunteers really need to be trained. I just don't think that you can tell a volunteer often enough how grateful you are for what they're doing for you. (Interview, parent)

And, as Van Galen (1987, 82) found, it is the working parents who are poor—and those needing child-care—who are not appreciated for their work by the school. Parents serving as volunteers are expected to commit themselves to consistent schedules and regular availability. Parents who can volunteer only occasionally, or for limited times, say they are not recognized in the end-of-year recognition awards. Only "good" parents (*i.e.*, those with considerable resources such as time and money) seem to feel appreciated.

Many parents perceive the school as an institution with bureaucratic procedures, and one that is not a place they want to be. The institutional nature of schools, with crowds of students, routines, rules, and an involuntary population, led Philip Jackson (1968) to liken schools to jails. Parents in this study did not use such a harsh metaphor in their descriptions, but they did argue that the idea of spending time at the school is not a particularly inviting one. As one high school parent put it, "Why would I want to be at school with my children? They wouldn't want me there and I wouldn't want to be there. Have you been up there for any length of time? It's a zoo." Willard Waller (1932) observed half a century ago that parents' recollection of their own school days may be enough to instill a dislike and avoidance of school: "It would require some generations of sensible and friendly teaching to remove the stigma from the occupation." Schools are often seen as intimidating places with their own unwritten rules, practices, and jargon.

An outcome is that many parents feel tentative about getting involved in school, not wanting to intrude on teachers' territory. A fear expressed is that if a parent is outspoken on issues or intrudes on a teacher's "turf," reprisals will occur: "Teachers will take it out on the child. I have seen it happen. If you want to make waves you think about it long and hard. Is it worth possibly causing problems for your child?" (Interview, parent).

CENTER AND PERIPHERY

Participation of parents in school and in parent groups (both formal and informal) is characterized by the invisibility of some parents (the periphery) and the centrality of a few (the center). Many parents do not feel included in the school, nor are they welcome in the parent groups. Parent groups that do exist do not always represent the larger parent body, nor are they perceived as open to everyone. Exclusionary practices are resented by some parents. Both formal (*e.g.*, PTA, Athletics Club) or informal (*e.g.*, the coffee klatch) groups can be elite:

> I felt excluded [from PTA] because this group of parents were involved and kind of assumed they knew everything. They didn't seem to be used to having new parents come in. It was the Old Guard that always worked on school activities. Some of these groups are pretty insular within themselves (Interview, parent)

Parents who are alienated from the parent groups feel powerless to participate in school activities and powerless to influence school policy or practices.

Parents also argue that there is teacher resistance to parent involvement, or at least a lack of respect for parents' important roles in the educative process: "At the high school frankly the teachers do not seem to appreciate the parents or want them around. Or they don't show they do. I think it's important that parents are appreciated and that people know that." (Interview, parent)

In Robertson School District, and in many school districts, formal participation of parents in many schools is limited to four main sources: PTAs (Parent Teacher Associations) or PTSAs (Parent-Teacher-Student

Associations); parent clubs (*e.g.*, athletics) or volunteer activities with limited decision making powers; school board or site-council participation (which is often limited to a narrowly selected elite); and parent-teacher conferences and/or consultations with the school principal—possibly when the child violates school rules.

In this regard, the handbook of Robertson High School refers to parents on only five accounts—four of them in relation to school rules, the other for parent conferences:

1. Parent conferences—"whenever possible appointments should be made ahead of time" (8)
2. Parents will be informed after the fourth unexcused absence from school—unless parents request an automatic telephone call the day after any absence from school (13–14)
3. Accusations of parents regarding students' substance abuse must be confirmed through investigation prior to disciplinary action (15)
4. Parents shall be notified in writing of all discipline which results in limitations on co-curricular activities such as athletics (18)
5. Parents (along with students) have the responsibility for dress and physical appearance (28).

Moreover, the Robertson School District organization chart illustrates the importance of the school board and site-based councils, but fails to include any reference to the general parent body.

Even those parents at the center of school life, namely the school board and site-based councils, may be managed in a bureaucratic way. A traditional administrative approach to complying with state law on site-councils is to carve off separate areas of responsibility for the site-council and the school board, while retaining professional administrative control. In this view:

> The key to avoid problems [in board-superintendent relations] is to develop a clear understanding of board and administrator roles . . . conduct board workshops and new board member workshops focusing on the organizational rationale for carefully defining and separating roles. The emphasis here is on a smartly designed management scheme. (Streshly and Frase 1992, 12)

A superintendent coming from this position argues, "our only hope is for bureaucratic leadership," and he uses the example of a school district that had clearly differentiated roles as a model for retaining administrative control. He believes that site-based councils should be responsible for program delivery, while the school board makes policy decisions with the leadership of the superintendent. In other words, the site-council's function is limited to instruction. Site-based councils are not able, for instance, to hire and fire the principal. The site-councils are aptly named "learning improvement teams," thus clearly differentiating their focus on learning from the school board's control over policy. The principal is seen as key in managing the site-councils by bringing together the "vision, research, resources, and support for meaningful site-based decision making." In the superintendent's words: "Tell them *your* vision. The parents haven't thought them through. Then they'll see you know what you're doing. It can be maneuvered." Similarly, teachers are involved in instructional issues, not administrative issues. Instructional issues are seen as non-threatening for teachers to be engaged in, from an administrative point of view.

In a competitive, bureaucratic system, even current reforms for collaborative, participatory decision making can thus be translated into competitive "turf wars," with each unit competing for access to the important decisions and the power (*i.e.*, the center). Thus, site-councils can end up competing with school boards. For instance, in Chicago, local school councils were required to meet in a public place where their meetings could be observed by the public, but "custodians refused to open school buildings at night without overtime pay, and the board refused to fund that cost" (Hess and Easton 1992, 160). Local site-councils had to scramble to find places to meet, and the situation was eventually resolved by negotiating with the engineers' union, not by the school board accommodating the request. Moore (1992, 148) calls for a decrease in the authority of central administration and the school board in order to allow for increased decision making by site-based councils. In Chicago, the school board is now responsible for centralized services (*e.g.*, transport and school construction) with each school taking on its own responsibility for day-to-day school operations and decision making. Also, in Chicago, site-councils and administrators have negotiated to define their separate roles and responsibilities. Site-councils select their principal, adopt a school improvement plan, adopt a budget, and advise the principal and staff on curricular, textbook, disciplinary, and attendance matters. Principals in turn, hire their own staffs and have authority to carry out day-to-day school management (Moore 1992, 147).

One of the fears of administrators, which contributes to preserving the tradition of carefully segmented roles and responsibilities and to keeping parents at the periphery, is that too much information given to parents and the community may make school operations unworkable. An administrator argues, "Parents will hold us hostage over choice, books in the library, and so on." The question is also asked, "What if a parent wants to see the most recent evaluations of all fourth grade teachers in order to place his/her student with the best teacher?" A recent case out of Seattle (Brown vs. Seattle School District) confirmed that evaluation and application records on teachers are not a matter of public record, and therefore are not available to parents. (On the other hand, records on teachers of misconduct and reprimands are available public information under the Cowles case) (AWSP 1994, 2). The assumption is that parents, if they have access to "center" knowledge, may use confidential information for their own interests and purposes, which may not be in the interests of the school—hence the restriction on teacher evaluations.

School board members and PTA presidents (representing parents) are also seen as needing to be managed by the school:

> One superintendent periodically reminds his staff that they should deal with board members as they do with their PTA presidents. In other words, treat them as special, influential, and very interested members of the community. But, just as an administrator would not allow the PTA president to rifle through the [students'] cumulative files, they must not allow individual board members to violate student privacy and record laws. (Streshly and Frase 1992, 6–7)

Thus, even parents with access to the administration, those in the center, are frequently viewed as different from administrators, and somehow as less disinterested than educators. The irony, to my mind, is that superintendents, administrators, and teachers are often also parents in the same school or school district, yet they are presumed to be able to set aside their personal interests from their professional ones.

GENDERED PARENT-SCHOOL RELATIONS

Given that the highest levels of leadership in public schools are most often held by men, and that men currently enjoy a high level of public visibility and credibility in our society, it follows that parent-school relations would also be gendered. Research has shown that "upper-middle class mothers are the most intensely involved in their children's schooling; working-class fathers are the least so" (Lareau 1989, 84). Women's greater participation in schools is a long-standing convention (see Lightfoot 1978). In this study, men and women also participated unequally in their children's education. Mothers more than fathers assumed primary responsibility for attending to both schoolwork and homework:

> It tends to be predominantly mothers who are involved (Interview, teacher).

> Ninety-five percent of the parents who come in and do the work are women. We do have a few fathers who are also willing to do that. (Interview, teacher)

> The majority of the work done at school is done by the women. But of course the men do things like for the plays; they make the structure, wood structures if they're asked. (Interview, parent)

> Dads usually do the big stuff, the large projects like building the bird cages, and women help with the homework and make sure everything is taken care of for the children. And of course we fund raise and bake cookies (laughs). (Interview, parent)

> Part of the tradition is that women volunteer. Men's time is more valuable (laughs). Although I must say that at the Athletic Club we have a lot of men who volunteer, and that's acceptable because it's athletics. They can go out and move the chains on the football field and it's sports related. (Interview, parent)

> I've always signed up for PTA and we try to attend the carnivals and the spaghetti feeds, and I go to all the parent conferences as the parent. Bill [husband] doesn't care to go to these things. It's still considered that the woman will be involved with whatever the kids are, and take care of all that. I think that it's just not high on his priority. So, I get involved with all those little functions with the kids. I've gotten involved a couple of times on assisting with field trips, just so I could be part of knowing some of the other parents, because I'm not really able to go to the classroom during the day and take part in that. So every once in a while I've taken off from work in the afternoon and gone on a field trip. But their dad has

come to Kathy's class when they have a musical thing, a skit, because I've never learned to run the camcorder. So he has to do that. He has to come. We've fooled him a couple of times. (Interview, parent)

I go to all the teacher conferences and my husband has never gone. He's never been involved. Of course, I think that's another one of these generation things and being brought up to believe a certain way. It's still considered the mother also who will handle the children in all aspects, let alone buying their clothes and making sure they're ready to go to school and any school functions that come up. We've never had any tall, mounting discussions, it's just been presumed. So the kids know by now that unless there's something absolutely specific at the school that asks only for their father to attend, they'll come to me first because they've just gotten used to the fact. I think that's the way he was raised and I think it still goes on to some point that men are supposed to do this, and women are supposed to do that, even though they've been trying to do a transition as women. It's easier to just do it than to fight about it. Just get it done. (Interview, parent)

My wife, Janet, is more willing to give of her time in supervising the boys' homework. She always has. I guess what bothers me is some of the old archaic things that schools do. Kids come home and they spend half the night copying the problem down, and then adding up the numbers, then half the time if not more, to copy the problem down. I resent that as a parent, when I see my kids doing that. I want them to come home and have a life like we do. Janet has always been more patient with all that and the schooling side of things. I have provided my expertise on the school district facilities, visioning and planning, and the economic support. (Interview, parent)

Mary Catherine Bateson told a wonderful story at the University of Virginia a few years ago. She described gender relations in a traditional tribe this way: The men sit around most of the time, and then when they do go out hunting, they come back with something spectacular, a giant eland or the like. The women, on the other hand, perform the work that sustains the people on a daily basis. They gather and provide 90 percent of the tribe's nutrition, but it is daily work that requires patience and maintenance, rather than a spectacular show. I am reminded of this in looking at patterns of gendered involvement in the Robertson schools. The women do the day-to-day work with the children, the work that goes unnoticed, but is vital to the children's well-being. In most of the families, including upper-middle class families, parent involvement in schooling is seen as women's work. Women are typically seen as having the patience, time, and inclination to undertake the task of monitoring children's progress, supervising homework (even if it is copying material down in an "archaic" way), and establishing and maintaining a relationship with the school. The men, on the other hand, pride themselves on their greater "expertise" and economic support (and men in this society do earn more than women, whether or not they are more productive or contribute more). Men's contribution is more spectacular in the sense of being visible and showy, whether it's athletics (which is sacred in the public schools), or making a building structure. Men see themselves as giving of their work-related expertise or economic support.

The historical tradition that working with children is women's work—frequently unpaid or lower-paid labor—has been largely continued. Teaching, itself, has been defined as women's work, although it is ironic that the very core work of schools, teaching, is also the least rewarded, with the position most removed from the classroom, the superintendency, the most prestigious position in U.S. public school systems. In 1905 there were no women superintendents; women made up 0.1 percent of superintendents nationally by 1972–73 (Tyack and Hansot 1982, 183), and nationwide today somewhere between 5.0 percent (Shakeshaft 1993, 86) and 6.7 percent (Sharratt and Derrington 1993) of superintendent positions are filled by women. Classroom teaching shows a different picture, with nearly "sixty-nine percent of teachers, women (85 percent of elementary, 53 percent of middle/junior high school, and 44 percent of secondary)," but the supervision and management of the women teachers undertaken by men (75.2 percent of administrators at all levels are men) (Shakeshaft 1993, 86). As one moves up the hierarchy, male dominance is even more apparent: nationwide 95 percent of superintendents are men, 88 percent of secondary principals are men, and 66 percent of elementary principals are men (Jones and Montenegro 1990, in Shakeshaft 1993, 86).

The demographic portrait of school administrators is thus one of upper-middle class males, primarily white, "who are out of touch with the academic needs of minority and/or lower social class youth" (Scheurich and Imber 1991, in Capper 1993, 57). The emphasis on administration and leadership as a science, with an upper-middle class norm to undergird school practice, rules and behavior (Parker and Shapiro 1993, 45) is not meeting the needs of many of the students. I would also add that the hidden curriculum of this organizational arrangement of white, male dominance in school leadership is that boys and girls and minority students are learning first-hand about inequitable life chances. For instance, students see their mothers doing the necessary but mundane and largely invisible work for schools, and they see teachers who are largely women being managed by principals and superintendents who are largely men. Schooling is thus, like the broader society, a gendered phenomenon.

With women given responsibility for education, they are also blamed when children do not do well in school. Rockhill (1987b) found that mothers are often *blamed* for their own inadequate education and for that of their children. Mothers, not fathers, are held accountable for the child's behavior in school (Van Galen 1987, 85). Moreover, women's lives as parents are becoming increasingly complex. Part of a woman's responsibility to the family today is as a wage-earner in paid labor, whether the woman is single or married. The new responsibilities for educating children and involvement in schooling are added onto women's responsibility for career advancement. Women must overcome barriers and prejudice in the workplace and in society, while forging new family structures and opportunities. Those mothers in Robertson School District who are students at the university, or are in the workforce, are seeking to provide for themselves and their children, and have found that the schools' agendas for parent involvement are not always responsive to their needs. For instance, child-care is not provided in all schools to allow low-income parents to attend parent-teacher conferences, or to volunteer in classrooms.

A STRONG AUTHORITY SYSTEM

Schools have organized a rather rigid authority system, which means that flexibility, change, and responsiveness are difficult to achieve. For educators, the bureaucracy of schools means that at the school level, educators' hands are often tied by the very structures and processes that were instituted for educational purposes. Curricular changes become a "lengthy process," and ways and means are sought to side-step the bureaucracy of schools. A principal in Robertson School District strategizes, "If we include Spanish instruction on our SLIGs [Student Learning Improvement Grants] through a partnership with the university's bilingual progam, we can make curricular changes without going through the whole system. So this allows us to do two things that we need to be doing: freeing up time for teacher collaboration during Spanish instruction, and also the language instruction for the students." Similarly, in Chicago a principal noted that school site-council decision making enhanced teaching and learning because she could sidestep some of the bureaucracy and "get things done more quickly because she did not need approval from various layers of the bureaucracy" (Hess and Easton 1992, 164).

Lack of responsiveness on the part of the school, stemming from a bureaucratic organization, is also a source of frustration to parents who do not always see decisions made in the child's best interests: "There's a great deal of dissatisfaction with the academic programs and with individual teachers but there's no action being taken. I know there are processes that have to be gone through, but nothing is being done." (Interview, high school parent)

When parents have a problem or complaint they must go through bureaucratic channels rather than receiving immediate responsiveness. Administrators, even when they agree with parents on a problem, such as the need to remove incompetent teachers, feel constrained by the difficulties involved in remedying the problem. Leadership has been defined in the bureaucratic system as non-collaborative:

> Gay Sanders is a particularly involved parent at Robertson High School. She wants to know how her kids are doing and does not believe that something as important as her kids' future should be left in the hands of professional educators. Unfortunately, Gay's interactional style is somewhat abrupt and she has a reputation as a pushy parent. Gay strongly criticizes the administration, for she perceives them to be blocking her participation, and she calls them "arrogant." What Gay perceives as an "arrogant administration" is, from the administrators' perspective, an administration that believes in "professional" rather than "lay" leadership. Listening to parents is the principal's main concession to their rights, but he

feels strongly that he has been given a mandate to lead—and anything less than strong and decisive leadership would be considered weak and ineffectual from his own, and from the parents'
perspective. Listening to parents works, to a degree, for parents
keep hoping that one day there will be some action and their voiced
needs and demands will be met. The mere act of providing a space
for parents to voice concerns works well in maintaining the status
quo and achieving an equilibrium in the balance of power. The
superintendent quietly reinforces a pattern of parental expression
yet professional decision making at the annual stakeholders meetings, where people are encouraged to voice concerns that will be
considered by the board and the superintendent. Superintendent
Carroll and the principals in Robertson School District are being
forced by shifting mores regarding parent involvement, including
state legislation, to review and reposition themselves as people
who are open to shared power and decision making, but they are
approaching it cautiously and using traditional administrative state-
gies. (Field notes)

In a traditional bureaucratic administrative approach the administrator exercises leadership, by which is meant power. For example,
one superintendent urges administrators to employ two kinds of power
in their leadership, expert power and referent power. Expert power is
explained as "based on the leader's possession of expertise, skill and
knowledge which, through respect, influences others . . . This respect
leads to *compliance with the leader's wishes*." Referent power is "based
on the leader's personal traits. A leader high in referent power is generally liked and admired by others because of personality. This liking
for, admiration for, and identification with the leader influences others"
(Simpson 1994b). In this view, compliance is seen as being achieved
through expertise and personal charisma. The superintendent explains
that "the community people we're working with understand this." Such
an approach is seen to work in the control and management of community people. In this view, the superintendent maneuvers to control
teachers, staff, parents, business, community, and student input into
education.

Another traditional and bureaucratic administrative strategy is to
"let the criteria make the decision" (Talmage 1994). Using this
approach, the administrator removes him/herself from responsibility by

devising criteria that make it look like an objective, fair, rational decision beyond reproach, instead of a personal and value-laden decision. This is part of the bureaucracy of schools. Most decisions are made by real people with real interests and purposes, but it is seen as necessary to avoid dialogue with parents and community on what those interests and puposes are. Devising so-called impartial criteria and then "letting the criteria make the decision," is a way to minimize conflict and exercise "leadership," but such an approach does not allow for decisions to be informed by collective voices and interests and concerns. Of course, not all administrators engage in engineering control of their constituents' voices, but it does happen, and is the antithesis of participatory leadership.

Also, in the traditional bureaucratic authority system of the school the superintendent has control over strategic planning (long-range facilities management, fiscal planning, and visioning), while the teachers have control over executing the superintendent's wishes and putting his or her ideas into practice (operational planning) (Simpson 1994). Teachers, principals, parents, community people, students, and the superintendent do not collaborate or work together on the ideas and practices of the school district. The irony is that traditional school administrators see themselves as heads of corporations operating in a top-down manner, even while instituting site-councils and shared decision making, yet many of the corporations themselves are no longer operating in such a bureaucratic manner. Boeing Corporation, for instance, is involving its employees and directors in collaborative teamwork.[1] To be fair, the superintendent may want to engage in more participatory leadership, but may be constrained by past practices, expectations of proper superintendent behaviors, and the way a school district is traditionally run. In addition, key players—influential people in the school district—help socialize the superintendent into the role, acting as "advisor."

POWER STRUGGLES BETWEEN PARENTS AND EDUCATORS

In Robertson School District, parents may once have been happy to leave decision making to professional educators and to be relegated to fund-raising. But today, parent groups such as the Athletic Club are beginning to demand greater input. Further conflict and competition is imminent between the administration and the parent group, particularly the upper-middle class influential members, as they negotiate to have their needs met:

> If we're going to donate eighteen thousand dollars to the school district then we want to know where it's going and we want to have a say. I don't think the school district is going to like anyone else involved in the budget process, but after all they are a public organization. Even if it weren't money given by the athletics parent club it's tax money, and so they are accountable to parents. There seems to be an arrogance in the administration that "this is none of your business." This is what we are dealing with, but the Athletic Club members have begun to feel themselves. People among the administration and coaches did not want to have a parent club because then they don't quite have the control that they had. I think they have good reason to be concerned (laughs) because people are about to challenge them. The parent club is going to demand to have a member to come and observe the budget process. We never have had a community member doing that before. (Interview, high school parent)

Parents begin to feel empowered (able to "challenge" and "demand") when they have resources with which to negotiate, and when they are working together around a common cause.

When parents are upset with the schools, typically a great deal of talk occurs and people may organize politically to strengthen their voice through numbers—sometimes forming a voting block against educators. As an example of political action by parents, when parent support is needed by the school district (*e.g.*, to pass a bond or levy), resistance can be high:

> Parents and the community are basically ignored by an arrogant administration. The rejection of the bond and levy the past two years is evidence of the failure of the administration to involve and listen to the community. There was an arrogance there that they could do whatever they wanted to. So they didn't think they really had to be responsive to the community. They just put in what they wanted. When it went down the first time they thought this is just an aberration and when it went down the second time they really stood up and took notice. It's the arrogance that's been

challenged. They finally began to involve the community and it passed this year finally because they did things a little differently (Interview, parent)

The bond is clearly a political issue. Parents felt ignored and negotiated by using an obvious yet overlooked political tool, their voting power.

Furthermore, informal meetings have proven to be an effective strategy, used by an influential group of parents to work politically to strengthen their position:

> There's a coffee klatch that meets downtown every morning, folks who own local businesses and key parents and they all talk about what's going on and the budget process and the school. People are very upset right now about the whole situation. Sam Phillips [parent] told me that he had approached the athletic director about the decision to send five kids on the cross country team to state [competition]. Sam said to the athletic director "I heard at coffee this morning that you were only going to send five. Why aren't you sending seven?" And the athletic director got very upset and he said "Well if your coffee klatch thinks that they can do my job better than I can then you can take over." And Sam said he lost his chance there because they are ready to take over (laughs). (Interview, parent)

Administrators and teachers feel vulnerable to both individual and collective parental disapproval. Parents are not unaware of the power they hold to influence school decisions. As one parent put it:

> What I will do if expectations don't rise is go and talk to people who are responsible for the curriculum, and I can't imagine that one person's voice is going to have much impact, and so you get a lobby out there. You get a group of people together and lobby to change the curriculum. (Interview, parent)

The media can also be used by parents as a lever for change, and in Robertson School District the local newspaper became a forum for both signed and unsigned "concerned parent" letters complaining about specific educational issues:

> If I'm really unhappy I would go public. First, I try to go through the proper channels, to the teacher concerned or the principal, then

to the school board members and the superintendent. But if that doesn't work I will use the media to have my voice heard. (Interview, parent)

Taking the complaint up the hierarchy can be a lengthy process, but if an unhappy parent starts at the top, and does not go through the proper channels, the teachers and administrators can be resentful. A pattern of defensiveness, competitiveness, and opposing interests can be established between parents and the school. The superintendent believes it is "teachers who are resistant to parent involvement"; teachers are frustrated with an administration that places more expectations for parent involvement on teachers than they feel they can reasonably manage without additional support; parents themselves blame a complex school system made up of athletic directors, superintendents, principals, and teachers. It is important to remember also that Superintendent Carroll is in a vulnerable position, able to be fired at the will of the school board—hence, his Achilles' heel is that for all his educational expertise and professional identity, he is nevertheless at the mercy of parents. Further, the superintendent feels pressure from the legislators who mandate school reform, "some people in Evergreen [the superintendency of public instruction] think it [shared decision-making] will just happen," but do not provide assistance with implementation. The outcome is thus one of more bureaucratic policies and practices, a "bunker mentality," interests divided between parents and schools, and acts of resistance on the part of parents.

CONCLUSION

Public schools are organized for "scientific management" with a separation of roles and responsibilities and specialized functions. Parents are defined and constrained by a bureaucratic system in a variety of ways that are not conducive to parent-school collaboration, including the following: (a) distancing of home and school, with separate and overlapping—not collaborative—spheres of influence; (b) center and periphery, the centrality of a few parents and the invisibility of the majority; (c) gendered parent-school relations, with women largely responsible for family educational concerns; (d) a strong authority system that can inhibit change or responsiveness; and (e) power struggles between parents and educators.

An openness on the part of educators to multiple perspectives and a commitment to meaningful communication would bring to the planning process more egalitarian—and I believe more productive—decision making. Top-down, bureaucratic decisions may appear to be more efficient, but the shortest way is not necessarily the most educationally sound. The intimate knowledge mothers and fathers gain in the course of rearing their children is valuable knowledge that is often neither respected nor utilized in the school setting. Professional educators have to be willing not to hide behind bureaucratic norms and a traditional "professional" cloak that distances them from families. We need to view the teacher as a professional who is enhanced by his/her community.

Another aspect of the professional context of the school is the changing level of specialization as children progress through the school system. Parent-school relations are very different at the elementary than at the middle or high school levels. The next chapter examines these differences, and the implications for more collaborative organizational structures. The chapter also focuses on the differential treatment of children and families from diverse backgrounds. Those children who do well in school typically come from homes where the concept of education and the school in which the child is enrolled is respected and valued. Students who do less well in school often participate daily in two quite separate worlds—compulsory schooling and the family. Educators have yet to find ways to understand the alienation of many parents from school and to establish relationships based on parents' and childrens' needs.

NOTE

1. The extent to which real collaboration is occurring is beyond the bounds of this study, but it would be a useful study for an educator to go to corporations and study through qualitative methods and extended fieldwork the leadership of corporations in changing times.

5

The Cultures of Schools and Homes

They don't really want people involved
other than a few hand-chosen old families,
people who think the way they do. There
are absolutely no foreign parents there.
They are invisible. It would be nice if the
schools were open to asking Mr. Abdul,
for instance, what they do for math
instruction in the home country and really
listen to what he has to say. There's not
really an openness to new ideas. (Interview, parent)

Typically, parents enter the contested
public sphere of public education with
neither resources nor power. They are
usually unwelcomed by schools to the
critical task of interrupting the educational
establishment and, typically represent a
small percentage of local taxpayers. (Fine
1993, 5)

Consistent with a system that characterizes teachers and administrators, parents and educators, as separate in their roles and responsibilities,
part of the organizational pattern of public schools is for increased levels of specialization and fragmentation as children advance through the
grades. It is helpful to further examine these structural arrangements, for
they powerfully impact interactions between parents and educators and
define the parameters of any possible collaboration.

SCHOOL LEVELS AND SPECIALIZATION

Horace Mann, Fairfield, and Riverview Elementary Schools

The elementary school classrooms are characterized by intensive frequency and duration of contact between students and teacher, particularly in kindergarten and grade one. In the classroom, teachers and students achieve a level of intimacy and emotional attachment rarely found at other levels of schooling. The elementary classroom becomes a personalized, *gemeinschaft* community (Treiman 1994). Parents participate more in school during the younger grades. In particular, it is mothers who are involved in school, more so when the child is young and when the child is male, a finding backed by other research (See Epstein 1987; Stevenson and Baker 1987).

In pre-school, kindergarten, and the first grades, parents say they feel welcomed by the school and able to participate more fully than at later stages:

> There are just so many things they need help with, just an extra pair of hands, whether it's for the Halloween party or putting together materials or helping out as an extra adult on a field trip. You're always welcome. (Interview, parent)

> In elementary school they're still your babies. There's still that close attachment, and you still have a high level of responsibility in raising them and loving them and nurturing them. And OK they don't have that level of independence yet. So you're almost kind of forced to be involved in the school. You should be there. (Interview, parent)

At the elementary school, there is much more reciprocity between home and school, and closer contact between teachers and parents, with parents more often dropping children off at school and picking them up in the afternoon. Parents are visible and physically present on a regular basis. However, even at the kindergarten level I saw teachers beginning to separate children from the family, believing that children will never grow up if the parents keep "babying" their children.

From about third grade on, the teachers' attitude seems to be "this is my class and these are my expectations":

> I tell them what my aims are for the children, what I want them to learn, what the objectives are, why I'm teaching something. So, just talking with parents and just letting them know those specific things is helpful, so that they can be supportive. (Interview, teacher)

In the present study, fourth and fifth grade students led conferences with parents, and then students wrote reflections on the conference. However, at this stage, fewer parents showed up for conferences, and parents explained that they had done all these activities before. Also, some of the distancing of parents from schools as the child gets older seems to come from the child. Students typically seek more independence from parents as they mature. Children want to have less to do with the parents and may be embarrassed by parents "hanging around" the school. Parents' inadequacies in being able to assist their children in school work may also become evident as children advance in the grades, and some parents may become less keen to be involved with schoolwork in general. In addition, by this time the schools have sorted students out into those who do school well and those who do not, and for those students labelled as less competent, their parents may give up at this point, having already given a great deal of time and energy that does not seem to be rewarded. During the early years, especially in kindergarten, parents seem to think anything is possible, and they may hold high aspirations for their children. Parents of young children are optimistic that their children will do well in school, and over the years as they realize their child may not be as successful as they had hoped, they may have less desire to be involved with school and school-related work. Parents can "burn out," and the novelty of helping out at school may diminish as the child gets older.

Reasons given by parents and teachers in this study for reciprocity between home and school at the early elementary level included: (a) teaching in the early grades is like parenting and therefore the lines separating parents and educators are not so clearly drawn; (b) parents often physically bring children to school and visibility leads to communication; (c) parents have a belief in their children, and have not yet been disillusioned by school "failure" labelling; parents still think their children can be successful. Another reason, not given by parents and teachers, but evident to me is: (d) the organization of schools at the elementary level allows for parents to be involved with their children's education.

At the elementary school the very organization of schooling facilitates a home-school liaison:

- Typically, elementary schools employ one teacher with a class of students, allowing for an extended relationship between one class and its teacher—compared to high school where many more teachers are involved and contact is fragmented.
- The elementary school embodies a more holistic and child-centered sense of education, and parents are a part of that child-centeredness.
- The elementary school has multiple opportunities for parents to do something tangible, for example "making materials, helping to put the activities together, the physical assistance, whereas in middle school they don't do all the charts and the bulletin boards and the kidsy activities" (Interview, teacher).
- The elementary school has more informal opportunities for parents to be involved with school, not just the traditional "open house."

Parents, teachers, and administrators repeatedly expressed the view that parent involvement occurs best at the elementary level, and decreases as the child moves up through the grades. At all the elementary schools I found strong parent-school connections, although framed in a traditional sense of involvement, with the school professionals controlling and responsible for education, assisted by parents. Site-based councils were beginning to challenge that pattern, although even here, traditional bureaucratic procedures, limited representation of parents, and limitations on the powers of site-councils kept parents in a traditional, supportive role.

Park Middle School

During adolescence, conflict with parents is likely to increase (Cauce *et al.* 1990) and educators may play a critical supportive role for students. Young people who are beginning to move towards autonomy and independence and toward forming their own values and identity need adult role models alternative to their own parents. Teachers and administrators are seen as able to nurture adolescents and as able to provide the disinterested care that is needed.

Yet even with the supposedly child-centered ethos of middle school education, parents may be noticeably absent from the school. At Park Middle School the lack of parents in the school is explained in the following way:

> For one thing, it is a time when youngsters don't want to see their parents at school. It's an embarrassment or they feel like they're being babied. For instance, when my son was in the eighth grade I was offered a job here, and he had such negative feelings about my working here that I didn't even take the job. (Interview, teacher)

The isolation of the middle school from parents and the community is also noted in the literature. From the upper elementary years on, parent participation diminishes and is almost nonexistent in middle level schools (Carnegie Task Force 1989; Epstein 1986).[1]

However, middle schoolers still need parental support and attention, particularly if the home culture is different from the school. One of the problems with the current isolation of the school is that middle schoolers could benefit greatly from parental support, despite their quest for autonomy and independence:

> Deep down the kids do want their parents to show an interest, it just has to be more subtle. (Interview, parent)

> In the elementary school the children tell you everything that's going on and they like you being involved. Now my children have always liked me being involved even at the middle school level. Some teenagers don't like their parents to be around. I think though that it's just a perception, and once their parents do get involved they realize it's nice and they like having them there, but a lot of parents stop being involved because of that. They say "Oh Mom, I don't want you around any more," and so parents don't push it any more. I think that's a big mistake. (Interview, parent)

Robertson High School

> *Question:* "How best can parents help?"
> *Answer:* "By not being here." (Teacher)

> The best parents know what's going on at school, but are not actually floating around the place. The kids don't want that. They provide a place and a structured time for homework. They turn up at sports or music or Back-to-School Night to show that what the kid is doing is important. One mother here at the high school is involved in every little thing. Wean your kids! She overreacts. He had a rough test and so she calls up. She babies him. (Interview, teacher)

At the high school level parent involvement occurred mainly in the extracurricular activities—athletics, music, plays—not in the classroom. A typical response to the question, how are you involved at the high school, was, "I find high school really hard to know what is going on. I feel very removed from the situation" (Interview, parent). Reasons for this given by parents and teachers included the following:

- Homework gets more difficult at the high school level and parents don't feel qualified to help: "I don't feel comfortable with algebra, and so I shy away from helping my kids" (Interview, parent).
- At the high school level, teachers view themselves as having a discipline- and subject-centered orientation (calculus, biology, composition, etc.). Teachers at the high school tended to see themselves as experts in knowledge, not experts in relating to kids or to their parents. At Robertson High School, teachers were divided on whether high school teachers should even engage in relationship work (as opposed to strictly academic work) with their students. On the one hand, "Life is difficult for kids. If we can help kids develop self-esteem, that's what we need to do" (Interview, teacher). On the other hand, "I'm here to teach physics, to make sure that I meet the needs of the advanced kids, plus the other kids, not to hold hands" (Interview, teacher).
- High schools are typically bigger in size. In smaller settings there are many more opportunities for intimacy. Some high schools in the state in which this study took place are experimenting with school buildings and organizations that faciliate more stable contact between students and teachers. In one school separate "pods" have been designed for the building, so that each pod of around seven hundred students becomes a school within a much larger school, with an aim of allowing a cadre of teachers to get to know students and their families more intimately, and of providing better learning opportunities for students. However, size is not the only influence on more detached relations between home and school at the high school level. Robertson High School has only seven hundred students altogether; one might expect teachers and administrators to be closely connected with families, but that is not the case. Parents and community people do hear gossip and stories about teachers and administrators, and they have some knowledge of what goes on at school from their children. However, by and large parents stay away from the high school except for sporting events: "On an average day there are no parents here" (Interview, teacher).
- By the high school level parents may also be tired of doing the same old thing, particularly if they have already been through several cycles of

school events with older children: "I feel more physically tired. It's real hard to go to those science fairs and things with my youngest one. I just have to push myself and say, "Go!" You know, "Oh God, not one more carnival! No!" (Interview, parent)

- Open House at the high school level is much more formalized, with carefully prepared "scripts" and a managed performance. At Robertson High School typically very few parents even bothered to attend open house.
- Students in high school experience fragmented relationships with a number of different specialized teachers. Some parents see this as the best way to achieve a high level of academic success and do not want this arrangement and the form of instruction to change, while others decry the lack of responsiveness to students:

> It's all lecture and paper. Boring. Lecture and paper. Boring! Make sure you quote me on this. Out of sync, not with the times, not twenty-first century. They just go behind closed doors with each teacher and get more of the same day by day right through high school. (Interview, parent)

Noddings (1988) suggests that this typical high school instructional arrangement could be changed to allow for a meaningful continuity:

> There is no good reason why teachers should not stay with one group of students for three years rather than one in the elementary years, and this arrangement can be adapted to high school as well. A mathematics teacher might, for example, take on a group of students when they enter high school and guide them through their entire mathematics curriculum. . . . Suggestions such as the one above for extended contact—or like Sizer's alternative idea that teachers teach two subjects to 30 students rather than one subject to 60 (Sizer 1984)—are not simplistic . . . we might do well to [also] suggest smaller schools . . . and work toward an educational system proudly oriented toward the development of decent, caring, loved, and loving persons. (pp. 225–226)[2]

One of the barriers to innovative and radical restructuring, such as this, is the bureaucracy of schools and the entrenched practices described earlier. As Noddings notes, we moved to large bureaucratic school systems because the influential Conant report, released in 1959, persuaded those in power that large schools would allow for more sophisticated academic offerings, a move that overlooked students', parents', and teachers' needs for community and connectedness (p. 226).

- The older students may want parents to stay out of the school context for their own personal and social development. While this study focused on parent, teacher, and administrator perspectives, students frequently asked me questions about what I was doing. At Robertson High School, a frequent response to my short answer that I was studying parent involvement in schools was that "my parents used to do all that stuff when we were little." One high school youth recalls: "My Mom came up to school once, I don't know what for, and I was so embarrassed that I went 'Who's that?' I pretended I didn't know her." Teachers concur, "Children and parents need to cut the umbilical cord at some stage." High school students want to be their own persons, without the expectations and demands of parents infringing on their "territory."
- High schools are more competitive and academic in emphasis, with less time devoted to social skills and less innovation in structure or programs: "At the elementary level parents are more willing to try new ideas or programs. They're more flexible. At the high school level they're more concerned that 'my son or daughter is going to Harvard' and 'don't mess with anything.' The stakes are higher. It's more competitive as you move through the grades" (Interview, administrator).

Throughout all these stages of elementary, middle, and high school, part of the motivation for educators controlling and managing parent involvement in school stems from the following concerns:

- Parents are seen as possibly having a narrow self-interested view, whereas the educator sees him/herself as doing what is best for the whole class, school, or school district. For instance, parents may insist on their child having a particular teacher, when the teacher may have other reasons for placing students (*e.g.*, discipline). Parent demands can be seen as a threat to educators' professionalism.
- Teachers and administrators experience anxiety over academic progress. They feel placed in a double bind or a no-win situation where they are criticized if they do not adequately involve parents in their children's education, yet to do so may make it more difficult to teach, since parents have their own agendas and demands that may conflict

with teaching and learning. Teachers, in particular, describe feeling added stress as a result of having parents around: they don't like the "fish-bowl" effect. Administrators were less anxious, for their job is defined in part by the requirement of parent and community relations.

- Teachers and administrators may do things differently if parents are around, just to please them, and this may not be good for the students or the class, as in the matter of discipline. Teachers feel that they may be pressured into making deliberate changes to accommodate the presence of another adult. This may also lead to conflict over goals. Teachers ask, "Am I teaching children, or modeling for parents and giving them what they want in order for them to see me as a good teacher?"

We might do well to ask, however, who is being served by the present bureaucratic organizational structures. Certainly, despite the stability of the public schools and their ongoing support, not all students are being served well. Issues of equity become even more apparent in the analysis of the differential treatment of individual families, and of their varied access to school knowledge and opportunities for success, which is the focus of the next section.

INSTITUTIONAL BARRIERS TO SCHOOL SUCCESS

While the organizational structure of schools is one potential barrier (or alternatively a potential facilitator) to parent-school collaboration, the human side of organizational structures also affects what is possible. By the human side I am referring to school leadership with regard to parent-school relations, and how school personnel perceive and relate to students and their families.

All too often, parents are not seen as equal partners in the educational process even though the family serves as the child's primary educator. Parents are educating children from the moment they are born, and parents continue instilling norms, expectations, and experiences that are not abandoned at the school door. The child brings to school internalized values and a range of influential experiences. Regardless of whether parents actually collaborate with schools, engage in school activities, teach academics, or supervise homework, everything they do prepares a child for the teaching and learning that goes on in the classroom. And the school also intrudes into home life.

The culture of the home has been shown to be of critical importance in preparing children for success or failure in the worlds of school and work. Home and school life are interdependent (Connell *et al.* 1982): the family "does not form a child's character and then deliver it ready-packaged to the doorstep of the school. The family is what its members do, a constantly continuing and changing practice, and as children go to and through school, that practice is reorganized around their schooling" (p. 78).

The school responds to the home context in either positive or negative ways. Cultural discontinuity exists for many children between home and school which plays itself out in helping to establish differential school outcomes (Connell *et al.* 1982; Heath 1983; Ogbu 1974, 1978, 1988). An abundant literature on cultural discontinuity has shown some of the reasons why "minority" children fail in school. The work of Au and Jordan (1981), Heath (1983), Philips (1972) and others have detailed the consequences of educators consciously or unconsiously viewing cultural and linguistic differences as deficits.

Schools support families who most reflect the school's intentions and purposes. Minority parents, for instance, may care deeply about their children's education, but they may stay away from school and traditional parent-school activities, such as PTA, because they feel uncomfortable at school (Comer 1986). The middle class institution of the school clearly has unwritten codes of behavior that may be a subtle barrier to some parents' involvement in school. Simply inviting parent participation, but not examining policies and practices that may be unwelcoming or unsupportive, guarantees that not all parents will participate. For instance, low socioeconomic status (SES) parents are often contacted only when the child violates school rules, leading to parents feeling alienated from the school (Calabrese 1990).

Even if diversity and cultural pluralism is evident in the school, schools can still effectively be alienating places for many students and parents whose cultures are different from the one celebrated in the school. Schools have a literate culture that typically has a white, middle, or upper-middle class perspective (Boykin 1994; Delpit 1988; Heath 1983; Mulhern 1994). Shirley Brice Heath (1983) has shown how working class cultures of both black and white families are at odds with the middle class culture of the school. In the community she studied it was the "townspeople" the middle class . . . whose values and interests were exemplified in the school. Schools reward those students "who demonstrate a knowledge and appreciation of upper-middle and upper class culture" (Parker and Shapiro 1993, 51). Black students may feel that they have to "act white" and upper-middle class in school in order to get ahead (Fordham and Ogbu 1987; Ogbu 1987).[3]

Lareau (1989) also argues that social class is critical in schools—that those parents who are most distanced from schools are working class. Working class families' great respect for the professional expertise of teachers may result in a separation between school and home. Unlike their more privileged counterparts, working class parents grant teachers full professional status: "From their position in the class structure, working class parents looked up to teachers; teachers had higher social and educational status than the parents" (Lareau 1989, 59). Rather than teach their children at home in a way that is at odds with school instruction, working class and some middle class families may prefer to leave schoolwork and school business to school professionals. Many families have faith in teachers' professional expertise and want the school to take care of the education of children.

Professionals, especially in a team situation, can also project the idea that schools know best, which can be intimidating to some parents, particularly working class parents or parents from nondominant cultural backgrounds. Parents who are intimidated by schools may buy into the idea of specialization and fragmentation by upholding the belief that it's the school's job to educate (Ogbu 1974). Once inside the school, the children may "belong" to the teacher, with parents relinquishing their offspring in exchange for the hope that new opportunities will be open to them through schooling.[4] Distancing of parents in schools is heightened by practices that emphasize the school as a *formal* organization rather than as a responsive one:

> In most schools parents who aren't educated are intimidated by teachers. When my kids were little I remember one time going to a conference when my son was in seventh grade and he'd had some problems, I guess his grades or something. Anyway there was this whole team of teachers of the seventh grade and so I sat down for the conference and there were six teachers and me. Now I'm a teacher too, but I was still intimidated by these six teachers standing there telling me things about my son. And I can see how it would be very easy to be intimidated if you weren't a teacher, if

you weren't in the system. You are trained from the time you are little that teachers are someone who is to be respected and believed, so there's definitely an intimidation factor. People who don't have degrees may feel somewhat intellectually inferior and a teacher is supposed to know it all. So why would you question what they're saying and doing? (Interview, high school parent)

It is necessary for schools to assemble teams of professionals in order to gain more complete knowledge and perspective, but the possible side effects, such as an unbalancing of the conversation, particularly with low-income or language-minority parents, needs to be considered carefully.

Upper-middle class parents appear to get the most attention in schools. As an administrator in this study put it, "If there's a request by two sets of parents, a lawyer or a migrant, and you can only satisfy one, what goes through your mind?" Political clout can become a silent factor in decision making. In Robertson School District an influential family (a major employer in Robertson) has become an "advisor" to the superintendent (Interview, superintendent). And in a study comparing parent involvement in schools in a working class community (Colton, California) with the same type of involvement in a middle class community (Prescott, Arizona), conclusions were drawn that school activities *penetrated* family life more in the middle class families than in working class (Lareau and Benson 1984).[5]

In Robertson School District, the enrollment of students is small enough that each school is an inclusive community school, not sharply demarcated along socioeconomic lines. Robertson High School, Park Middle School, and the three elementary schools all have the full range of socioeconomic and ethnic backgrounds of students and parents, with the elementary schools showing some differentiation by socioeconomic status. Horace Mann Elementary School serves primarily children of university staff and workers; Riverview Elementary School is made up of the children of professors and a few farming families; while Fairfield Elementary School draws on the children of students at the university, which includes a substantial international population and more ethnic diversity. Nevertheless, in all schools, high levels of parent involvement are consistent with high socioeconomic status.

From the point of view of the civic elite and of the faithfuls who are always up at the schools working tirelessly, "those other people" who are not also have the opportunity to participate, but they simply abnegate their responsibility:

> Every time it's the same old people who turn up and do all the work. We want to work with the school, but at the same time we can't help wondering why so many other parents don't make the effort. You get tired of trying to do it all. (Interview, parent)

Parents participate very unequally—some are highly involved in school and others are not at all. Schools tend to leave it up to families to decide how much they want to be involved with their children's schools, and some families have more resources available to participate. Clearly there are many issues involved as to why SES is so important—for instance, time off work for parents, confidence to participate in school, and "cultural capital."[6]

Educators themselves may hold classist views which carry over into an unbalanced situation, with the school holding power in relation to working class parents. Even if educators have initially come from low-income families themselves, their education has put them in an advantaged position: many teachers and administrators are "thought to be a more elite social class than the majority of the population in the United States" (Parker and Shapiro 1993, 42). And, as Grant and Sleeter (1986) found in their study of school and community, educators may not be sensitive to social-class issues. Inequality with regard to social class was heavily inscribed in the culture of the school: "When asked what classism was they [the administrators and teachers] could not define it or describe it in much detail. In discussions of the students' home background and on the attitude assessment scale, they expressed many negative stereotypes related to social class . . . It seems as though their acceptance of an unequal social class structure was so entrenched that they did not regard it as inappropriate to hold and voice these beliefs" (p. 240). There were teachers in Robertson School District, however, who did have a more critical perspective:

> In this district the well-educated and important parents get the most attention. You only need a couple of the right parents to complain and

the superintendent listens. The wrong parents of lower class drop-out kids get marginalized and complained about. (Interview, teacher)

Moreover, teachers may frequently develop a relationship with the child based on parental characteristics that further disadvantages lower class students. Teachers may perceive children as an extension of the family:

> When you meet the parents you can see why the kids are the way that they are. Some kids are good and some aren't, and a lot of it is the parents. Mostly it's what parents do at home that makes the difference. Those parents who are involved, their kids are not a problem. The ones who show up for the Drug Night, their kids are not druggies. (Interview, teacher)

What goes on in school in teacher-student and student-student interactions is heavily influenced by the perceptions of teachers about families and family life. Victoria or Vincent do not leave their family identities at the classroom door. Perceptions and biases about class, race, ethnic, religious, or other cultural differences play into school life in powerful ways. One of the problems with teachers identifying children with their parents' socioeconomic status is that teachers may raise or lower expectations for educational performance based on perceived parental status.

Becker (1986) further argues that even if schooling were not biased against low-income students, "a school is a lousy place to learn anything in" and that it is actually the home environment that most influences student learning:

> The spectacle of elementary and secondary education gives credence to James Herndon's wry hypothesis (1968, 79) that nobody learns anything in school, but middle class children learn enough elsewhere to make it appear that schooling is effective; since lower-class children don't learn the material elsewhere, the school's failure to teach them is apparent. (p. 174)

It's not that "lower-class" children don't learn material outside the school; it's simply that what they do learn is not always consistent with the content and type of learning valued by schools. Upper-middle class parents engage in educational activities in the home: "the curriculum of the home" (Walberg 1984a, p. 25). These parents read to children, question them, extend their "school" knowledge through travel, trips to museums and the like, and they affirm the importance of education. Working class families may also believe just as strongly or more so in education. They may aspire to overcome poverty through education (Ooka Pang 1988). Like the middle class, working class families may also engage in "school-like" activities at home, but the school typically affirms the language and culture of the middle and upper classes. The daily life, knowledge, values, and language of the working class is devalued in school, as children are socialized "up" to middle class culture. Those students whose home culture is discontinuous with school may find it more difficult to do well in school, and their parents may also find the school more distant.

Differential treatment of parents across different class orientations of public schools has also been documented. In schools with a high level of parent involvement, resources are channelled into further encouraging strong home-school relations. Schools with low levels of parent involvement appear to do little to establish stronger links, and few resources are made available (Koza and Levy 1977, 78; Lareau 1989). In other words, those schools that are populated by high SES families, and already advantaged by parent involvement, receive additional advantage and incentives, and those schools with little parental input receive disincentives. Further adding to some students' disadvantage in the system is the tradition of reliance on local property taxes as a chief revenue source for education (nearly half the budgets in most schools districts), leading to gross inequities in schools. Such a financial structure has on one hand created school districts with healthy property tax bases, but on the other hand, it has also created an underclass of schools—those without a strong financial base and few resources.

Social class also affects school-parent relationships in that upper-middle class parents believe they have a right to challenge professional decisions and a right to participate equally in educational decision making. They seek to "ensure" their children's success. For these parents, involvement in school by providing goods and services (*e.g.*, becoming a reading volunteer) is a way to ensure access to the school, to see their children, to be physically present, and to be given information that helps them to understand the system and therefore to be in a better position to manipulate it. In the words of one high school parent:

> Mainly my activities have been being involved in whatever my children are involved in. I'm very involved in sports because my sons are both athletes. One of my main reasons for getting involved is to have the opportunity to get to know their teachers and know what they are doing. When I was new in the community I didn't know what was going on at the high school. Coming to the schools makes a big difference in how your kids are treated, the opportunities they get. (Interview, parent)

Those parents with time to donate to the school are in a privileged position to use that time to negotiate for additional resources for their children, such as teacher attention and desired placement in classes. Time is an important resource closely connected with power. Upper-middle class parents (and this is particularly helpful to those whose children are low achievers in school) are able to spend time advocating for their children (Lareau 1989). A teacher in Robertson School District put it this way: "They know how to advocate. Some do it with a smile and others not, but they all know how to advocate for their child." A strong motivation is to help the child do better—to improve his or her life chances. The advocacy role is taken on comfortably by these parents because they know the system, and they believe they can make a difference in their children's life chances through active participation in school:

> Families may be very similar in how much they stress the importance of education or how frequently and diligently they attempt to teach their children new words, but they may differ in how closely these activities are tied to the school's curriculum, how much they monitor their children's school performance and how much they complain to educators (Lareau, 1989, 170).

Education, occupational status, income, and the characteristics of their work provide parents with unequal resources in both educating their children and advocating for them in the school.

It is argued that *all* parents can talk to their children and participate in their learning at home, and that this kind of parent involvement "does not limit working parents and does not place less-educated parents at a disadvantage" (Ames 1993, 44). I disagree. All parents can talk to their children and they can participate in their learning at home, but they do so with varying degrees of support by the school system, with various degrees of confidence, with varying knowledge of the school system and how it works, and with varying resources to contribute to their child's efforts. If, for instance, as Fordham and Ogbu (1986) argue, some black children feel they have to "act white" in order to get ahead in the school system, and some working class children find their home cultures are devalued in the school (Heath 1983), they are disadvantaged by the system. Less educated parents may be at a disadvantage to help their children, although they frequently can and do encourage high aspirations and achievement, against all odds.

With a recognition of the unequal playing field, we can begin to frame home-school relations and parent-school collaboration in a manner that reflects the realities of families in all their configurations and cultures. Educators' understandings of cultural patterns and valuing of ethnic and cultural differences are critical if we are to establish parent-school collaboration. As an example of insensitivity on the part of the school, parent education is frequently done with missionary zeal and an intent to "fix" parents that is disrespectful to working class parents. Parent education in some cases has become a volunteer scheme, using middle class mothers who visit poor, usually working class mothers, possibly from minority ethnic groups, to educate them on child-rearing practices (David 1993, 165). Finch (1984) points out that an unintended consequence can be that the gap between school and home seems even wider to the working class parents than they had thought, and they may choose to stay away from the school, given the perceived cultural discontinuity or "dissonance."

Another factor that may need to be taken into account is that working class parents may give too much respect and deference to educators, which precludes the possibility of joint problem solving. On the other hand, upper-middle class parents may not collaborate well with educators if they view educators as school functionaries and fail to give adequate weight and attention to working with teachers towards a common end. Joint problem solving is unlikely to occur if one party does not respect the other, as seen in the following interview with a teacher feeling "used" by parents and feeling as if she were being treated like a "slave":

> Some of the parents are very demanding. Those parents who are
> very wealthy are quite used to getting things done their way "yes-

terday." I'm sure they think I'm terrible when I don't cave in on every demand. But I have more to think about than their own personal wants. So I am working hard to teach them the word "No." It's a new concept for some of them. (Interview, teacher)

When the upper-middle class mothers start climbing your frame you go, "Oh, Here we go again. I know I'm not being paid enough to do this job." (Interview, teacher)

Anxiety, fear of ignorance, distrust of school authorities and lack of respect for educators' competence can all contribute to an impasse or an inadequate collaboration. If parents and educators each feel superior in their relations with the other, or, alternatively, angry, powerless, incompetent, or guilty, such feelings seriously jeopardize collaborative teamwork.

CONCLUSION

School organization, with increasing levels of specialization as students advance through the grades, means that possibilities for parent-school collaboration change in character and tend to diminish as the child matures. While we cannot ignore the concerns expressed by teachers and students that parent involvement needs to be appropriate to each grade level, with student autonomy an important consideration, I agree with Nell Noddings (1988) that smaller, more intimate class sizes and continuity of teacher-student relationships over a number of years (*e.g.*, keeping the same math teacher through high school), even in the high school, have merit and are worthy of further consideration. We also have to work to reframe school organization in general as less bureaucratic and more responsive. The nature of parent-school collaboration can change as the student matures, with middle school and high school parents working with educators on such projects as curriculum committees, providing vocational experiences, and acting as consultants on educational matters concerning the student.

Most importantly, we need to address the fact that many students experience a radical disjuncture between home and school life. Schools do not always attend to the diverse cultures, goals, talents, and needs of *all* children and their parents, not just those who recognize themselves in the culture of the school. A shift must occur to constitute a pluralistic community and to balance power more equitably between professional educators and parents. We need collaboration and problem solving for the schools of the future. Ways to balance power, to enhance continuity between home and school, and to work constructively with diversity are available to us.

Teachers and administrators who have a better understanding of family cultures and an awareness of how parents are distanced from schools will be able, I believe, to interact more thoughtfully with parents. An equal-status interaction between parents and school professionals is likely to benefit students and to improve school practices. Further, if parent participation is seen by teachers as a legitimate part of the social and academic culture of the school, then parents are more likely to participate fully. Building a culture of inclusive community has to be a key goal of administrators and teachers. With site-based management and the inclusion of parents in decision making, new demands are placed on administrators to approach school governance from a participatory stance. This is where a feminist perspective has much to offer. Women's ways of leadership embody collaborative and community-building styles (Helgesen 1990; Shakeshaft 1987, 197).

As an antidote to the organizational mentality, continuing bureaucratization of schools, and the current disadvantaging of whole classes of students "at risk," a feminist agenda for change includes making schools more responsive and more concerned about equity and students' needs. All participants in public education—educators, researchers, activists, parents, and community people—are urged to work towards recreating a "democratic, lively public sphere within public education . . . with and not on the backs of parents" (Fine 1993, 7). When administrators and teachers have authentic connections with the communities in which they work, they can not only be better advocates for working class families, but can work with people from all SES strata to promote parent and community involvement.

The dialogue between the school and its community is ongoing. The community becomes a part of the conversation about what education should be. If we are to bridge the gap between reluctant and possibly alienated learners and an imposing school that is seeking to take the student out of the familiar into remote subject matter, then we must involve people in the course and direction of their education. Greene (1973; 1988) quite rightly points out that it is not enough for professional educators to decide what is best for a community of learners; the people themselves must be brought into the debate about the various possibilities in curricula and what each will mean for their lives. The educator must be both self-aware—"wide-awake" and constantly grappling with personal growth and freedom—and also aware of the needs, interests, and perceptions of the students and their families. The next chapter explores the question of building school cultures that celebrate diversity and allow for multiple interests and purposes, and that includes those whose voices have typically been silenced.

NOTES

1. The Carnegie Task Force (1989) blames school administrators for discouraging parent involvement, and urges that some of the feelings of "isolation" in middle schools could be improved through attention to inclusion of parents and community in the school (p. 36). Similarly, NASSP's Council on Middle Level Education (1985) stressed that since the public and the school's "constituent community" had become distanced from the school, it is necessary to "work hard to maintain relations" (pp. 18-19). But even in many of the efforts to restructure middle schools, parents are still defined as the group that is to be informed by the school, rather than as being included in decision making. For instance, Clark and Clark (1994) in *Restructuring the Middle School Level*, suggest that "with a well established sense of purpose, teachers and administrators can articulate *their* program to parents, community members, and school boards" (p. 98). Parents are seen as "stakeholders" (Clark and Clark 1994, 213) to be informed and involved, but "professionals," and particularly administrators, are assumed to take leadership and move the organization in a professional (meaning efficient and harmonious) direction. I am arguing that we have to go far beyond this to a point where conflict is embraced and many more voices contribute to schools, and that the outcome will be improved learning opportunities for students.
2. For those interested in an extended-teaching organizational arrangement, which is a common practice in Waldorf Schools where students stay with the same teacher from grades one through eight, see Henry (1993).
3. As an example of cultural discontinuity between home and school, Wolcott describes and analyzes his own difficult time trying to teach antagonistic youngsters in the Blackfish (Native American) school, an outcome of powerful cultural differences between the school and its Native American community. Wolcott (1987, 145) found it useful to regard *the teacher—himself—as the enemy*, that is, for the teacher to regard his own culture as the

alien one: "I was not assigned to the village to teach villagers their way of life, I was assigned to teach them something about mine." Wolcott's is an evocative telling of the interface of an alien school with a culturally different host. The gap between school and home cultures is a vital issue that needs to be addressed in all school contexts. In another example, from a public television documentary that I show in my university classes, an Hispanic girl from the Bronx, Jo Vegas, is awarded a sholarship to Groton, an exclusive eastern college-prep school. Jo finds herself educated out of the Bronx into the upper-middle class norms, language, and behaviors. Yet she can never totally be a white girl; she finds herself torn between two worlds and never properly fitting into either. To her Hispanic family and friends she has become very different, a "white girl"; to her preppy school mates she is still Hispanic, which is seen by them as undesirable. The documentary shows the distance that can exist between school and home cultures, and how racism and classism subtly poison social relationships and the educational process.

4. In Robertson School District, even some middle class parents argued that parents ought not intrude in professional decision making. Professionalism, as it has been traditionally constructed in schools, is a position of authority. Teachers and administrators seem to feel duty-bound to have all the answers, or feel that they *ought* to have all the answers, and parents may feel acted upon and disadvantaged in the conversation.

5. Community-studies literature also shows that "the public schools will often act heavily in favor of residents from the "right side of the tracks" (See Cicourel and Kitsuse 1963; Connell *et al.* 1982; Crowson 1992, 84; Havighurst 1962; Rist 1970).

6. Bourdieu and Passeron (1977) argue that those students from upper or upper-middle class homes have access to "cultural capital"—books, travel, visits to museums, theatre, and so on—which allows them to experience greater success in school. The deeply internalized values or "habitus" which arise from "cultural capital" are rewarded in schools and in the wider society. But as Boykin (1994, 250–252) quite rightly points out, "when we fail to acknowledge the integrity of the cultural capital" African American and other students bring with them to school, we are failing to educate well. Ways have to be found to connect students with their heritage (ethnicity, social class); to demystify and provide access to the culture of power; and at the same time contributing to changing the culture of the school to be more representative of the people.

6

An Ethic of Care—Celebrating Diversity

> Twenty years ago we had many more parents in the schools. But it just isn't possible now. We talk about partnerships and collaboration more today, but we actually do less. (Interview, teacher)
>
> We still don't know very much about how to be in schools. Schools weren't designed for parents to be there. (Interview, parent)

The speaker in the quote above, noting that "twenty years ago we had many more parents in the schools," refers to "parents" when it was largely women—women who did not work outside the home—who volunteered their time and energy in schools as a way to be close to their children's education and to maneuver politically to have their needs met. However, schools are no longer populated by as large a proportion of children who grow up with two biological parents living together—and a mother who stays at home—as was then the case. Patterns of divorce, more inclusive social mores about what it is to be a family, and the increasing employment of women in paid labor have meant new family configurations. These include dual-wage families,[1] single-parent families, and blended families, among other family structures, in addition to two-biological-parent families. Instead of viewing the new families from a deficit perspective, we need to find ways to enrich schools with their different perspectives and needs.

Given the diversity of parents and community and the tensions between the public school and parents, an ethic of care is needed to inform educational policy and practice. If the only people whose voices are heard in school and the only people represented on school boards and on site-councils are those who most reflect the school's interests and intentions, then we have failed to provide for *public* education. A traditional administrative approach is to control or limit the number of voices that can be heard in the school. In this view, "multiculturalism" is something that is done at a certain time slot in the school day where children eat with chopsticks or listen to Peruvian music, rather than something that is infused throughout the school culture and practiced daily. Thus, administrators are urged to "balance cultural diversity values and a multicultural curriculum with common core values" (Interview, administrator). But whose core values are they? What is meant by "common core values" is most likely the *status quo* of white, upper-middle class dominance. Non-dominant groups representing diversity in the school whose voices have traditionally not been heard include those defined by race, language, gender, sexual orientation, alternative family structures, social class, disability, bilingualism, and those with alien or refugee status. While I cannot address here the intersection of the public school with all the diversity represented in the schools, I can show the range of viewpoints and perspectives that are frequently marginalized or silenced by the schools, and point the way toward an inclusive and caring standpoint.

At the same time that I highlight categories of parents, I want to point out that there may be as much diversity within as between groups. Not all single parents face the same problems, particularly when that status is complicated by economic or cultural differences. However, it is a useful heuristic device to take the particular situations of diverse groups of parents in order to understand how and why it is that the civic elite has such a dominance in U.S. public school systems. Of course, there are exceptions, where public schools are buzzing with the input of diverse parents and multiple perspectives; but the dominant culture of the public school is white, male, and heterosexual (Shakeshaft 1993). For instance, even today in many states an administrator or teacher who is openly gay can be dismissed and not protected by the law.[2]

The concept of school as a community representing a diversity of interests and beliefs is tied to the social and political climate of the times as reflected in Supreme Court decisions. During conservative eras, schools are portrayed and legally sanctioned as homogeneous; during more liberal times schools are seen as housing dissent and unpopular views in addition to the dominant perspective. Thus, during the McCarthy era, teachers were required to sign loyalty oaths attesting to their patriotism and swearing that they did not belong to any "subversive" organizations. Those teachers who were not prepared to work on such terms established by the school district were dismissed (Adler v. Board, 1952). In the late 1960s this decision was reversed, and First Amendment rights to free expression were upheld in Keyishian v. Board of Regents in 1967. The battle between state and individual rights in public education continued in 1968 in Pickering v. Board of Lockport, where an individual teacher won the right of free expression in speaking out publicly against a board of education decision. The tension between the image of the school as a collective authority versus seeing it as a group of individuals with conflicting and diverse views has not been resolved, and continues to be an issue for litigation and changing legal rights. As long as schools, constituted by the law, continue to uphold the *status quo* and dominant perspectives, and to be intolerant of alternative views, we are losing some of the richness of the school community.

THE WHITE MIDDLE CLASS CULTURE OF THE SCHOOL

Schools in the United States were never monocultural in their constituencies. Schools represent a diversity of cultural traditions, ceremonies, perspectives, values, and languages. For Hirsch, the solution to cultural pluralism is to give everyone access to literate culture, by which he means a middle class Euro-American perspective:

> Literate culture is the most democratic culture in our land: it excludes nobody, it cuts across generations and social groups and classes; it is not usually one's first culture, but it should be everyone's second, existing as it does beyond the narrow spheres of family, neighborhood and region. (1987, 21)

Hirsch's rationale is that those students who are culturally diverse are socialized into the mainstream culture of schooling through access to key bits of knowledge (some fifty thousand schemata). The "minority" becomes a member of the "majority" culture. One of the problems with this thinking is that it emphasizes homogeneity at the expense of the richness and value of multiple cultures and ways of being. This is not to argue that literacy ought not be part of everyone's life, but to highlight the value-laden, white, upper-middle class bias of Hirsch's literacy, and of many of our public schools. The language, rituals, and symbolism of schooling is no-one's first language, but it is more closely synonymous with, for instance, white rather than black culture, middle class rather than working class. In addition, if "minority" students have to learn to use a "majority" cultural code, the cards are stacked against them in terms of ease of access to knowledge and self-esteem, which is linked to school success. Furthermore, changing demographics in this country point to a future in which minorities may well be the majority: "The United States Census Bureau (1988) projects that 33 percent of the school-age population will consist of minorities by the year 2000" (Chavkin 1993, 1).

However, the notion seems to have persisted in schools that white male leadership is the best, and that a Eurocentric curriculum is acceptable. An administrator in the school district studied states, "We hire minorities and women because it is the law, not to be altruistic." Unfortunately, too often schools attempt to diversify simply on the grounds that it is politically correct or in the interests of justice and affirmative action—because minorities or women have been oppressed for too long. What they fail to acknowledge is that it is in the school's best interests to do so. Diversity enhances schools. Teachers can benefit enormously from the new knowledges and perspectives of administrators, staff, teachers, and parents from a range of cultural and linguistic backgrounds. Parents, too, can assist in promoting a multicultural curriculum and in eliminating racism in the school.

Even when schools attempt to diversify and to include outside perspectives, they often end up reproducing a white, upper-middle class perspective. As an example, if selection on committees is based on "expertise," those people considered the experts are those most like the dominant power structure in the school. The following excerpt is evidence of one state's attempt to diversify and involve parents and community members in curricular and instructional planning, but it implicitly excludes many people:

> All committee members and chairpersons will be selected based on their knowledge, experience and skill in the disciplines outlined in Goal II of ESHB 1209; their ability to communicate their knowl-

edge; and their ability to work well in groups . . . Each committee
will have between 25-45 members including the following stake-
holder groups: Approximately 60 % educators . . . Approximately
40 % community representatives including parents, and business
people with expertise related to the disciplines in Goal II. (Memo,
State Commission on Student Learning, March 1994)

The very criteria for inclusion in decision making means that a somewhat homogeneous group of middle or upper-middle class parents are
likely to be the ones who will be involved.[3]

PARENT AND FAMILY DIVERSITY

The demographics of this country make it imperative that schools attend
to racism and classism, and that schools change organizationally to better reflect the student population: in most urban districts around the
country, the trend is towards school-age children from single-parent
working class homes. Many of these children are non-white (Education
Week 1986, 186; Lareau 1989; U.S. Department of Education 1988).
The states of California, Florida, and Texas are projected to have a 60
percent Hispanic school population by the year 2010 (Hodgkinson
1987). The majority of children in kindergarten in Texas (51 percent) are
Hispanic, and the majority of elementary students are students of color
(Yates and Ortiz 1991). In other states, not just the Southwest, the proportion of students of color in school is increasing. By the year 2000 the
number of Spanish-speaking people is projected to increase to more
than twenty-two million (Reyes, Velez and Pena 1993, 67). The number
of limited-English-proficient (LEP) students in California public schools
rose from 376,794 in 1981 to 986,462 in 1991; Caucasians are below the
50th percentile in the school population (California Department of
Education 1991), with 3.5 million LEP students in U.S. public schools
(Boyer 1995). The higher the social class, the lower the birth rate
(Lareau 1989, 119).

The so-called "Leave it to Beaver" family (father at work, mother in
the kitchen) and the type of society associated with it, is gone, and with
the changes have come exciting new possibilities for people, and also
challenges. Many children live, and will live in the future, in single-
parent families: one of four white families and one of three black fami-

lies are single-parent families (Martin 1993, 57). Single-parent homes are often also low-income homes. For many, poverty and single parenthood go hand in hand. In addition, two-thirds of mothers work outside of the home (Snyder 1991, 1). Telephone companies report that "at 3:00 P.M. each working day, the nation's phone calling system peaks as the children get home from school and call their parents: 'Hello. I'm home and I'm safe' " (Snyder 1991, 2).

Statistics also tell us that the concerns of safety and youth crime are increasingly important educational issues: Many of the youth in jail are high school dropouts. More than 80 percent of America's one million prisoners are high school dropouts. Typically, states with the lowest high school dropout rates also have the lowest rates of prisoners per 100,000 people. With two exceptions, states with the lowest educational levels—indicated by graduation rates—have the highest rates of prisoners per 100,000 people (Hendrick 1992, 50–51). Schooling, or lack thereof, appears to be linked with youth crime.

Many of the parents with whom teachers work are of lower occupational status. The local systems are unprepared to deal with these social and demographic shifts. If teachers and administrators see themselves as professionals and "live in upper-middle class neighborhoods where they socialize with other upper-middle class families" (Lareau 1989, 118) then it is likely that the gap between teachers and working class families will widen, with negative educational consequences for children.

In terms of representation, there is a gap between schools and homes. Schools fall short in addressing the needs of children by not having sufficient role models as teachers and administrators for many students. The teaching work force has historically been white and continues to be white: there is one teacher of color for every ten white teachers and few school administrators of color: 3 percent are Hispanic and 8 percent are African American (Digest of Educational Statistics, 1990). These statistics on changing demographics will eventually force schools to change in order to better respond to the needs, interests, and nature of the students. Schools will have to be more representative of their communities, and the institutions of school and family are going to have to find ways to work together better.

Even in the somewhat monocultural university town of Robertson, family diversity is a part of the social fabric, as can be seen in Table 1.

TABLE 1
Fairfield Elementary School Demographic Survey
Robertson School District 1993-94

Categories	*Percentage of Students*
Speaks English as second language	24%
Rides bus	40%
Lives in apartment	30%
Is member of racial/cultural minority	27%
Eats free/reduced-price lunch	35%
Has child-care after school	25%
Has parent(s) who is a student	34%
Has parent at home after school	59%
Lives with two parents (includes blended families)	78 %

And in the accounts of parents which follow, there is clearly a wide range of needs and perspectives in the different types of parents and families that has not yet been adequately represented and given voice in the schools.

Social-Class Diversity

The following interchange took place at a local site council meeting:

Parent: Do we want to include "free/reduced lunch" as a category on our report?

Self: Who is this going to?

Principal: The parents, and it's also made available to anyone in the community. It's required by law.

Self: Well I think we should be thoughtful. As soon as you start sorting people into "free/reduced lunch" or "lives in apartment" then it can become a case of measuring people against a "right" standard. Is there a stigma attached to receiving free/reduced lunch?

Staff: Yes, there's a stigma. There's definitely a stigma.

The existence of social class has been called the "dirty little secret" of American social life. The U.S. was founded on the principle of democracy and on the right of all citizens to participate in access to the American dream of social mobility for all, irrespective of background.

The myth is that the U.S. is a classless society (Parker and Shapiro 1993, 45). The reality is that some people are advantaged by social-class privileges, while others are not. Some families' values are consistent with school culture and they are provided advantages. Poverty puts other children at a distinct disadvantage:

> I have done home visitations only on very rare occasions and in this school you need to be really careful and pick and choose the home you go to because some of these kids come from poor homes and very abusive situations. A couple of my fathers are very defensive about how they're raising their children. We tell them at school how to practice literacy skills with their child when they come to kindergarten, but you have to tell them, and tell them again, and it doesn't happen. (Interview, teacher)

> Some of these parents [low SES] don't even know where their head is, and you can see the effects on the child. (Interview, teacher)

> It's very obvious who the children are whose parents are reading with them. The other thing that I encourage parents to do, because so many of these kids are in daycare, is to talk to the kids. I know parents are overworked, and it's so much easier just to plug them into Nintendo or the TV, and that's what those parents do. (Interview, teacher)

Across the nation, various school districts are trying out various parent programs which may further advantage upper-middle class parents. Some programs *mandate* specific hours for family involvement. For example, in one school in Washington State (West Valley School District, Spokane) "90 hours of volunteer time per family is required. A general rule-of-thumb is 30 hours minimum classroom hours and 60 hours in committee work, events and activities" (Brumback 1992, 25). Such requirements often preclude involvement from single and working parents and tap into the resources of upper-middle class women—married to professionals—who are devoting their time to parenting.

In response to the patterns of low participation among working class parents in schools, other schools have set up "school-based mutual-support groups (MSGs) for low-income parents, with an emphasis on reaching out to ethnic minority parents" (Simoni and Adelman 1993,

335). The idea of community-based mutual-support groups is to encourage two-way, participatory parent involvement rather than top-down parent "training" led by professionals, which has been criticized as paternalistic and insensitive to cultural and social-class differences (Mannan and Blackwell 1992; Nieto 1992). Research by Simoni and Adelman (1993) provides preliminary support for the concept of mutual-support groups based on a study of an elementary school in a low-income area in urban Los Angeles. The groups were able to provide parent-run collaborative support in such areas as child-rearing discussions, academic assistance, and needs for the school and families (*e.g.*, cafeteria and playground monitors, classroom volunteers, financial and emotional aid to families in need). However, further research is needed to explore the benefits and difficulties of MSGs and to discover how MSGs differ from traditional parent groups.

In Robertson School District, a variety of parent education programs, parent evenings, seminars, and activities were conducted by two of the elementary schools—with mixed success:

> We provide parent seminar opportunities and we may have from five to fifty parents at any one of those. They're not necessarily overwhelming in their attendance, but they are offered. Such things as Children and Stress; Gender Issues; Reading with your Child; Self-Concept; Technology; Sibling Rivalry. Sibling Rivalry was a big one we did last year that got a lot of attendance. (Interview, principal)

The question of inclusiveness—who attends, the target audience, and the assumptions behind such education—still needs to be addressed. For instance, some parents (particularly the well-to-do) praised the efforts of Horace Mann Elementary School for providing parenting classes for parents "needing some assistance in that area," while others do not believe it is the school's business to be teaching parents how to parent: "parenting classes should be left to the social agencies. That's what they're there for. We're here to teach children."

Cultural and Ethnic Diversity

A disproportionate number of poor children are also of color (Scott-Jones 1993, 250): 40 percent of children of color live in poverty compared to 14 percent of white children (Hodgkinson 1985). Since the school has been shown to typically embody white, middle class values, the lack of involvement of parents from poor families and families of color in schooling can be seen as an outcome of not feeling welcome at school. It is often assumed, and backed by some research, that low-income parents and ethnic minority parents are not well-involved in their children's schooling (Ascher 1987; Davies 1988). But this does not mean these parents are not interested in schooling. Many "minority" parents hold education in high esteem as the hope for a better life, to move past the condition of inequality. However, for those parents who have not been highly educated, they may hold the school to be the "expert" and still may not be properly included in school affairs.

The alien and unfamiliar *cultural practices* in schools can inhibit some parental involvement. For example, the PTA often with its white, middle-class agenda and structure and articulate speakers may not be welcoming to parents whose own culture is quite different. In addition, the ongoing persistence of a white teaching and administrative force means that minority children face the barrier of a lack of role models and representation of their interests and purposes in school. Erickson and Schultz (1982) in *Counselor as Gatekeeper* show how counselors can differentially give or deny access to meanings based on social interactional patterns and expectations. In the study, white counselors during counseling sessions gave advice that put up barriers to black students, perhaps unwittingly, pointing to the need for the hiring of counselors, teachers, and administrators who represent a variety of ethnic and cultural interests and purposes. Scott-Jones (1993, 245) notes that the proportion of educators of color is sadly decreasing so that it appears likely that nonminority teachers will have to learn to relate to and collaborate with minority families in the educational process:

> As the proportion of minorities in schools has increased, the proportion of minorities in the teaching force has declined sharply. In 1971 almost 12 percent of teachers were minorities; by the year 2000 that proportion is expected to drop below 5 percent (Nicklos and Brown 1989).

The issue of under-representation of people who are ethnically and culturally diverse in teaching and administration is an important one. Students and families need to see themselves reflected in the structure and culture of the school, and this is unlikely to happen if the dominant cultural group is not well-educated in cultural understandings and pluralistic perspectives. (See Hollins, King and Hayman 1994; Bowers and Flinders 1990.)

Also included in cultural diversity are people who are recent immigrants to the United States, including myself, for I came to the U.S. from Australia less than ten years ago. Cultural isolation and alienation are common difficulties experienced by families in this category, as they struggle not only with unfamiliar cultural rules and norms, but also quite frequently with marginalization. For some newcomers the home country they have left behind represents connectedness and the good life, even though they had good reasons for immigrating. Schools play a significant role in the well-being, and the social and academic success of students from new immigrant families. Immigrants should not be treated as marginal to the concerns of the country. They have chosen to make the United States their new home, and are contributing to the society through their lives and work; they may also bring fresh perspectives and insights from a comparative cultural viewpoint that can be useful for schools and society. When I came to this country I came with a belief that this was a country where all views are accepted. Instead I found that a "live and let live" philosophy was not always practiced here. My experiences of marginalization are, most likely, not unique to me, but common to many women and immigrants who start new lives in a new country, many of whom do not have my educational advantages and my whiteness to ease the transition.

Parents of Special-Education Students

In the United States, special-education students have historically been marginalized. Like African Americans, for whom separate and unequal school systems were provided until the passing of Brown v. Board of Education in 1954, special-education students were also segregated. The segregation continued until 1975 with the passing of PL 94–142, the Education for all Handicapped Children Act (now the Individuals with Disabilities Education Act) which established the inclusion of children with special educational needs in mainstream classrooms.

Early on, in special education, discrimination occurred with regard to social class: "children with clear-cut, though relatively mild learning problems were often classified as mildly (educable) retarded if from a lower socioecomic class, but classified as learning disabled if from the middle class" (Mearig 1992, 211). The advocacy of middle class parents, who were able to exert an influence on school research and practices, was helpful for all children in moving away from a stigmatized "mildly (educable) retarded" label to a position that put the responsibility on schools to provide for specialized and individualized learning differences. "Learning disability" became included in PL 94–142, and parent input and collaboration for individualized education services was seen as a key toward academic improvement. Parent involvement was mandated for the developmentally, emotionally, and socially disabled.[4] School staff are now required to work with parents in devising an individualized educational plan (IEP) for disabled students. For years, parents of children with special needs were only able to participate in schools on the terms of the professionals, who held the power and were privy to classified information. The new ethic has made professionals accountable to parents; parents are involved with professionals in assessing children's needs. However, even in situations of parents and teachers collaborating together to devise IEPs, parents' voices can be muted, and in turn upper-middle class parents can also be intimidating to some educators. A parent of a special-education student at Fairfield Elementary spoke up at the Second Annual Stakeholders Meeting:

> My son has a hearing impairment and he is not qualified for special services. At a meeting with the principal, the teacher, my husband and myself we were told this. I found the process very painful. I couldn't find out what could be done. I felt the teacher was trying hard but didn't have the information. The new guide book for 504 is dry and doesn't tell you much of anything. The process is painful and mystifying. I'm shaking just like you were (turns to another parent who had also spoken to a different problem with her child's schooling). We're so invested.

It takes new professionals who know how to communicate extremely well—to collaborate and value diverse perspectives—to really problem-solve with parents in a way that places the child in the center.

Parents of Gay Students

One parent, whose son attended Robertson High School, told the following story:

> When my son was in high school one of the teachers said to him "What is that earring you have on? You're a faggot." Now it turns

out my son is not gay, but that kind of behavior was extremely hurtful to my son at the time. And that teacher's attitude is condoned in
the school. To this day the teacher remains on the faculty at the high
school. And I'm sure he has not changed. (Interview, parent)

Even in books and studies that focus on diversity and pluralism (*e.g.*,
Chavkin's *Families and Schools in a Pluralistic Society),* the voices of
gay, lesbian, and bisexual students and their parents are noticeably absent.

The fact that homosexuality was classified by the American
Psychiatric Association as a "mental disorder" until 1973 is evidence of
the homophobic heritage of our society. And as Sears (1993) shows in
his study, the general climate of the public school is one of discrimination against sexual-minority youth, who are two to three times more
prone to suicide than other youth (p. 112). Homosexual students are an
invisible minority in the school and homosexuality is a taboo, non-discussable topic in the school (with some exceptions).[5] Not only must
students struggle with their own identities and relationship concerns,
they also find themselves outside the discourse of the school and often
faced with ridicule in public settings, such as the anti-gay jokes bandied
about at a Robertson High faculty meeting. In addition, we need to
remember that all students are affected by a rhetoric of hate, and that a
number of children who may or may not be homosexual live in family
arrangements where one or both partners is a self-identified lesbian,
gay man, or bisexual person (Sears 1993, 118). The number of children with minority-sexuality parents is speculative, ranging from six
to fourteen million children (Rivera 1987; Sears 1993).

In Robertson, the general conservatism of the public schools and the
local people means that homosexuality is pushed to the margins in the
discourse:

> The Robertson Daily News ran a cartoon strip called, "For Better or
> Worse," and in that one of the characters, male, tells one of the
> other characters that he's gay. And they're both very young boys at
> school, and it was, I thought, very sensitively done, very under-
> stated. The two boys talked a bit; the one who was gay I think had
> trouble describing his gayness to his parents. The first criticisms
> that started to come in were that these cartoon strips are supposed
> to be funny and there's nothing funny about that. And of course
> that's a good point, except that these cartoon strips go way beyond
> being just for laughs. But then the whole homophobic community

> started to write about how they were dismayed that the newspaper
> would run a cartoon strip that would show homosexuality in this
> light. (Interview, parent)

With homosexuality often an undiscussable topic in school and
community, and homosexual students, teachers, parents, and administrators not adequately protected by the law, relations between home
and school are likely to be far from optimal. Laws need to be changed
to provide the conditions of safety necessary for discussion of needs.
If good teaching is embedded in good relationships between all concerned—teacher-student, parent-teacher, teacher-administrator, and
so on—and I believe this is so, then the stress put on such relationships is likely to have an adverse effect on teaching and learning.
Sears (1993) notes that gay teachers may separate themselves from
students and their families using "psychological distance," and hide
their own private lives in order to put up barriers and protect themselves (p. 122).

In addition, if there are teachers or administrators in the schools
who are openly homophobic, as in the case of the teacher at Robertson
High School, then there is much work to be done in advocating for the
rights of all children, not just those who most conform to the stereotype
of the so-called "average" student. And difficulties for homosexual students are heightened if they also differ on other counts, such as cultural or ethnic-minority status, or poverty.

Dual-Wage Parents

The dual-wage family—both parents working outside the home in paid
labor—is now the norm in U.S. society (Trudel *et al.* 1992, 31). When
both parents are working outside the home the school can buy into the
myth that parents don't care about being involved with their children's
schooling. In response, a parent has this to say: "It's not that we don't
care about our kids and how they're doing. But we're very busy just
keeping it all together and we don't always have time to do these
things." (Interview, parent and site-based council member)

The school does not always take into account the busy lives and
multiple demands being made on parents as a result of their employment. In this study, it was clear that parents will be involved if it is a positive experience for them—with rewards such as an opportunity to get to

know a teacher. Educators who are prepared to think through problems such as why parents are not currently involved are more likely to achieve collaborative relationships with parents. Often, both parents are working and schools are not accessible to parents. As an example, in some of the schools in Robertson, parents want to be able to visit the school during the work day, without formal appointments, so that every class is observable at any time. Problems of disruption and security would then have to be overcome, but the advantages may well outweigh the inconveniences. Other strategies for parent involvement might include, for instance: scheduling informal meetings at school, with parents encouraged to attend at their convenience; establishing resources for parents in the school; using videotape to document student participation in school; collaborative projects; and so on. I believe it is also important for schools to provide child-care and after-school programs. Business and industries have shown only minimal interest in providing child-care and after-school programs in the U.S. (unlike European businesses). It is time the public schools and the corporations begin to fulfill these needs. We cannot ignore the needs of children and still expect to have a thriving economy and nation.

Single Parents

Today it is no longer customary for children's parents to necessarily be married. In the U.S. and Britain, births to single, unwed mothers were almost one-third of all births in 1990 (David 1993, 199). And with the increase in divorce in society, a *majority* of school-aged children now spend some time in a single-parent family (Lareau 1989a, 254). However, educators can sometimes continue to hold a deficit view of the family that is not a two-parent traditional family. In Robertson School District I heard many stories about those "poor children" who had "uncles" who changed frequently, with connotations of sexual impropriety on the part of the mother, and a view of marriage as the only way. Another example: "Single parents in particular are going to school or working and the child is in day care all the time when they're not in school. And these kids suffer" (Interview, teacher). The irony is that some of the deficit-view stories came from teachers who themselves had lived, or were living in families constituted differently from the traditional two-parent family. The research literature is also replete with examples of negative value judgements placed on single-parent families:

"broken homes" (Wadsworth and Maclearn 1986, 151); "irresponsible families" (Murray 1990, 3); "narcissistic families" (Lasch 1980); "latchkey" kids (Clark and Clark 1994, 219).

Women and men who have taken on parenting without the support of a partner are strong in the face of social and economic difficulties. The demands made on these parents are multiple, and much research and conventional wisdom continues to view children from these primarily mother-headed families as deprived. For instance, father-absence is thought to lead to academic decline over time (Shinn 1978); less competitiveness in boys (Fry and Scher 1984) (which is perceived as a negative outcome); and lowered school performance (Guidabaldi, Perry and Cleminshaw 1984). However, other research associates children of single-parent families with positive educational outcomes (*e.g.*, Weiss 1979). Interestingly, it is social class, not marital status, that is most often linked with student achievement in school (Carlson 1992, 45). But since single-parenting often goes hand in hand with poverty, children from single-parent homes may be disadvantaged in school. Furthermore, in Robertson School District, single parents face not only many of the difficulties faced by dual-wage parents (lack of child care, lack of time off work, *etc.*) but also a remaining stigma attached to single parenthood. Officially, the schools hold no such view, but in talking with single parents and listening to teachers and administrators describe parents, I am convinced that in this particular school district, one's status as a parent is enhanced if one has a husband or wife. Some examples include the following:

> Parents, married couples that have been around for a while, parents that are part of the core community, old timers in other words, they have the ways and means to influence and they're prepared to use that lever. They're prepared to say OK, we'll give you money for this, or maybe the district gets it for science or math education. So that kind of parent has power that they can exert. And they have status and respect. For a single parent, like myself, there is an entirely different set of expectations. (Interview, parent)

> Megan's teacher last year said, "Come in whenever. We would like you to be a part of such-and-such." But I couldn't because I'm a single parent and I had to work. I couldn't have just decided to have, say, Wednesday mornings free in order to go in. I think the

first-graders and the second-graders sometimes measure their family success by the number of times and the number of opportunities their mother and father is seen in and around the school. (Interview, parent)

Blended Families

In addition, with the rate of divorce in U.S. society, many children are coming to school from blended families. Fifty percent of all marriages end in divorce and 70–83 percent of these people will remarry (Norton and Moorman 1987). Also, with a 60 percent divorce rate for second marriages, many children "will experience the divorce and remarriage of their parents two or more times before they become adults" (Bray and Berger 1992, 58). I have used the term "blended family" because the common usage of "step-family" (see Anderson and White 1986; Bray and Berger 1992; Norton and Moorman 1987) carries with it pejorative overtones, perhaps stemming back to an older social and moral order that placed sanctions on remarriage (hence the folk stories of the "wicked stepmother"). Illustrative of the new situations created by blended families is the following account:

> When the teacher asked a student, Paul, if his parents would be coming to open house, he looked confused and asked, "Which parents?" "Both parents," replied the teacher. An even more perplexed Paul asked the teacher, "Does this mean my other parents can't come?" (Bray and Berger 1992, 57)

Even in the case of reporting to students' homes and notification of school events and students' needs, teachers do not always respond to all the people who have a legitimate claim to matters concerning the child.

CELEBRATING DIVERSITY THROUGH AN ETHIC OF CARE

So how do we begin to create a more inclusive school community that works for everyone? This is not an easy task, but we can start at the level of conceptual change—a new way of perceiving parents and community in relation to the school. In this section I want to highlight some of the conceptual change informed by an ethic of care that is necessary for collaborative relationships between parents and schools.

Caring is defined as essential relational work done by educators to promote the growth and well-being of students:

> Caring . . . is a form of what may be called relational ethics. A relational ethic remains tightly tied to experience because all its deliberations focus on the human beings involved in the situation under consideration and their relations to each other . . . One who is concerned with behaving ethically strives always to preserve or convert a given relation into a caring relation. (Noddings 1988, 218–219)

Following feminist theorists Nell Noddings (1984, 1988, 1989, 1992, 1994), Charol Shakeshaft (1987), Lynn Beck (1994), Prillaman *et al.* (1994) and Carol Gilligan (1982), I am arguing that an ethic of care is a necessary underpinning of all educational and social work. Gilligan's work (1982) argued not for a different morality for men and women, but that our moral domain as human beings should be extended to include care/connectedness, a feature strongly evident in the female population she studied, as well as justice/rights. Whereas Kohlberg (1976) saw moral development simply built on an ethic of principled justice (*i.e.*, socially constructed rules), Gilligan (1982) showed that a strong morality can be based on care, a responsibility to engage in service to others, to see who is suffering, and to work to alleviate suffering. If we consider parent-school relationships, an educator using an ethic of care would recognize, for instance, the diversity of parents in the schools, and that some parents and their interests and purposes have been marginalized by the school. Ways and means would then be found to validate and work with and for students and their families, whatever their culture, ethnicity, social class, or family configuration. Caring, community building, and focusing on the core technology of teaching and learning would become the essential work of all educators.

Tronto (1987, 647) suggests that the ethic of care may be created in modern society by the condition of "subordination." In other words, the less powerful group, such as women or minorities, learns to attend to and read the dominant group so that their needs are taken care of, trading care for benevolence. This view contains a kernel of truth, for it is well-known that the less powerful group always has a more intimate knowledge of the dominant group (their needs, desires, interests). However, I differ with Tronto in her assumption that therefore an ethic of care is utopian and only deserving of further reflection and moral and political theorizing before it can be applied to institutions. We already have a situation in schools where new approaches to school organization and leadership are needed. Parents and schools just don't collaborate in the way that they ought to. Many children are dropping out of schools, or stay in schools with daily feelings of inadequacy—alienated from schools and society. I do not propose discontinuing philosophizing for a full theory of care, but we can begin with an ethic of care as an organizational principle to reframe parent-school relations. The concern that an ethic of care can become insular (*e.g.*, we only care for members of our family) is also valid; but I propose that a universalistic approach to morality and an ethic of care need not be mutually exclusive. Native peoples' care of the earth is one example of an ethic of care applied in an equitable and universalistic manner. Similarly, in schools an ethic of care could help address many of the problems shown in this book—the gap between schools and homes; social-class inequities; cultural, ethnic, and linguistic differences; and power-related difficulties.

Establishing Links

As an initial step, the school counselor can be an important link, providing care, providing essential knowledge, and building trust between parents and schools. The counselor typically has a close knowledge of kids and their families, particularly with regard to social and academic needs. Such knowledge is invaluable in establishing trust and in strengthening communication between schools and families. A counselor describes his work in the following way:

> With the parent liasion group I try and get a two-way communication going. We meet once a month for an hour, the first Tuesday of every month at noon. We usually start with just a very open forum. We just open it up to parents in terms of questions that they have about the programs, or things they have heard about the school, or programs that they would like to see us offer. I think it is real important not to be defensive about what we do, to be open-minded. We can identify some things that need to be changed. The other thing we do is the group becomes a sounding board, particularly for programs we're in the process of developing, so that they can come back and ask good questions and help shape it. (Interview, counselor)

Community-minded folk, such as senior citizens who have a sense of the history of a community, can also be helpful to schools searching for a strengthened school community. Locating key individuals and enlisting their support is likely to assist in establishing stronger parent collaboration with schools. However, it is not enough to leave the work of community-building to counselors and community folk. All educators can work from a position of understanding the contexts of schools and homes, and of understanding the need for an ethic of care and collaboration. Realistically, not all educators will buy into this idea, but even the die-hard supporters of the *status quo* can learn from examples of classrooms or schools where care and collaboration works, and they will begin to see differently.

Sharing the Power

Working from an ethic of care, intervention projects such as parent training, parent centers, and parent leadership cannot be top-down processes, with outsiders demanding ever-increasing levels of commitment from parents. Instead, the process should begin and end with care and respect. It is simply not fair for the conceivers of parent involvement to impose their views on parents, when parents in turn can ask so little of organizers. Family privacy may also be at issue here, with well-intentioned reformers intent upon forcing parent involvement "for their own good," without considering how that feels to those being coerced and losing their privacy. Collaboration is two-way, not an imposed relationship. Home visitations seem like a harmless and well-meaning intervention, and there are many situations where home visits will provide educational benefits, but if the impetus for home visitation comes solely from the school, and is conducted by educators holding consciously or unconsciously classist or racist views, the outcomes of such visits can be more harmful than helpful to the child. As Garlington discovered in her attempt to conduct home visits in an African American neighborhood in Baltimore, Maryland, which took place through screen doors, windows, and using family members as buffers, "visits cannot be forced regardless of the sense of urgency the program staff might feel" (1993, 14). In using an ethic of care and in sharing power the educator seeks to come to know the family and community through attending to their perspectives. If students and their parents discover that their voices are heard, and their lives validated by the school, some of the distance between home and school will likely be bridged.

Authenticity and Cultural Knowledge

Schools, their teachers, administrators, and parent leaders do not always represent the racial and cultural composition of the community. Of course race is not the only criterion for successful relationships. The more important issue for families is "not race but rather the ability to trust motives and intent" (Garlington 1993, 9). Nevertheless, racism in schools and the lack of role models and mentoring are important issues with strong implications for students' success. Capper (1990, 22–23) compares and contrasts one school community ("Deerfield") that is caring and responsive to the Native American cultural values of its clientele, with another school community ("Dover") where school was held "without ceremony" on Martin Luther King Day despite a significant African American population. Insensitivity to the school population, ignorance on the part of school officials, or racist practices, such as the example just given, can lead to tensions, hostilities, and distrust. Whose school is it, if the only norms, values, and traditions that are celebrated are white, middle class ones? Every school has a reason for celebrating Martin Luther King Day, for it is an important part of the nation's history and its lessons in social responsibility and humanity. To ignore the significance of messages sent through the use of symbols (*i.e.*, not to recognize Martin Luther King Day) is to ignore the powerful effects of school culture.

The issue of authenticity and cultural knowledge is critical. Women; African Americans; Chicanos; Latinos; disabled; and working class kids, need people in leadership positions who understand their cultures and can role-model success. At the same time, educators have to understand the characteristics of the home cultures represented in the school: Is education valued? How do men and women relate to each other in the culture? Each teacher seeks to get to know what is valued in each family. Rather than getting to know about cultural differences in a stereotypical way, teachers can connect with families and learn first-hand about their issues and concerns. An appreciation for variability within and across cultures will be developed. For instance, it may be that American Sign Language needs to be taught in a school with a deaf student, and connections or a partnership formed with a school for the deaf. All children can benefit from such diverse educational experiences, not just the individual student concerned.

Mulhern (1994) found that parents in the Latino community she studied in Chicago viewed the school as the expert and saw themselves as providing support for the school in the home setting. However, the school did not communicate with the homes about the methods of instruction used in the school, and parents had very different expectations. To the parents the "emergent writing" of their children looked like a bunch of letters with no meaning. The school had not educated parents about what holistic literacy would look like. In other words, working from an ethic of care it becomes clear to the educator that parents need to be invited into student's educational experiences.

CONCLUSION

Given the diversity of parents and students, it is not enough for schools to continue to pitch their language, goals, policies, and practices at a white, middle class audience. Schools are not currently attending adequately to the full range of parents. I have argued that schools can be more inclusive, and respect and value all parents and students, not just those who most reflect the school hierarchy's interests and purposes. Students are not well-served by being labelled as at-risk or deficient, or by being educated in isolation from their families. As Noddings (1984) points out, a caring, empathic, or responsive relationship is interactive, not one-way. For schools to be caring, which they must be in order to address current needs of children, conversations would occur. Parent-school initiatives, communication, and collaboration must be, by definition, two-way. Part of the problem to date has been that schools have been able to operate in isolation, with policy and practice carrried out on the school's terms without taking into account diverse perspectives and needs. Care and respect comes first, for all people, not just for those parents deemed worthy. Parents want very much to be appreciated and listened to, but even more importantly, they want to be respected. Policymakers and educators who take no account of the complexities of family life and the unique needs of particular social groups, including racial and ethnic minorities and/or single-parent households, will continue to reproduce entrenched patterns of social class. School is a place where children should be able to participate without the signifiers of family configuration, social class, gender, race, or ethnicity being used as gatekeeping devices to a full education. In the next chapter we further explore the ethic of caring, taking up the important issue of collaboration and community-building. The process of collaboration poses many challenges to all concerned, not least of which is how to work together when there are so many conflicting voices and interests. One of the critical considerations—if we are to move successfully in a more democratic direction—is how can schools begin to frame parents as educators and view home and school cultures as inter-dependent?

NOTES

1. In 1940 fewer than 9 percent of all women with children worked outside the home, a figure that jumped to 70 percent by the 90s (Trudel and Fisher 1992, 17).
2. The United States Supreme Court has refused to rule upon constitutional claims regarding homosexuals in education, which means that homosexuals are dealt with differently in each states' lower courts (Valente 1987).
3. Similarly, Scheurich and Imber (1991) showed how a school district's civic elite, composed of real estate developers and wealthy, white parents, worked in collusion with the school administrators to exclude participation by the low-income minority school population, who were not considered "experts" and therefore not given a voice.
4. Interestingly, parent involvement was first mandated in Head Start early childhood programs funded by the federal government in the mid 1960s. Parent involvement was then mandated in the mid 1970s for special education, but not for general education.
5. The first public school specifically addressing homosexuality in its curriculum and serving homosexual students was the Harvey Milk School in New York City (Rofes 1989). As Anderson (1994, 153) points out, this school is an attempt to "salvage the lives of gay and lesbian students who have been bashed and damaged in our school systems." Some school districts do include units on homosexuality, although in many schools homosexuality is a "non-discussable" topic (Sears 1992).

7

Collaboration and Community-Building

> The feminist framework focuses on
> female leadership as community building,
> which increases levels of job satisfaction.
> (Ortiz and Marshall 1988, 137)

> The Rainbow Coalition specifically pre-
> serves and institutionalizes in its form of
> organizational discussion the heteroge-
> neous groups that make it up. The aims of
> equality and respect are met by highlight-
> ing differences, not by transcending them
> or looking beneath them for a common
> foundation. (Welch 1991, 83)

It makes good sense for schools and families to collaborate—to work together around the common mission of the education of the child, rather than operating as separate entities—for schools occupy only a portion of a child's life. Walberg (1984, 397) argues that twelve years of schooling equal about 13 percent of a student's waking life over the course of eighteen years. Thus, parents and the peer group are involved with 87 percent of the student's waking time. And many students do not get twelve years of schooling. Clearly, schools need to tap into the knowledge that parents have of their children, for reasons of sharing knowledge, enhancing learning for students, and building support for schools. However, relating to and collaborating with parents and community is a challenge. Today more than ever, educators must be committed to communicating with parents from an ever-increasing variety of cultural, ethnic, language and social-class backgrounds, and orientations. The Eurocentric, middle class culture of the public school can no longer remain detached from its pluralistic clientele—expecting them to change while the school remains the same.

An important part of administrator and teacher preparation is now the competency to: (a) engage in creating community spirit and a strong school culture that celebrates pluralism and diversity; and, (b) communicate and work together with diverse individuals from a range of perspectives and backgrounds. Educators have to go out into their communities with empathy, and interact meaningfully with their constituents. Being professional can no longer mean remaining isolated in the school. Traditionally, public schools have used parental involvement for their own purposes—to maintain "control" over how the community relates to the school (Van Galen 1987). If parent involvement in public schools is defined in terms of the way the school wishes to be supported, then this is a top-down or one-way relationship. The caring ethic and interdependent relationships discussed in the previous chapter work best in environments that stress a sense of community (Beck 1994, 11). Trust, which is so essential, is achieved in a community setting that values diversity and pluralism.

Mark Twain's *The Adventures of Huckelberry Finn* ([1885] 1981) illustrates an ethic of care necessary for community building:

> Huck Finn learns to see his companion and runaway slave, Jim, as a person with human needs and feelings, and he learns to care for Jim even as Jim cares for him. At one point in the story, Huck contemplates turning Jim over to the authorities. His culture has taught him that this would be morally right. Indeed, Huck has been led to believe that he risks punishment in hell if he does not turn in Jim. In a moving passage of the novel, Huck grapples with his culture and his conscience and finally decides, "All right, then, I'll go to hell" (206), rather than betray his friend (Beck 1994, 19).

Through the act of caring, Huck Finn in fact finds not hell, but peace and satisfaction. In giving to the other and risking his personal life, Huck is rewarded. Schools can also create conditions where people are aware of their interdependence, and seek not to dominate or compete with others, but rather to work together in collaborative projects—to care for and about one another while respecting each others' freedom and wishes. Education is about teaching students to be members of a community, not to embrace think-alike, look-alike values. And it is about teaching students to work with and value those who are different as well as those who are most like ourselves. A community can thus be an interesting multiplicity of voices held together by a commitment to care and collaboration, and in the case of schools, by a commitment to students and to their learning.

Collaboration is built on cooperation, group effort, and a sense of belonging to a caring community: you work with and for others, and they look out for you. Such an approach has been displaced in many of our institutions, including schools. Individualism, personal success and competition have been rewarded (McCaleb 1994, 45; Bellah *et al.* 1985; Etzioni 1993). Alienation, atomism, and aloneness result when there is an over-emphasis on doing things alone and when there is an absence of caring, nurturing communities. Bellah *et al.* (1985) suggest that a misunderstanding of the intentions of America's founders has resulted in extreme individualism: personal rights at the expense of others; independence and competition with an impoverished sense of community. Competition may seem like a motivating force, but students and their parents can give up the struggle if it appears that the game is stacked against them, as it must seem to so many children today. If students learn to work collaboratively in problem solving, they are not only generating new knowledge, but learning to live and work together across cultures and languages.

IT TAKES US ALL

In tribal societies all members of the community are involved in the critical process of bringing up the young, so that they may, in turn, lead and govern and contribute to the good of the community (Davies 1991). Modern schooling, with its specialized functions, has much to learn from tribal societies and the education of their young, and from the nineteenth-century integrative community schools of the rural United States. If parents are involved in the life of schools and given a direct voice in governance and other key decision making, schools will benefit in a number of ways.

First, students learn by example that the school is an institution to be valued. Even if students do not actually receive parental help and guidance academically, the collaboration of parents with schools sends a powerful message that school matters. The carryover of parent-school collaboration to student achievement is considerable. Studies of recent immigrant families, in which parents value schooling highly, provide evidence for the value of school-home connections (Gibson 1987). If families support the notion of schooling, this in itself, I believe, will yield positive results for school performance. One way to transform education, I believe, is by practicing feminist ideals in leadership. Significantly, feminism is a political movement that has advocated for and gained legal and social rights for women, and it is also an intellectual school of thought grounded in principles of equality, respect, and humanity. Feminism thus offers a philosophical approach and strategies for organizational structures and leadership to help frame school-parent relations.

Second, as we have seen, parents represent a large body of human resources that is currently untapped. Parents represent a wide variety of backgrounds and interests and occupations, from the unemployed single mother to the CEO of a major corporation. Every parent possesses knowledge and skills that they use in their day-to-day work. While the children in each particular family benefit from the worldview and experience of their parents, this expertise could be brought into schools to provide a sharing of perspectives. Schools have become caught up in the fallacy that they represent learning environments in and of themselves, with one group of students taught by one professional educator. Opportunities exist to open the school doors to the many parents and citizens who have much to teach students, and not just as reading volunteers or people to be used on the school's terms. Parents possess knowledge and skills and ideas that they are able to share with children and youth. All the adults in traditional societies teach the younger generation ethics and wisdom for their future survival. But our schools today have become isolated from their communities to such an extent that this often creates a bureaucratic difficulty or a legal standoff with teachers' unions when attempts are made to open the school doors to alternative conceptions of organization and multiple learning opportunities.

Third, better decisions can be made if contributors to schools represent diverse perspectives. Education has become inbred and inward-looking to the extent that educators talk mostly to other educators. The lines of professionalism have prevented cross-linkages and openness to new ideas. Schools can, however, become *more like communities* through an emphasis on personalization, collaboration, and a feminist ethic of care. One parent puts it this way: "You can't input [sic] a computer if you don't know how it works. It's the same with kids. Teachers today have to be more like parents and they have to know the parents, because kids are dealing with many more issues and losses—divorce, drugs, you name it. Young people need teachers who can relate to those feelings and turn them into something positive." All educators need not only to understand students and the social context in which they work; they need to be invested in the "whole village" of the community (Oliver *et al.* 1994).

Nevertheless, we also have to remember that while parent involvement appears to be good for children, parents, and educators, we also need, as Lareau (1989b) points out, to consider the "dark side" of parent involvement. The dark side is that the culture of the school is more supportive of upper-middle class families than of working class families. Families are unequal in the social practices and resources available to them to intervene in their children's schooling. Further, when parent involvement is seen as the "proper" relationship between the family and the school, a two-track system is established of the "haves" and the "have nots" which may accentuate stress between families and schools. Thus, in advocating for educators to work with parents and schools, the ethic of care must underpin all policy and practice, for we need to be aware of the implications of what we are doing, continually asking, Is this best for the student? Mandating parent involvement, for instance, without providing needed resources to enable full participation, may further tip the scales in favor of those already advantaged.

CREATING COLLABORATIVE ORGANIZATIONAL STRUCTURES

So, how do we begin to turn the tables on traditional patterns of bureaucracy and defensiveness? A starting point is to acknowledge that reproducing the *status quo* is grounded in a fear of change. As we can see, schools remain remarkably unchanged, "intractable" in Seymour Sarason's words (1990). Many educators in this study call them "dinosaurs." Reducing fear, building up trust, and risk-taking are necessary first steps towards establishing authentic parent-school collaboration.

The following strategies are just some of the many that educators, parents and others can employ in working towards a more inclusive collaborative relationship between parents and educators.

Reversal as a Communication Device

In anthropology, in order to gain an "emic" or "insider's" perspective, the researcher engages in fieldwork—living amongst the people. Walking in the shoes of the people studied is necessary in order to reconstruct how the world works for them. If educators want to understand how it feels to be a parent (and many of them *are* parents in other contexts), it is a useful exercise to reverse roles, even if this is simply a visualizing exercise and not acted out. An example would be to reflect on the current pattern of professional staffing around special education, where a team of five or six different service providers meet with the parent(s) of a particular child to lay out a plan. As we saw in chapter 3, a parent or parents can feel intimidated by professionals, who seem to know what is best for the child and may not listen well to the issues and concerns of the parents. If we reverse the situation mentally, with one teacher and five or six parents advising the teacher on how best to teach their children, we gain a sense of the one-way nature of the communication.

A parent voiced the following concern at a parent meeting in Robertson School District:

> The school bus transfer at the park is just not working well and needs attention. At the park there are kids of all ages, with very little supervision. I know you hired one person recently to do that, but I'm not sure she can handle all the disputes. The other day a first grader was very distressed. The little kids have no shelter, there is no phone if anything goes wrong, there is no bathroom. When the kids get on the bus at school I'm not sure they always realise that it's gonna be a long while till they can go to the bathroom.

In response, Superintendent Carroll wrote on the overhead projector—for he was recording the comments—"A concern with liability." The parent was concerned with children's safety and happiness, but the superintendent translated the issue into one of liability. Both concerns are valid, however the parent needed to be recognized for his focus on the children.

Another example of educators needing to take the other's perspective comes from Robertson High School:

> They have a freshman program of sending the students out on adventure training, and it's a bonding process and they send all the freshmen to this two-day adventure. Students go on ropes and all that and it's a great program. Well the counselor approached me and he said, "I want to talk to you about getting the PTA to take on the adventure dynamics." He said, "PTA says that they don't just want to be baking cookies and raising funds, so this is your opportunity to get involved." Now immediately I was turned off. It really made me mad when he said "You *say* that you want to be involved." I was insulted because in the first place we do much more than bake cookies and raise funds. And he was asking for probably ten days with four people volunteering all day, so this is a major undertaking. Asking volunteers to do that just to save them money—and "we're not going to pay you to do this because your time isn't worth any more than that." If it were initiated by the parents, something the parents wanted to do, and they got involved and organized and did it, that would be different. But in this case the school started it and then they just wanted to pass it off. (Interview, parent)

Both sides—parents and educators—need to be able to genuinely appreciate the other's expertise and contributions, and have respect for the efforts of the other. Language is critical. In the case above, the one word used by the counselor, "You *say* you want to be involved," carried with it the implication that parents are not sincere in their claims, and the parent reacted with further alienation.

Shared Decision Making

In traditional professionalism, school administrators act as "trustees" rather than as partners in their relationships with parents. Trustees see themselves as professionals—authoritative experts who are able to make the best decisions for children. Thus, in a traditional view, superintendents see themselves as heads of quasi-corporations, and pride themselves on the fiscal management and directing of those corporations. As an example of the corporate model, an announcement of a meeting for Robertson School District (described in chapter 1) reads as follows:

FIRST ANNUAL ROBERTSON SCHOOL DISTRICT
STAKEHOLDERS MEETING

All patrons of the Robertson School district are invited to the
First Annual Stakeholders Meeting. The School District is a $16
million corporation, and like many corporations we will be holding
a meeting of those who have a stake in the organization — that
means all citizens, staff, students and interested parties.

As part of our new goal-setting process, we are initiating this
meeting so that the School Board may hear from the constituents of
the School District.

Particulars of the meeting:

Wednesday, February 16
Scott Auditorium, 7:30 PM

Agenda
State of the District
Financial Report
Presentation of Ideas for Improvement for the
1994-95 School Year
Public Input

We are hoping for an excellent turnout.

Traditional administrative practices for school-community relations
are thus aimed at disarming critics, "selling" the school through public
relations such as newsletters, activities, and the like, and teaching parents and others how they should relate to the school (Morris *et al.* 1984).
The hierarchical, top-down, trustee model of administration is also frequently the norm in administrator preparation: "Educators seldom are
trained in, or have opportunities to observe, delegatelike [partnership]
administration" (Crowson 1992, 9). Bottom-up, responsive administrative strategies, as opposed to hierarchical strategies, are often thought to
be too "weak" to be effective in today's schools. Thus, in Robertson
School District, to implement "shared decision making" in line with
state legislated reform, Superintendent Carroll set up a committee which
was answerable to him, and which had limited decision-making powers:

The shared-decision-making, or "reform" committee as it is called,
is comprised of two community members, a school board member,
three teachers, two principals, the superintendent, his administrative

assistant, and myself. It is very difficult, however, for a group like this to sit down and try to talk about something like this within a bureaucratic setting because everyone knows how open the superintendent really is by saying this is what we're going to try. Everybody knows there are strict parameters, and until you get the superintendent to actually tell you OK these are the decisions that I am going to let you have a go at, and those that you are not able to, you can't go forward. (Interview, team member)

To help close the gap between the intent of the reforms and actual practices, feminist leadership is long overdue, and we cannot ignore its potential to impact schools powerfully. Feminist thought on administrative practices has been and will continue to be critical in shaping the new administrative directions (see Capper 1993; Grogan 1994; Harding 1993; Marshall 1992; Noddings 1991/1992, 1992, 1994; Ortiz and Marshall 1988; Shakeshaft 1993). Actual shared decision making, as opposed to the current androcentric organization, which is bureaucratic and hierarchical, can be a vital part of the new innovations.

Parent-school collaboration can become an authentic process—not merely a public relations exercise. "Listening" to parents and giving them window-dressing roles on committees is not collaboration with parents. Work with parents is best done not simply from the school's perspective or for parents, but by and with parents. It can include matters of importance, such as having a say in financial decisions and in the hiring of personnel—not just the token participation that sometimes occurs. Some of the work that can be done together, in addition to policy work, includes: joint projects of parents, board members, teachers, and administrators; collaborative planning and visioning; engaging in child studies; teaming around student-centered problems and issues; and jointly celebrating students' successes.

A Standpoint of Respect

Administrators and teachers do not always *respect* parents as partners in the educational process. Educators may do nothing to inform parents adequately so that they can engage in useful discussions, and then may complain because the resulting discussion is trivial, focusing on matters such as dress and discipline.

Ziegler *et al.* (1977) argues that in the present technological age the superintendent is propelled into a dominating role because school board members are faced with educational knowledge too complex for them to understand. This is part of the mystique of professionalism. Giving a structural "voice" to parents without providing the knowledges, norms, and political base to effectively become an equal collaborative partner in the educational process is little more than a token gesture toward parental involvement. Educators are able to mystify education and the school system by making problems inaccessible to parents. As Reed and Mitchell (1975, 202) point out, even the superintendent often mystifies educational practices for parents on the school board: "He [sic] can usually gain control over most policy questions by simply defining them as technical questions requiring [his] expertise. Thus the superintendent is as much a 'separator' of the board from the school as he is a link between them." And as we have seen, a dominating role often leads to miscommunication and alienation.

Communicative competence for teachers and administrators also means being sensitive to the educational levels of parents. As one working class parent in Lareau's study noted, educators can be inclusive or exclusive in their language and communicative style:

> It all depends on the person and how they treat you. If they start using big words, you think, "Oh God what does that mean?" You know, it is just like going to the doctor's. And it makes you feel a little insuperior to them. Because I don't have the education they do. You know, I just don't. (1989, 108)

Parents can feel vulnerable to the impenetrable cloak of the professional educator's jargon and terminology, including pedagogical terminology, state and federal rules and deadlines, policy statements, and guidelines and the "expert" opinions of educators. Ignorance on the part of parents about school programs may contribute to parents' unwillingness to speak out, even on issues that concern them. Educators, in turn, play a part in maintaining parents' ignorance by mystifying school goals, policies, and processes, thus distancing parents and minimizing potential conflict. As Foster (1986) notes, hierarchy and language distortions are common in relations between educators and parents.

It is not only parents and educators who talk in different languages. Professionals sometimes cannot talk to other professionals. Each profession has its own language and its own sets of rules, professional assumptions, perceptions of clients needs, and approaches to service delivery that may not be intelligible or acceptable to others. These differences sometimes occur even between administrators and teachers. In the service-integrated schools of the future, public service professionals, such as educators, public health nurses, social workers, law enforcement officers, child psychologists, parents, and community organizers may all be working together. In some schools this is already happening, in what are known as full service schools. The various professionals who work in schools are going to have to find ways to work with each other, with parents, and with community people so that the whole is more than the sum of the parts. Finding a common language, or at least being able to understand the other's perspective, is essential.

Seeking Outside Perspectives

Administrators and teachers are also going to have to learn to communicate effectively with leaders in the community and with a wide range of parents. Recent reform efforts to involve businesses in schools have met with resistance on both sides. Business people and educators are often distrustful of each others' expertise and commitment (Jones and Maloy 1988; Trubowitz *et al.* 1984). "Different workaday . . . languages, traditions of decision-making . . . competing interests and perspectives" result in distrust on both sides (Crowson 1992, 15). Business people do not always respect educators, viewing many practices in state organizations and schools as inept and sloppy by private business standards. Indeed, the way that schools do business in attempting to mimic business practices, (*e.g.*, "We are like a corporation") sets them up for failure. Schools are not businesses. The central work of schools is the education of children, and children are not goods to be processed and sold, but humans to be nurtured and brought up to be creators of and participants in the wider world. If schools focus on their central work, the education of children, all else will fall into place. If students are to be educated well, then it makes good sense to be responsive to family contexts and to form collaborative partnerships with all those who have an interest in education. From this perspective, business people, among many others, have something to offer schools. We have to be careful, however, that schools are not "bought" by business interests and turned into commercial ventures. And we also have to be careful that the central *public* mission of the school is upheld.

Collaborative work can be done around the development of a school's mission and purpose. Parents, teachers, and principals who work together to create a mission are more likely to be invested in the school. The school becomes *their* school. Such work is never completed, but rather is part of an ongoing process of clarification of these questions: What does the school stand for? What is worth standing up for? Dewey (1938) showed the importance of constantly revisiting one's mission in order to renew commitment and ensure that one is not merely pursuing a mission that is no longer passionately upheld. Instead of trying harder at the same goals, we need to be constantly asking, Are we going in the right direction?

Consideration also needs to be given to the values that are upheld in the school community, so that they are inclusive and not exclusive. Welch's (1991) discussion of the assumptions underpinning Jesse Jackson's Rainbow Coalition is useful here. Welch points out that uniting for a common purpose can be oppressive, since only certain dominant interests are served. Instead, community is needed that has the means to criticize injustice, forms of exclusion, and limitation in any given social system (86). A community becomes more vital with multiple constituencies, and with divergent principles, norms, and mores. Interaction and collaborative projects—doing things together—are essential for the creation of such a community.

Informal communication can be a useful means of building trust. Daily, weekly, or monthly interchanges between parents and teachers help establish a view of the school as supportive or critical of the home culture. Students learn through these interchanges whether the school is valued by the parent: "These daily (chance) interactions certainly had weightier significance than the vacuous, ritualistic PTA meetings scheduled by the school. They were more highly personalized and direct, and they often evoked strong emotion and passion" (Lightfoot 1978, 11). Or, in the words of a parent in Robertson School District:

> Being at the high school a lot I know what is going on, and so it's very helpful to me. I know all the teachers by name and so I interact with them better. They come up to me. I feel much more that we are on the same team. Being known, being around, has a lot to do with it. (Interview, parent)

As administrators and teachers tend to these seemingly unimportant interactions, lines of communication, trust and supportive relations can be built.

The View that We Cannot Teach Kids in Isolation

At the end of my fieldwork in Robertson School District I was able to study an alternative, inner city Milwaukee public school with an 86 percent African American student population. I was one of a team of seven researchers from across the country (San Francisco, New York, Columbus, Denver) who had previously studied the alternative form of education (Waldorf) that was being implemented in this inner city public school. What was fascinating was the use of Waldorf education for African American, inner city, low-income students; until then it had been used exclusively with largely white, upper-middle class (and frequently rural) children. Part of the Waldorf philosophy is a commitment to parents. How would an inner city school achieve a good working relationship with parents? Seventy six percent of the students were on free or reduced lunch, and the neighborhood was characterized this way by the principal: "[It's] a high crime and depressed area. Killings and violence and drug situations do happen. The area can be considered unsafe, just as the world itself is often unsafe. It's good to be aware of that. This is a more depressed area than other parts of the city."

Nevertheless, while being "careful and alert" to danger, the principal encouraged her faculty to go out into the community, to work with parents, because "you can't teach kids in isolation." Teachers did not set out to change parents, but rather to meet them halfway, to show them that the school is a comfortable place to be, that they would be listened to, that there were important tasks that they could do, and that parents are valued. Some teachers practiced regular home visits and even took children and parents on weekend trips and other excursions. Not all faculty bought into this. Many did live out in the suburbs far away from the school. Other teachers, both black and white, worked with families, getting to know their issues and concerns and respecting their perspectives. From the principal's viewpoint, it is "not a racial thing or . . . suburbs versus inner city. Those teachers who are here are supposed to be here. It isn't for everyone, philosophy or location, and the ones who are here are here for a reason." What was remarkable was an understanding and intent on the part of the principal and many of the faculty to teach kids: not in isolation, but in relationship to their families.

Schools that isolate themselves from the community they serve have been written about in the literature. Rosenfeld (1971, 103) describes a Harlem school and community:

> Though Harlem School belonged to the neighborhood, it was not psychologically a part of it. On the contrary, teachers felt unwanted, estranged. Perhaps this was why few ventured off the "beaten paths" to the "hinterland" beyond the school, into the side streets and the homes where the children played out their lives. Some teachers at Harlem School had never been to a single child's household, despite the fact that they had been employed at the school for many years. Nothing was known of community self-descriptions, the activity and social calendar in the neighborhood, the focal points for assembly and dispersal, or the feelings of residents toward the "outside world." Teachers could not imagine that they could foster a genuine coming-together of neighborhood persons and themselves. They hid behind their "professionalism."

If teachers and administrators are not part of the school community psychologically—caring about the lives of the students and the cultural baggage that they bring to the classroom—how can students' needs and interests be met?

In Robertson School District, teachers and administrators are very much a part of the community. For instance, when a local parade was held, teachers from Fairfield Elementary School formed a marching band, complete with baton twirlers, and joined in the festivities:

> Besides being real personable and always getting people involved in what's going on, this is a really family-oriented place. I've just always liked it and had a good feeling here. I mean teachers and everything are totally committed and involved and you get that feeling that they all work together. It's just a nice place to be involved with, and so you feel like you want to be involved more. In bigger places you could get swallowed up. Here everyone's involved in education because that's their life. Some of these people have never had kids of their own, but they're devoted to the cause of what they're doing. (Interview, parent)

Nevertheless, there are sectors of the community that are alienated and isolated from the schools—typically single parents, those on welfare, the working poor, and low-income ethnic minorities. Spindler (1987, 165) notes that disarticulation or separation between school and community occurs when teachers and the school are from a different subculture than the students and their parents, a finding that is supported by the present study. This has implications for the hiring of diverse faculty and for preparation programs that teach educators about the educational issues of culture, language, and learning.

Diverse Membership Patterns

One of the key barriers to school change is the tendency toward social reproduction. The *status quo* is maintained even while instituting supposed reforms. Parents may be listened to and serve as token members on committees without sufficient leverage to really influence important decisions. For example, a parent representative serves on the selection committee to hire new teachers at Robertson High School. The committee includes the principal, the vice principal, a department head and a university professor. And there is a concern that one parent voice may be "window dressing" and that "if it's not a strong individual who can stand up and fight for what they believe in then they could easily be intimidated by all those professsionals and teachers" (Interviews, high school parents).

Another example is that site-based councils can simply reproduce traditional governance methods (Malen, Ogawa and Kranz 1990). How is this achieved? Principals are able to retain their authoritative roles by monitoring and controlling a membership pattern that discourages conflict and initiative. In Robertson School District, as we saw earlier, parents and community people who serve the schools were sometimes selected and encouraged for their potential for supportiveness. Supportiveness itself is not a negative quality, but it could prevent necessary changes and new directions.

One of the strategies used across the country to enhance more diverse participation in schools as well as interaction between parents and educators is the establishment of parent (or family) centers. Parent centers are spaces in schools where parents, teachers, and community people can meet to talk, gain information, and generally interact. Funding for such centers has come from a variety of sources, including school operation funds, Chapter 1 federal funds, fundraising carnivals, foundation grants, and donations from school partners. Most of the parent centers have paid staff or are in the process of fundraising in order to pay volunteer staff. Paid staff serve as linkage agents in the schools in order to move schools and families toward collaborative relationships (Johnson 1993, 1994, 1994a). While the idea of parent or family centers has merit, and is proposed here as a possible change toward establishing open lines of communication, the parent centers ought not merely reinforce traditional parent-school relationships. One problem evident in reports on family centers is that those parents and community people who are involved in the centers—who drop by to have a cup of coffee, visit with other parents and teachers, and so on—are the converted, not those who are culturally/linguistically different, or those distanced from the school.

This strategy of setting aside space and resources in the school to reach out to parents is commendable, but it must not simply be a place for the valued parents. All parents have something to offer schools. Teachers, staff, and administrators who are themselves representative of the diversity of the neighborhood and whose hearts and minds embrace diversity in all its manifestations—social class, ethnicity, gender, and so on—will help foster diverse participation in schools.

Developing a Shared Language

The language of educators and parents is often worlds apart, exacerbating the gap between the cultures of schools and homes. Just as Tannen (1990) shows that men and women experience communication difficulties because they are often working from different cultural assumptions, rules, and understandings, so too are parents and educators coming from quite different perspectives. The language of educators is riddled with jargon and acronyms for "new" programs, unintelligible to the uninitiated. For example, OBE, ELRs, TQM, SLOs, SLIPs, SLIGs, HB1209, are just a few of the terms bandied about in the Robertson public schools that I have been in for these past two years. Parents can feel uninformed when they hear these terms used without explanation:

> A lot of jargon was used in the survey that was sent out, and I understood it because I'm also trained as a teacher, I know that language, but I don't think the average person does. I don't think there's any opportunity for real input. (Interview, parent)

> You don't have the same base of experience there, and we've got to
> be very careful we don't come on too teachery. We have to kind of
> fill them [parents on committees] in on what's going on building
> wide, district wide. You have to fight being teachery because we
> really get into it when you just meet with teachers year after year.
> You begin to speak that common language that only teachers
> understand. (Interview, teacher)

The irony is that there is nothing so difficult about any of the terms, but
they can be used in such a way as to alienate and exclude people who do
not have access to their meanings. You can't even look up many educators' terms in a dictionary, for they are coined words or acronyms that
have become part of "professional" educators' knowledge base.

Parents may then defer to professional educators, even when they
have an important contribution to make. As Nemzoff (1993, 62) notes
with regard to legally mandated parent-school collaboration in devising
Individual Educational Plans (IEPs) for special educational students,
the professional use of jargon can have the effect of "precluding real
maternal [and I would add "paternal"] participation" in educational
planning. Accepted practices of using so-called professional language
and the language of rationality means that only part of a parent's voice is
brought into the conversation:

> Professionals often view mothers as foot soldiers in their treat-
> ment plans . . . The IEP setting is one in which the mother must
> curb her emotion and speak in a controlled fashion. Yet deep emo-
> tion is a necessary component of her maternal work. Protocol
> demands that the mother participate impartially and with great
> control. Thus the mother may speak with only part of "her voice."
> (1993, 63).

The new ideas and wisdom that could be generated by parents using
emotional as well as rational knowledges may be subordinated to the
commonly held "expert" ideas and practices of teachers and administrators. If the different perspectives of parents are not given a chance to
spark new initiatives, then site-based management and reforms for parent-school collaboration will fail to have any real impact on schools.
When educators are truly sincere about shared decision making they
will find ways to communicate clearly and effectively with all types of

parents. Educational language is only a tool for precise use of terms to deliver better educational services. It should not obscure knowledge or alienate people. Well-educated teachers and administrators are able to communicate readily with a wide range of people and to use the parents' knowledge to inform educational practices.

New Knowledges and Skills

To employ the strategies that I am advocating, schools would have to learn to educate not only from within themselves, but also in collaboration with parents. Training for teachers and administrators to work with parents would become part of professional development. Currently, school-community relations are dealt typically with in one or two courses designed to teach administrators and teachers how to engage in successful public relations. Partnership of schools with parents will require quite different knowledges, skills, and abilities in educators in the following areas:

• *Communication.* Schools engage in a two-way conversation and reciprocal dialogue through such means as newsletters, written reports, parental access to records, meetings in school, home visitations, and PTAs. In addition, competence and sensitivity is needed in understanding the cultures of the home. Heath (1983) shows how important this is. The style of communicative competence of principals and teachers may vary with the socio-economic profile of the school or of subgroups within the school. For instance, a school with a predominantly upper-middle class clientele is likely to have parents who do not automatically defer to the teacher's authority (Lareau 1989, 164). This is the case in Robertson School District, where some parents argue, "I feel sorry for the teachers, because here everyone's an expert. They all think they know better than the teachers." Many of these parents are willing to offer direct criticism of the school or teacher. Educators thus must not only be competent, but able to articulate in a number of different linguistic codes the rationale behind their thinking, and to inspire the confidence of parents.

• *Concepts and Perspectives.* All too often, parents are seen as "advisory" or "helpers" in a supportive role to the school. Reframing the views of educators towards a more inclusive view of partnerships and collaboration around the education of the child can be attended to by beginning educators. Attitudes of the veteran teachers and administrators in the schools may be more difficult to change than those of new teachers.

- *Diversity in Child-rearing and Parenting Practices.* Educators, through their interaction with families, need to come to see that when they complain about working parents they are out of touch with current realities, and that when the school only validates white, middle class forms of child-rearing, it is perpetuating racist practices.
- *Shared Decision Making.* Educators are going to have to become competent in working with parents on matters of significance, such as policies and operations of the school—assessment, school mission, curriculum, finance, personnel searches, and so on. The sharing of decisions between educators and the laity can be studied and practiced throughout professional preparation programs. Learning to trust the expertise of collaborators—whether families, neighbors, businesses or university professors—in making important school decisions is critical. Each collaborator represents different interests and perspectives which must be equally valued if decisions are to be made collaboratively. Those in schools thus need to learn how to work collaboratively, and not just impose school-based views and practices on parents.
- *Inter-Agency Collaboration.* The ability to work with government services and other social agencies and to educate parents about these services is today important knowledge for educators.
- *De-mystifying and De-bureaucratizing Education Systems.* Educators can problem-solve and work on ways to create more informal contact with parents. In other words, educators can experiment with ways to work well in an educational setting that does not need mystification to make itself look better than it really is.
- *Non-Sexist Education.* Sexist policies and practices continue to this day in public schools. Every time I heard administrators and teachers using sexist language in Robertson schools (*e.g.*, the so-called generic "he" and "mankind") I realized how far we still need to go in addressing this problem. Modelling of non-sexist, non-racist, and non-classist practices in a school environment teaches students much more than the formal curriculum and will stand students in good stead as they go out into the world.

CONCLUSION

Work for community-building includes: the process of reflecting on current patterns and listening to the voices of parents and community people; reframing the school-community as an ecology of people and events that interrelate; and developing new practices and approaches, such as participants getting to know each other through common activities. Strategies that can be implemented include the following: (a) reversal as a communication device; (b) shared decision making; (c) a standpoint of respect; (d) actively seeking and valuing outside perspectives; (e) the view that we cannot teach kids in isolation; (f) diverse membership patterns; (g) developing a shared language; and (h) learning new knowledges and skills. The ecology of the school-community thus places children in a social context and begins from a foundation of the quality of *relationships* between parents and educators.

Parent-school collaboration will occur only if a responsive community built around public values has been formed, and if parents' needs are taken into account. "Common values" does not mean homogeneity. The commonality may well be a commitment to public values such as diversity, equity, and social change, but it is important that the school-community is a viable group with a sense of itself *as* a community. Community ought not preclude discourse, debate, and conflict. On the contrary, the *status quo* is that matters of conflict are not discussable or are dealt with covertly through silent negotiation (*e.g.*, a "no" vote on the bond or enrolling children in private school), which leads to further resentment and hostility. Conflict between parents and schools needs to be embraced as an avenue toward growth and enhanced educational practices. An open door policy is needed and a demonstrated commitment to not only listen to all perspectives on an issue, but to seek to make changes in new directions—always bearing in mind what is in the student's best interests. While public schools are often large and unwieldy, they can be scaled down into smaller teaching and learning units and become more flexible and more accepting of different views.

Teachers and administrators are encouraged to actively seek out ways to get to know parents and to make them feel genuinely connected with the school. Teachers cannot effectively teach kids if they have only limited knowledge of the students they teach. The process of competent communication with parents begins in teacher and administrator preparation and should continue throughout educators' careers. Schools and teachers do need to be sensitive to cultural differences among students and parents. Developing strategies for communication with all parents can be made a central part of the school's mission, and attention can be given to creating a welcoming school environment for all. Issues of multiculturalism, diversity, and equity are particularly important here.

Traditional administrative practices in public schools aimed at creating an impenetrable mystique. Parents were to be managed by the competent administrator. Parents were to be involved in ways that helped reflect a positive image of the school, not necessarily in ways the parents themselves wanted. Distancing between educator and parent was sought. Similarly, traditional practices for teachers include isolation and autonomy. Teachers teach in the isolation of their classrooms and are able to make autonomous judgements based on their professional expertise.

Today, administrators are beginning to reframe their relationships with parents. Administrators must not only engage in discourse with parents, as we saw in chapter 1 with the annual stakeholders meeting, they must actively collaborate and consult with parents on educational matters and be prepared to share administrative power. New structures mean new skills and approaches. Teachers must forge new relationships with parents, and begin to see them also as educators. It is critical that administrators and teachers know their school community well, in order to be able to build collaborative relations based on the character and strengths of that community, so that educational accountability is enhanced. The next chapter focuses on the attention of teachers and administrators to the core technology of teaching and learning. As one teacher put it, "Teaching kids today is more challenging, but it's what keeps me, every day of my life, happy to get up in the morning and coming to work. I love it. But you can't teach well if you know nothing about the kids, what matters to them, where they come from, what's going on in their lives."

8

A Focus on Teaching and Learning

> Leaders would be intensely involved in
> the actual production units of the organi-
> zation (teaching and learning) and serve
> the organizational workers by resolving
> conflicts and coordinating resources.
> (Ortiz and Marshall 1988, 138)

> Ultimately, the focus for professional
> work and discourse, for study and growth,
> will be teaching and learning . . . others
> besides principals fall into the noninstruc-
> tional category—testers, counselors . . . I
> would make the same argument regarding
> them: they should not be permitted to flee
> the classroom if they want to work in
> schools. (Sacken 1994, 670)

Competition is embedded in public school practices and in approaches to
teaching and learning. Teachers compete with one another for status and
merit pay, and to be promoted out of the classroom and into the administrative ranks. Students compete with one another for desirable labels,
(*e.g.*, "honors student"). The notion of competition is of course central to
the competitive marketplace economy of this society. A competitive
view considers schools primarily in relationship to the marketplace.
Schools are to sort, classify, and credential students for their roles in the
productive labor force (Bowles and Gintis 1976). However, schools also
can be viewed as places where social values are nurtured so that an ethical and democratic citizenry, who are also competent and well edu-

cated, are prepared for their world. Considerable evidence in recent years points to the harmful effects of a single focus on competition, and supports instead school cultures based on an ethic of care. Studies have shown a link between noncompetitive school environments and students' academic achievement (Beck 1994; Dillon 1989; Grant 1988; Lightfoot 1983). Thus, the marketplace, business-economic model is brought into question. Perhaps business principles dominated by a profit motive are not the best ones to apply to the education of children. Bad products can be forced out of the business marketplace and replaced with more competitive ones. But schools ought not be in the business of labeling some students as bad products, for students are not products that can be thrown away. They will stay with our society for a life span and will educate their children to be either for or against the system.

Instead of a goal of competition, I am advocating for collaboration informed by an ethic of care. Beck (1994, 64) notes that:

> A caring ethic does not negate the importance of academic achievement, vocational competence, or economic health, for these contribute to both personal and community well being . . . the values of caring actually subsume those held by leaders accepting a competitive ethic. The latter would consider the achievement of dominance in the marketplace to be the chief reason for education. The former, on the other hand, emphasizing the worth of persons, would view anything that promoted personal development— including academic and vocational competency—as being of value.

Is this simply idealism? Can students benefit academically and socially from a collaborative community? I believe they can. When relationships in a classroom, school, or community are built on a foundation of caring, trust and self-respect, which are necessary for learning, follow. Caring educators do not allow students to compete on a zero-sum-game basis. Rather, ways and means are found to promote *all* students' wellbeing and to validate their concerns. If schools adopt a collaborative approach to school organization, teaching, and learning, then two key things are likely to happen: (a) parents and community become part of the school; and (b) all work of the school is focused on teaching and learning and how best to facilitate an educative learning environment that meets the needs of all children, not just those for whom schooling has always worked.

From the feminist standpoint advocated in this book, schools are informed by an ethic of care; schools are communities of learners, and focus on the core technology of teaching and learning. Many teachers argue that they do not actively seek administrative positions—the principalship and the superintendency—because this takes them out of the classroom and out of contact with children, where the *real work* is done. The small numbers of women in the superintendency, 5.0 percent nationwide (Shakeshaft 1993, 86) may be explained by sexism and barriers to women, but an additional and unresearched piece of the puzzle may be women's undivided loyalty to children, and a mindset that views work outside the classroom as disconnected, and therefore not important. Currently, the superintendency has been constructed as a public and political role, not one that focuses on teaching and learning. I am arguing that the superintendency can be reconfigured instead as a teaching and service role, and that we need to reconsider the separation of administration (predominantly male) from teaching (predominantly female) so that *all* educators' work is more closely aligned and focuses on the core technology of teaching and learning. By contrast, in the current dominant structure of schooling, administrators protect teachers from parents and the community.

Focusing on teaching and learning does not mean that educators would shut themselves in isolated classrooms unaware of the lives of their students, and live apart (physically and/or psychologically) from the community. As Dorothy St. Charles, a dynamic African American principal leading an inner city alternative school in Milwaukee put it: "They [the community] love us here. They love their school. We have taken kids who were hostile, aggressive, and alienated, and now they want to come to school. The parents are grateful and they know us." This, in one of the poorest neighborhoods in the country, with crack houses and brothels near the school yard. The fence surrounding the school, the security system, and a full time security guard, are necessary. But at the same time, the school is seeking ways to reach out to families. In both Robertson School District, a predominantly white and middle class community, and in the inner city Milwaukee school, 86 percent African American and low-income, notions of community are vital to educational success. Furthermore, one cannot teach without taking into account the lives of students. If the bureaucracy of schools is preventing educators from meeting the needs of children, and if schools need more autonomy to meet those needs, we must reshape the character of schools. In the case of Urban Waldorf, the Milwaukee school, plans are being made to gain the status of a charter school—like a private school—in order to have the freedom from the bureaucratic system to do what needs to be done for children. (Typically, charter school status allows exemption from all public instruction laws except health, safety, civil rights, and finance.)

The administrators of Robertson School District are also constantly seeking ways to circumvent the bureaucratic system, seeing it as restrictive, even while contributing to its maintenance. As John Dewey (1938) suggests, our work in schools, building community, is never done. We have to constantly examine our aims to see that we are headed in a fruitful direction. Bureaucracy has been helpful in bringing some standardization and "professionalism" to education, but it has also been restrictive in emphasizing competitive—not collaborative—relations, in fragmenting classrooms and schools from the community, and in separating administration and management from teaching and learning.

If we begin our work from the standpoint of teaching and learning, then educators will do whatever they can to work together and to know their students and families—establishing relationships premised on what is best for the child. These relationships between parents and educators, teachers and administrators, students and their fellow students, do not always look the same. Parents do not necessarily have to be invited into classrooms, for instance, if to do so would not be helpful to the education of particular children. Teachers and administrators would be sensitive to and knowledgable about their students and their families, so that education would be done with—not to—children. Wolcott's (1987, 136) experience in a Blackfish Native American community, where it helped for him to view himself as the "enemy," would be less likely to happen if the educator represented some of the interests and values of the community. Education needs to be relevant to and connected with the lives of the participants. A bridge can be provided between the community and the school so that multiple ways of seeing and knowing are possible.

What I am advocating is a standpoint of mutuality and respect between parents and educators, and for educators to be well educated in understanding class, ethnic, language, and other social and cultural constructs that undermine student success. Even the corporate business world no longer invariably uses the kind of specialized, hierarchical organizational structure that public schools have maintained (see Charles Heckscher and Anne Donnellon's *The Post-Bureaucratic Organization: New Perspectives on Organizational Change*; Levering's *A Great Place to Work: What Makes Some Employers so Good (and Most So Bad)*; Peters and Waterman's *In Search of Excellence: Lessons from America's Best-Run Corporations*; Michael Schrage's *Shared Minds: The New Technologies of Collaboration*; and Thayer's *An End to Hierarchy and Competition in the Post-Affluent World: New Viewpoints*). While hesitant to be prescriptive about the kinds of collaborative relations that work, for these must be contextual and created by and with parents in the particular situation, this chapter outlines some possibilities; derived both from the fieldwork I conducted in Robertson School District and from the literature. Some of the things that I learned in fieldwork were the negatives—cautions and what not to do—which sent me looking for other alternatives: the positives and what works for schools.

CONNECTIONS THAT ENHANCE TEACHING AND LEARNING

Public schools, despite the leadership of well-intentioned and talented people, are often entrenched in bureaucratic norms and ethics. Most schools in our individualistic society are hierarchical bureaucracies. Schools are stable organizations that preserve these existing institutional orders and practices (Smylie 1994, 39). Yet the structure of schooling is outmoded and restrictive for current needs. A bureaucratic notion of professionalism—with separated roles and responsibilities—extends down the hierarchy to the classroom, where teachers view parents as "lay" people separate from "professionals," and parents are seen from a deficit perspective. An example: "I see more desperate, exasperated parents than ever, wanting help and advice on how to deal with their kids. They're crying out for help" (Interview, teacher). The teacher views parents as clients needing help, not as collaborators in a joint endeavor. Another example: "Parents should be more involved in their kids' education, not so much in their school" (Interview, teacher). In the current practices, the professional knows best, and hopes for families to do *their* work as a separate community, or as a community overlapping with the school. In the view that I am proposing, administrators become educational leaders, not managers. They teach classes and encourage others to take responsibility for decision making and problem solving. People who care about education—teachers, certificated people, students, parents—engage in participatory work for their schools.

Sensitivity to Social Class

Lareau (1989, 180–191) suggests that teachers seek working class parents' participation in schools through a different set of strategies than that used for upper-middle class parents. For instance, instead of assuming that parents should read to children, she urges that educators encourage other avenues, such as older siblings, cousins, or neighborhood children: "[Teachers] might encourage parents to ritualize these experiences as when cousins read together every Sunday after church, siblings read before bed on Wednesday nights, or children read every afternoon for twenty minutes with the babysitter" (Lareau 1989, 181). Lareau also argues that grades are very important for working class parents, and that teachers should therefore make grades an integral part of their connections with parents. Schools do sort children along the lines of success or failure, and parents are quite rightly unhappy if they receive only positive feedback on a child's progress, only to discover much later that the child, though making improvement, is lagging way behind his/her peers.

The important point, to my mind, is not that working class or upper-middle class parents be treated differently (although this may need to be the case), but that teachers and administrators know their context and their students and families in-depth, what works and what doesn't, so that strategies and policy reflect each particular school and the needs of particular children and families. For instance, it may be necessary to create an open door school policy for parents to allow for the possibility of spontaneous and incidental meetings in addition to formal parents' evenings. As we saw earlier, formal parents' events can be highly ritualized and not very informative for parents, since they are controlled by the school and can be a one-way transmission of predetermined information. Given parents' work situations, a more flexible visitation policy may be necessary. Each school's needs or ways to establish collaborative relations with parents is unique, depending on the school's culture and the individual players making up the school.[1]

Consider the expectations, often presumed to be unproblematic, with regard to: (a) homework and home-based learning; and (b) certain parental behaviors and volunteering in the classroom. Homework, "proper" parenting behaviors, and volunteering all presuppose considerable resources being available to parents. Some of the resources presumed to be available for homework include the following:

- *Communications.* Do parents have a telephone? Are they contactable? Do students have a computer or access to one? Child-care. Do parents have child-care or other alternatives available to allow them to visit the school to attend parent-teacher conferences and the like?
- *Transportation.* Do parents have a car or other means to get to school?
- *Knowledge, Skills, and Confidence.* Do parents feel competent to work with children on school-related work such as math, language skills, and science activities? In Robertson School District, the higher the grade level, the more intimidated parents became, and the less confident they were in helping their children. Also, high school teachers say they prefer that parents not "help" with the content matter, but rather engage their children in discussions about what they are learning and how they are responding to it.
- *Time.* Do parents have time off work to participate in school, or time in the home to engage in learning?
- *Energy.* Do parents have the energy to set up a learning environment? Do they have the energy after a long day at work (perhaps working double shifts or "graveyard" hours) to do more work with their children at home?
- *Assumptions.* Are parents motivated to work with the teacher on educational issues, or do parents believe that schoolwork should be done at school and that home is for other things? Do parents want to engage in a school-like teaching role with their kids?
- *Language.* Do parents have the language skills to speak to the teacher? Does the teacher have knowledge of the parents' home language? Is language a barrier inhibiting a free flow of information between home and school? Are parents able to initiate contact with teachers and administrators?
- *Materials.* Do parents have the materials that the schools expect them to have?—for instance, dictionaries, encyclopedias, books, paper, pens, paint, and scissors?
- *Space.* Do parents have the space to allow children to make a mess and spread out with their work? Some children have their own bedrooms and desks, while others share rooms with siblings or other family members and relatives, and may not have any work space. Even in the well-to-do Robertson School District there are homeless families—

some children living out of cars and trucks; these children face a social stigma in addition to being at a distinct disadvantage in terms of the physical and other resources needed for success in school.

Such considerations are not trivial. Schools typically have a comprehensive view of what the ideal parents look like which ignores differences in families and continues to stereotype "good" families as those with considerable resources and skills at their disposal. Every time an educator places certain expectations for school-type learning to occur at home, the family is impacted, and the child whose family does not meet school expectations may be disadvantaged.

Learning about Parents, Families, and Schools

When I was a graduate student at the University of Virginia, Pofessor Ray McDermott, then at Teachers College, Columbia and adjunct professor for UVa, taught a course in which I participated entitled "The Family as Educator." In this course we explored, from an anthropological perspective, some of the social and cultural processes that families engage in, and we also looked across cultures, reading for example, Tanizaki's (1982)*The Key*, and David Plath's (1980) *Long Engagements*. The course outline read, in part, as follows:

> Although it is clear that the family remains our most important and most cherished institution, it has been sadly neglected by educators. Worse, the only attention the family receives from educators is negative. How can we educate children, goes the current refrain, if they come from terrible homes? How can we overcome in a few hours a day years of deprivation at home? How indeed? Are these the right questions? Are schools really so free of guilt? Are families really such a mess? Are not families and schools both cut from the same cultural cloth? Behind all these questions is the more basic question: How can we understand life inside families? How can we think about families in ways that are fair to everyone involved, in ways that reveal the strengths of the people and illuminate at the same time the enormity of their problems? Does anyone know how to do this? Do social workers know? Sociologists? Psychiatrists? You or me? . . . Everyone makes sense once we look at how closely their behavior is tied and well tuned with the behavior of those around them. We are part of the world that is around all these troubled families. So are our schools part of the

trouble. How might we clean up our act? How might we help, rather than hinder? . . . This kind of work is too difficult to do alone. It takes courage and much hard work. . . . For help we can turn to each other. The interactional analyses and the papers are written in concert by a few people working in a group. . . . One grade is given to the whole project. It is almost as difficult as living in a family. It is also sometimes as rewarding. (McDermott syllabus, 1989)

McDermott is a gifted teacher who teaches his students to see the world differently, as interactional and relational. While every university may not have a McDermott in its midst, PK–12 teacher and administrator programs—for both undergraduate and graduate students—can focus on parent and family contexts in order for educators to be better prepared to lead and to teach. Traditionally, school and community are part of social foundations courses, and typically foundations people have a good understanding of the interrelationship between school and community and of the social context of schooling. However, not every department in the university has a social foundations course as a requirement, and at a time of restructuring and economic cutbacks there may be even fewer social foundations positions. We need more, not fewer social foundations courses. We need people who are able to interpret education in light of critical and interdisciplinary inquiry, and to relate schools to their social contexts. How can we have change in schools if people simply go on reproducing the same way of doing things year after year, and do not examine assumptions and directions critically and reflectively? In order to enhance teaching and learning in schools, attention to family and social contexts is central, and this work should be ongoing.

University-School Partnerships

A question that might quite rightly be asked of the university is: How can we teach teachers how to teach, or administrators how to administer, when we don't have any kids around? In response to this question, many colleges and universities have begun forming professional development schools, wherein the university forms a partnership with a particular school with an aim to revitalizing university courses by using the input of real classrooms and real children. This idea is not new.

Historically, "normal schools" or "laboratory schools" performed the same function, since the teacher training was conducted in actual schools (see Tyack and Hansot 1982). Universities moved away from the normal school concept in order to focus on scholarship, which is the work that the university has traditionally valued and rewarded. The rationale was that if people in colleges of education in universities were to achieve some form of parity with other colleges and departments they needed to publish and to engage in scholarly endeavors, which they could not do if they remained school practitioners. However, as professors of education have moved further and further away from the practitioner's perspective, they are sometimes isolated from practice and out of touch with life in schools. While we do not always need a formal university-school partnership in order to do collaborative work with schools, what matters is that university faculties are engaged in improving their own knowledge about teaching and learning through working with schools and families, and are engaged at the same time in working with the schools for improved policy and practices.

Collaboration with Social Service/Community Agencies

Responsive schools attend to the needs of parents and children, whatever those needs may be. The school may not work independently in this effort. For example, if parenting programs are needed, collaboration may be necessary with health and social services, with voluntary and community agencies, with police organizations and businesses, and with federal, state, and local governments. But this ought not be a school-imposed program; rather, it arises from parents' needs. That way, parents who need help in their parenting, or teenage parents who are themselves in need of additional support to complete schooling, are not left to struggle alone. Responsive schools closely monitor the needs and interests of their clientele and provide services accordingly. Crowson (1992, 232–233) reports that in Chicago, after-school and weekend programs in the city's parks department were little used by children, who were unaware of these activities. Schools, youth organizations, and the park employees failed to work together. Discontinuities in educational and social programs for children are a problem, and partnerships between schools and other agencies are a first step in a new direction for an inclusive and interdependent network of social and educational services for children. The school can thus be made the major site for providing a range of social services, as in full service schools. Teachers and administrators who teach well see students as holistic beings whose needs are much more than academic, and will find ways to provide services as needed.

Self-Study/ Evaluation of the School

It is helpful to invite someone, perhaps a graduate student from the university or a community person, to do an evaluation of the school setting in terms of its inclusiveness toward parents. The evaluation can be either informal or formal. The important point is to get an out-side view of how the school looks from a parent perspective; does it look inclusive or distancing. Parents themselves may be reluctant to give an honest evaluation because they may fear reprisals if their evaluation is unfavorable. The kinds of things that the evaluator(s) would be looking for would include, for instance, whether the sign on the front door says "Welcome to parents and visitors" or "All visitors must report to the school office!" Does the school have an open door policy by which parents and visitors are welcome at the school without a special invitation? Do parents have access to information on their child? Are parents able to complain and voice objections? Are parents consulted on all matters pertaining to the child? Does the school have a faculty-parent lounge where both parents and faculty can work and socialize? In Robertson schools, some teachers are very territorial about "their" faculty rooms, quite often resenting intrusions by parents. But if schools accept parent volunteers, they ought surely to be accorded the status of collaborators in the educational endeavor. Of course, the signs that are posted in the schools, visitation rights, and inclusion in the meeting room are only a small part of whether a cul-ture is really inclusive, but they may be signs of the deeper pattern of relationships. Once a school has a view of itself as seen by an outsider, it can build on those practices that work, and begin to create a more inclusive teaching and learning culture where there are difficulties. If schools establish a culture in which parents are able to spend a lunch hour with their children, or visit a classroom, the ownership of the school becomes more evenly balanced between parents and educa-tors. Furthermore, teaching is likely to be more effective, since kids see that schooling is valued. We need to be careful, though, that it is not only the white, upper-middle class parents whose presence and voices are heard in the schools. Ways and means must be found to include all types of parents, even those who are "difficult" and who challenge existing practices.

Self-study can be another useful exercise. At Robertson High School, it was found through a self-study survey administered to all parents, faculty, and community members involved with the school that a weakness in the school was lack of "a positive learning environment." Students ranked it at the 9th percentile, parents at the 30th, and teachers at the 60th. Only the teachers saw the school positively—and even they were not very enthusiastic—with regard to learning environment. This information was then taken to the site-council meetings, so that members could help devise ways to turn the situation around. Other means of school evaluation and review include questionnaires, structured interviews, and open-forum meetings. Whatever the approach taken, parents' voices and their perspectives on the teaching and learning going on in the school can be useful. Administrators need to ask parents what they think about the schools their children attend (Wolfendale 1992, 109).

Daily and Weekly Communication

As a teaching strategy, students can be encouraged to take ownership for developing their own newspapers and journals, which can also be a link between home and school. Parents can see and experience the concerns of their children as expressed in their own literature. This is quite different from newsletters used as a public relations tool. In the former: the students' work shows parents what they are thinking and doing in school, the latter is sometimes a school-owned mechanism for showing only those students whose work reflects positively on the school. At Robertson High School, the student-produced newspaper was seen by parents as critical for their understanding of their children. One parent noted wryly: "He tells us less and less every year about what he's doing in school, so we value every piece of evidence we have about what he is doing, and the school newspaper is part of that." Newspapers and newsletters done by school people, noting such things as students' learning achievements; class projects; calendars of upcoming events; ideas for parents on how they can help with student learning and homework assignments; sporting honors and events; teacher profiles and recognitions; and so on, can also be helpful.

Communication is fundamental to teaching and learning, and telephone calls can be a vital link between parents and educators. Of course, telephones have to be accessible. At Robertson High School, teachers could be found making calls to parents from their desks in their offices during free periods and recesses. In contrast, at Park Middle School and in two of the three elementary schools, teachers do not have their own telephones (other than the ones in the faculty lounge and the main office), which seems out of touch, to my mind, with present day needs. Teachers must be the only professionals to have computers before telephones. Robertson School District allocated large amounts of funds for computer upgrading, but not all teachers have telephones. If teachers did have phones, and made the time (before school, during recess, or after school) to confer with parents on educational decisions, or even to celebrate students' achievements, this could do much to establish more collegial relations. Face to face contact is good for meaningful communication, but is not always possible. Given the time factor and other constraints, the telephone can be an effective communication device, and is quicker and more personal than notes sent home. Written communications, while sometimes necessary, can be misplaced or overlooked, or the messages can be misinterpreted. However, leaving a message on an answering machine, particularly if telephone contact is not the norm, can lead to panic on the part of parents, who may tend to think that if the school is calling, something must be wrong. Direct communication allows for both parents and educators to contribute to the discussion. And this would work both ways; parents feeling free to call administrators and teachers with their own concerns.

If communications between home and school seems like an obvious point that hardly needs underscoring, Epstein (1986) found in one statewide survey of parents that 16 percent had never received a memo from their child's teacher, over 35 percent had never had a parent-teacher conference, 60 percent had never spoken to their child's teacher on the telephone and 96 percent had never been visited at home by their child's teacher. And if Van Galen's (1987, 88) analysis of the lack of parent-school collaboration is correct, it is the educators' need for control and fear of intrusion by parents into their "professional" domain that underpins lack of communication. These studies and the present one stress the need for attention to communication as a beginning step toward better teaching and learning.

Parent-Teacher In-service and Social Events

The aim of holding combined parent and teacher in-service and social events is to establish conditions wherein teachers and parents can relate to each other as people on an equitable footing. Also, by engaging in joint learning activities, teachers learn to see parents as teachers and learners. Topics of interest could be: shared decision making; child development seminars; and multiple learning styles and strategies. Lectures, seminars, luncheons, field trips, clothing drives, science fairs—indeed any activity or project that gets parents and educators working and relating with each other on a more even playing field—can only be positive for the school culture. It may be necessary to move these events off the school grounds to establish a more neutral territory where both educators and parents can form a coalition around a shared project.

Programs for New Students and Families

Fairfield Elementary School in Robertson School District pays considerable attention to new students and their families. With an ever-changing student population (the school serves the children of university-student families, with a high rate of turnover), the faculty, and particularly the principal, became concerned about facilitating a positive transition into the school for new students. The principal first conducted a qualitative study of these new students to see how the school looked from their perspective, in order to develop strategies that would ensure that these students are integrated into the school setting. In collaboration with teachers, she then implemented tours of the school, special orientations, and services to new students, to help with their transition and to facilitate their learning opportunities. (See Pierce [1992] for strategies and considerations.)

Site-based Councils

In many states, including the one in which this study took place, site-based school councils (variously named, *e.g.*, parent advisory councils, school improvement councils) are being implemented and/or mandated by the state. As we have seen in this study, parent advisory councils are no panacea. The people who serve on the councils may be the same groups of people whose voices have always been heard in the school. And their decision-making powers may be limited.

At Robertson High School, school improvement council meetings were largely dominated by the principal and the faculty—the faculty typically presenting a united voice and the principal attempting to lead faculty in quite a different direction. Parents, students, and community people were responding to the issues set by the educators' discussion, rather than being given an opportunity to shape the discussion collaboratively. As an example, the principal had a vision of the school as following Ted Sizer's "essential schools" model. He distributed to the site-council copies of the documents from the Coalition of Essential Schools entitled "Diverse Practice, Shared Ideas: The Essential School" and "The Common Principles." Participants were asked to read the documents and to come back prepared to discuss them at the next council meeting. Teachers, with back-up support from parents and community, spoke strongly against using the coalition documents as a guide, since the school already has a vision statement, and the principles in the coalition documents were considered "too broad" and not specific enough to really make a difference at the level of instruction:

> We are really not interested in a broad overview. We want more specific and concrete things. We're not interested in sitting around and talking, philosophizing. The impression I'm getting from everybody is that people don't care for Ted Sizer's coalition of essential schools. Let's do something for this school. (Interview, high school teacher)

Another teacher argued that the "hoary old chestnuts" that Ted Sizer is championing in the document are traditional principles of good teaching and that any one of the specific suggestions that teachers wanted to implement, such as an integrated curriculum or a three- or four-period day, "would fit in with the hoary old chestnuts." The principal was thus left with an empowered faculty with a strong voice who moved in a somewhat different direction than he had intended, and with parent, community, and student voices that were less distinct.

Holding such meetings at school and on the school's terms is likely a contributing factor in the educators' dominance, and I suspect that the professional/lay distinction is also at play here. To the principal's credit, he did attempt to invite parents and community people to ask for clarification of terminology: "We'll be talking a lot of educationeze.

If you don't understand the jargon please ask." Nevertheless, the use of "SLIGs," "mastery learning," "integrated curriculum," "senior project," and other terms without clear explanation, may have served as a barrier to full and equal participation. This is where joint activities and in-services involving parents and educators can help establish a common knowledge-base and terminology. What is sought is a more equal dialogue between parents and educators. Another consideration is the facilities and resources available for site-council members. Some schools allocate an office—for the use of the council members or for the chair of the council—near the principal's office in the school in order to facilitate communication. However, if the chair of the council is in paid employment elsewhere, then the office space may be more symbolic than practical.

Despite these difficulties, and despite the fact that site-based councils are not always broad-based, they can be an effective means toward shared governance of a school. An example of parent involvement in low-income "minority" elementary schools that has been written about and received much attention is the Accelerated Schools Project developed by Henry Levin of Stanford University. Two schools, Daniel Webster Elementary School in San Francisco and Hoover Elementary School in Redwood City, California, have reported high success with a site-based management approach. Parents reportedly became involved in a variety of school, home, and community projects which grew out of their own interests once the structure (site-based management) provided the space for parent initiatives and empowerment (Seeley 1989, 47–48).

The example of Chicago schools is also noteworthy. Since the 1989–90 school year, local school councils composed of a majority of parents and community members (rich and poor, least and most highly educated), and a minority of teachers and administrators, have exercised control over budgets, curricula, and personnel for each of the city's 540 schools (Crowson 1992, 262). In the Chicago school-site councils, parents are in the majority, with a parent as chairperson. The councils are made up of six parents, two community members, two teachers, and the school's principal, with a student included on the high school councils (Berman and Gjelten 1983; Hess and Easton 1992, 176). Thus, the situation in the Robertson High School improvement council, which has equal numbers of educators and parents/community people, allowing educators to dominate the conversation, would be more balanced with a greater representation of parents. Since school staff are often in a more assertive position, it makes good sense to balance the conversation. The fears of both educators and parents (chapter 3) may be alleviated, and communication may be improved through the collaboration. In Chicago, 65 percent of teachers on the site-councils reported improved parent-teacher relationships (Richard Day Associates 1990).

Educational Resource Centers for Parents and Educators

"Invite us in, give us space in the school, and talk to us, don't treat us like we're in the way. At present we don't always feel welcome," argues one parent in Robertson School District. I was not surprised that all parents don't feel welcome because some teachers argued loudly that they wanted their space to be kept "parent-free." One teacher said, "I personally don't wish to see parents in the teacher's room. If I go in there I want to know that it's safe. Sometimes I'm just letting off steam and the way I talk is awful and they would misunderstand." This is part of the tradition of teachers work being conducted in a professional arena without the scrutiny of parents.

If the faculty lounge is not yet a territory that can be shared, a space can be created in the school that is safe for both parents and educators. For instance, a school- or district-wide educational resource center can be set up, stocked with curriculum materials, multi-media resources, computers, video recorders, compact-disk players, a satellite receiver, a scanner, and other technological aids. Such a center can be a useful resource room for teachers, and can be a bridge between parents and educators if it is well used by the community and if it meets their needs. Once again, however, the impetus, design, and implementation of the resource center and its programs would be a collaborative endeavor, not simply a matter of educators deciding what the community needs. And educators as a group would also need to be committed to the project.

Computer Linkages Between Home and School

In an age of advanced technology it makes good sense for teaching and learning to use the technology that's available and to establish computer linkages between home and school. Parents can be encouraged to work with students, accessing on-line information to conduct research from home. My only caveat here is that if this is implemented it is done across the board, using grants or assistance from computer manufacturers and businesses to provide computers for all students, not just for those whose families have disposable income.

At Park Middle School, a computer-based telephone system provides daily information to parents on homework assignments, upcoming school events, excursions, and so on. Parents can call in to find out specific information from particular teachers. The only drawback in the system is that not all teachers participate fully in updating voice-mail messages and in ensuring that the information is complete and current. What matters most, however, is that communication from school to home and vice versa occurs on a regular basis.

Bringing the Community into the School

Fairfield Elementary School reaches out to the community by inviting a constant stream of visitors, speakers, contributors, and guests into their classrooms who not only add a vital element to the educational program but who also help with the school's reputation in the community. Also, at Park Middle School many guests, including the president of the university, have visited classrooms and talked about their work and their passions; among them have been a pediatrician and various businesspeople, artists, and photographers. The teacher who initiated the program explained, "I think the kids really need to make connections with personalities and positions. This is an opportunity for them to see that the president of the university is a real person. In every walk of life, people are reading." As Heck and Williams (1984, 37–38) point out, "people who talk for a living—such as beauticians, barbers and bartenders—should be included; they sometimes represent the single most effective grapevine system in any community." Newspaper coverage of such events can provide the community with a needed focus on the school.

Other credible people in the community are the school's own employees—including bus drivers, kitchen staff, and secretaries. They are an integral part of the community, and administrators can learn from them both positive and negative perceptions of the school as seen by the community. They can also be a sounding board for new ideas. Administrators themselves may be seen as "front" people, always representing a positive view of the school. Therefore, trust has to be built. Key community people can do much to strengthen school-community connections.

Parents' Involvement in Policy Making

Depending on how the school district goes about defining the work of site-based councils and the school board, the general population of parents may or may not have a say in the creation of policy and procedures on such matters as student tardiness, absences, discipline, and grading (see Marburger 1990; Epstein 1985). My own belief is that parents have much to offer in the establishment of policy in a broad-based manner. For instance, parents can provide a voice in the development of policy on discipline and curriculum. Policy should be a mechanism for fair and just treatment of all, and for defining an inclusive school culture, not simply a tool for limiting parent power. As we saw earlier, administrators can sometimes hide behind policy, and develop criteria and policies to avoid being accountable to parents for their own personal agenda in the public world.

Communication in Home Languages

The language of educators and the jargon that is used by educators can sometimes create a divide separating parents from schools. Also, the use of English as the only language of communication with homes can be alienating to some parents. Administrators and teachers need to know their communities well, and to provide multiple languages in all newsletters and in other communication with culturally diverse communities. This is an obvious point, but sometimes overlooked. The children may be fluent in English, but the parents may not. Even if the parents are competent in English, the use of a home language by the school can do much to show that the school cares, that the school knows its community, and that it is responsive to the home context. Use of the home language may enhance possibilities for teaching and learning. As Ernst (in press) shows, to develop a sense of belonging to the community, ESL students and their families, for example, have to be able to "integrate their backgrounds, interests, strengths and prior knowledge of language with sound strategies that promote second language and literacy development." Teachers acknowledge that the cultures and languages of students and their families affect their worldviews, and that they provide opportunities for students to "perceive the significance of what they have and know" together with "what their new school, language, and culture offer them." In helping to provide meaningful experiences, the school works closely with a local Senior Citizen Center that provides volunteers for the ESL program. And as one delightful "grandpa" (an elder from the culture) testified: "Every week I look forward to coming to class. Even when I wake up and my knees and back are hurting, I still want to come. By the time I get here and see these kids and see their faces, I feel great" (Ernst, in press).

Home Visitations

Sensitivity of educators toward the feelings of parents about home visitations is essential. Much of the literature on parent-school relations urges that teachers and administrators take responsibility for home visits. Home visits can facilitate strengthened relationships between parents and teachers, but they are only helpful if the condition of trust between the two parties has already been laid. The school cannot simply go knocking on doors expecting to "fix" recalcitrant parents and bring them around to the school's agenda and the school's point of view. In some neighborhoods where the school is viewed as a distanced—and, I would add, white and middle class—institution, it is not enough to send out a teacher in the role of quasi-truant officer. Much work needs to go on prior to home visitations to establish trust and open lines of communication, and teachers need to be *invited* into homes, and not simply invade other people's privacy on the pretext of better relations.

Reporting on Students' Academic Progress

All parents are interested in their children's learning. One has only to see the enthusiasm in kindergarten mothers and fathers as they enroll their children in school to be convinced of parental concern that children learn and do well in school. Participation in school is never higher than at the early level. During these early years parents hold high hopes for their children and expect that they will do well. Disconfirming evidence often starts to come in, for not all children do well in school. The school labels some children as successes and others as failures. Participation of parents in school starts to drop off as parents become less starry-eyed about a child's potential in school. This is where continual feedback to parents is so essential. A written report sent home needs to include not only standardized test results, but also observations and discussions of student work. Parents want to be shown what their kids *can* do as well as those areas they need to work on. In addition, parents need feedback on the contributions they can make, guidance on how they can help their children to do better, plus how the school intends to approach any areas that have been identified as lacking. Some parents in this study felt that the school had "written off" their children as "drop-outs" or "problem kids" without any discussion taking place with the family. Parents were shocked to find, at a certain point, that their children had become alienated from school, without them ever having been aware that this was happening.

Other States' Research and Reform Efforts

James Comer and his associates have worked for the past decade on an innovative plan to restructure schools around parent involvement (Comer 1980). The Comer plan, which is now being developed on a national level as the School Development Program, includes three levels of parent participation: (a) broad-based activities for large numbers of parents; (b) a one-to-one ratio of parents to teachers in the school, with parents working as classroom assistants, tutors, or aides; (c) a few highly involved parents participating in school governance. The schools in which Comer has implemented the plan serve low-income "minority" children, and the results have been significant. Comer writes of the New Haven schools:

> The students had once ranked lowest in achievement among the 33 elementary schools in the city, but by 1979 without any change in the socioeconomic makeup of the school, students in the fourth grade in the two schools ranked third- and fourth- highest on the Iowa Test of Basic Skills (Comer 1988, 48).

In addition, parent-school partnerships instituted in New York, San Diego, Houston, Boston, Milwaukee, Indianapolis, and Los Angeles provide examples to learn from (See Davies 1991; Epstein 1991). Educators who take advantage of reports of innovations in leadership, teaching, learning, and research and reform efforts in other settings— whether through personal contact, research reports, journal articles or conferences—will have a variety of tools for discussion and for implementing change.[2]

Equity in Leadership Positions

The message sent to boys and girls in our schools is often one of inequity in leadership and in positions of power. As noted in chapter 4,

but repeated here for those reading isolated chapters, the superintendent is typically male: nationwide the number is somewhere between
95 percent (Shakeshaft 1993, 86) and 93.3 percent (Sharratt and
Derrington 1993); high school principals are mostly male (88 percent);
elementary school principals are mostly male (66 percent), while the
bulk of teachers are mostly women (69 percent) (Shakeshaft 1993, 86;
Jones and Montenegro 1990). Once again, social reproduction occurs
whereby people in the position to alter the staffing patterns nevertheless
reject any notion of change because it challenges them to rethink current
practices. Hiring committees may reproduce themselves and select yet
another white male heterosexual administrator for the position of superintendent, rationalizing that he is the "best fit for the job." Indeed, he is
the best reproducer of the *status quo*, and anything different poses a
threat. Change is uncomfortable for some people, particularly those
whose positions may be threatened by new ideas and practices.

But we cannot revitalize schools if we continue reproducing an
exclusionary power structure. Nor can schools be places where all are
given equal opportunity. This is not a treatise against current leaders.
Many are deeply committed and talented leaders and educators with a
genuine concern for the education of all. Nevertheless, as members of
the dominant cultural group and as symbolic reminders of patriarchy,
white men who want to do things differently may be hard-pressed to
inspire a belief that things will indeed be different. It is challenging for
someone who has blindly or consciously lived his whole life with cultural approval and enhanced life opportunities to conceive of the lives of
African Americans, Chicanos, Latinos, Native Americans, Asian
Americans, gay people, women, and so on. From the time they are
enrolled in school, girl and boy children are treated differently. Men in
our society rarely get raped; women get raped and violated every day.
Men do not bear children, and may not engage in child-raising in the
same way as women do, or experience the same degree of limited
opportunity in the workplace and society. Sexism is as much a part of
life in schools as it is in the society in general. Such life experiences, or
the potential for these experiences, creates a different mindset, a different way of looking at the world. Studies have indicated that women are
more likely to use collaborative decision making, to attend more to
community-building, and to play a more assertive role in instructional
leadership (Shakeshaft 1987). Schools and school districts that take up

the challenge to diversify leadership positions will, I believe, be rewarded with different and new approaches to the school as an organization, to the school's relationship with the community, to the work relationships and roles inside the school, and to the ways teaching and learning are conceptualized.

CONCLUSION

This chapter has outlined a variety of ways that schools can focus on teaching and learning by connecting with families and the community. Following these recommendations, administrators would concern themselves not with the management or direction of a "corporation," but with students and families, where the real work needs to be done. Students' families would be invited into the educational experience, not by demanding that they participate, but by showing that the school is *their* school, relevant to their needs and purposes.

The ideas presented in this chapter will not automatically be useful in all settings. What matters is the standpoint of administrators and teachers viewing schools as being about teaching and learning, and of schools as being connected with families and community. Teachers cannot teach students well if they know nothing about them. To focus on teaching and learning means that administrators and teachers organize their work taking into account the unique needs of students, as well as the influences, educational and otherwise, that come from parents, siblings, peers, the media, and organizations. Focusing on teaching and learning does not necessarily mean that all those not currently engaged in instruction in schools—principals, testers, counselors—would be sent back to the classroom, as Sacken suggests (1994, 690). There are good reasons for allowing some professionals in schools to specialize. But this specialization ought not become too precious and isolated from children and their families, or too important and removed from the central work of schools, which is teaching and learning.

Principals' and teachers' work is changing with the changing times. Now educators need to work with the community and to become more like liaisons in working with parents, police officers, and other community members. Educators thus have to become part guidance counselor as well as part teacher. Academics is only part of our work: teachers also take care of young people socially and psychologically.

Principals, testers, counselors, and teachers cannot do their essential work of teaching without looking outwards towards the home and community and making connections and links with these vital settings. In the words of one insightful school counselor: "None of us who work in isolation live in isolation. There are a lot of inter-relationships, and if you ignore those you are not only in for trouble, you are also missing out on some real opportunities. That is how I approach my job and also my relationships with parents. And who is more interested in students than their parents."

NOTE

1. For those interested in the concept of school cultures, see Henry 1993; Page 1990; Wyner 1991.
2. Of course it is important to also critique others' efforts, and to customize educational plans for each school setting. For instance, despite the apparent success of the Comer schools, as King (1994, 39) points out, success seems to be premised on re-socializing poor Black children to be aligned with the culture of the school. But as I have argued throughout this book, the process ought surely be two-way, with schools enriched and influenced by a variety of cultural patternings and understandings.

9

Parent-School Collaboration

For Hannah Arendt, "power corresponds
to the human ability . . . to act in concert.
Power is never the property of an individual; it belongs to a group and remains in
existence only as long as the group keeps
together (1972, 143). Power may be
thought of, then, as "empowerment," a
condition of possibility for human and
political life and, yes, for education as
well. But *spaces have to be opened in the
schools and around the schools; the windows have to let in the fresh air.* (Greene
1988, 134)

Schools are part of the fabric of society, and given the individualistic,
competitive, rationalistic values of the wider U.S. culture, it follows
that schools would also embody these values. How then can we have
reforms to build inclusive community when the means available to institute them are bureaucratic, and often premised on exclusivity? This
book is about new possibilities, a new way of looking at schools and at
the work they do. Am I and other feminist educators proposing something unworkable? Is a feminist model for organizational structures and
school leadership out of step with current cultural realities? A feminist
mindset that is not competitive, bureaucratic, hierarchical, and exploitative is indeed at odds with the dominant culture. "Winners and losers"
are inscribed in our cultural realities and in schools. However, I do not
believe that this means we can't push at the edges and work from inside
organizations to promote change. If one microorganism can affect a

species, so too can individuals, working collaboratively, bring about cultural change. The costs involve a willingness to risk—to take chances and trust the process. While it will initially be harder to involve people outside the current framework, the benefit will be schools in which parents, teachers, and others can contribute to the common good.

The participants in this study at Robertson School District showed over and over, in various ways, that schools are segmented, hierarchical, bureaucratic organizations and that despite moves toward site-based management and shared decision making, and despite a desire for collaborative partnerships, the mindset and the technology continue to divide teachers as "professionals" from parents as "lay" people. Feminism is a useful analytic framework to help explain the gap between the intent of the reforms and the actual practices of real schools, and to point to new directions in organizational structures and school leadership. My informants did not generally espouse feminist thought. Indeed, a number may not even have read any feminist scholarship. On the contrary, professionals' work in schools, as principals and teachers, tends to be informed largely by traditional management theory, by the constraints of rules and regulations, and by the "way things are done" in public schools.

What I heard during the study was that even from a position inside the system, as administrators or teachers, all is not well. Things don't quite work the way they ought to. Parents "should" be involved but we "don't quite know how to do that yet" (Interview, teacher). Much research already shows teachers and principals "working very hard to do their traditional work better" (Smylie 1994, 39). What I have tried to do is to move away from the "traditional work" and reconceptualize the public school's notion of professionalism, particularly as it relates to the schools' relationships with parents and community.

FEMINISM TO RESHAPE POLICY AND PRACTICE

This brings us to the feminist framework. How will this work when so many people in power positions are helping to reproduce the *status quo*? First, a new cohort of leaders are poised to take on key leadership positions in the nation's schools—particularly women, who have been kept out of the superintendency by social and cultural practices defining them as women first and administrators second (Grogan 1994). Women and underrepresented groups need equal representation in lead positions such as the superintendency in order to effect change. These new leaders and superintendents may bring with them new ideas and possibilities and a mindset that is more participatory, collaborative, and socially concerned; they may reach out to parents and the wider community. In Marshall's (1992a, 370) words: "Numerous scholars (*e.g.*, Bell 1988; Marshall 1988; Schmuck 1981; Shakeshaft 1986) have compiled evidence that women school administrators' views of schooling, priorities, ways of managing, and ways of structuring interactions have elements that hold great promise for improving school leadership."

It is sometimes argued that power is power, whoever holds it, women or men, and that power leads to dominance and hierarchy. And of course, some women accept an androcentric (masculinist) view of the world. But feminists, building on women's quite different experience of the world, including attention to those marginalized, offer a different *view* of the world as well. Leadership by both women and men can be informed by the feminist ideas I am proposing here, which offer exciting new possibilities for the education of children. Educational leaders and teachers can learn from feminism—learn a different mindset, a way of relating that will help bridge the gap between parents and teachers, teachers and administrators, schools and communities. We need to move beyond gender differences (in the sense of pitting one gender against the other) and toward a theory of care that is inclusive and places caring in all our daily experiences and patterns of thought.

In other words, education is no longer seen narrowly as a set of managerial and pedagogical skills, but rather as a caring, collaborative profession which works with families and others to make decisions about pedagogy and curricula in order to best meet the needs of all children. Following this view, schools would be child-centered, collegial cultures, operating as small units, where risk-taking and creative ideas and actions are valued. Parents and educators would be working together for such goals as: building trust; creating a safe school environment for children; enabling academic, athletic, and personal successes; supporting teamwork and collaboration between school and community; and taking care of buildings and finances. Hierarchy would become something to overcome. In a feminist view of organization, face to face discussions and collaborative decision making take precedence over bureaucracy and formal rules. Administrators seek to engender collective empowerment among teachers, parents, and students and to avoid hierarchical domination (Ferguson 1984). As Noddings (1986) puts it, dialogue is critical: "true dialogue is open; that is conclusions are not held by one or more of the parties at the outset. The search for enlightenment, or responsible choice, or perspective, or means to problem solution is mutual and marked by appropriate signs of reciprocity" (223). In the words of Margaret Wheatley:

> Earlier, when we focused on tasks, and people were the annoying inconvenience, we thought about "situational" leadership—how the situation could affect our choice of styles. A different understanding of leadership has emerged recently. Leadership is always dependent on the context, but the context is established by the relationships we value. We cannot hope to influence any situation without respect for the complex network of people who contribute to our organizations. Is this a fad? Or is it the web of the universe becoming felt in our work lives? (1994, 144–145)

Table 2 shows the contrast between current school organizational structures and feminist structures.

So how does a feminist perspective inform the future direction of education with regard to parent involvement? Since I am in an administration department, my students always want to know the bottom line: "How can these findings help what I do on Monday morning?" In other words, how does theory inform practice? First, I urge that administrators and teachers critically examine their own school settings in light of the findings of this book. How much of what I have reported here about "professional" versus "lay" distinctions, and schools as competitive bureaucracies, adequately reflects what goes on in your own school? Are some of the same barriers and constraints to collaborative work in place in your school or school district? Can a feminist orientation be useful in your setting to transform practices and to begin to close the gap between the intent of reforms and actual practices? Second, the book includes a number of suggestions of possible ways and means of establishing more credible and meaningful collaboration with parents and community. Are these strategies, or adaptations thereof, useful in your particular setting? Have some of them already been tried, and if so, what are your conclusions for improvement of policy and practice? In the following section I will recap the main arguments.

TABLE 2
Organizational Structures and School Leadership

BUREAUCRATIC HIERARCHY	FEMINIST STRUCTURES
Metaphor Industrial model (military, banking, factories)	Organic model (nature)
Organizational Boundaries Only insiders ("professional educators") involved in decision making; strong boundaries around classroom and school	Outsiders are brought into the decision making process, including "lay" people; school is open to the community
Communication Channels Restricted information	Shared information; participative systems
Curriculum and Assessment Specialization and standardization	Relevant interdisciplinary connections; authentic assessment and communication
Relationships Relations of power; individualistic, isolated	Negotiated solutions; shared decision making; peer networks; dialogue; partnership
Decision Making Top-down decision making	Focus on the core technology of teaching and learning; student- and family-centered; flexible, adaptive, horizontal/lateral structures
Ethics Ethic of justice and competition; survival of the fittest; winners and losers	Ethic of care and collaboration; community-building; attention to equity, justice and fairness; interconnectedness of everything
Leadership Management and direction of a "corporation"; segmented roles and responsibilities; rigid, authority-based hierarchy; bureaucratic control	Holistic; customized (child centered); relations of collegiality, trust, discussion, and influence; collegial, collaborative

AN ETHIC OF CARE

First, *all decision-making, policy, and practice start from a notion of caring*. Rights and rule-making typically govern the current masculinist notions of justice. But as Gilligan (1982) points out, a feminist theory and practice begins and ends with the notion of caring; one always asks who's hurting and what can be done, rather than asking what rule is being broken. Interpersonal relations, intimacy, and connectedness take precedence over traditionally defined professional relations. You will note that Noddings (1994) calls her work "feminine" rather than "feminist." I have characterized her work, however, as feminist, not to differ with her own view of her work, but because I believe she is offering a critique of the dominant paradigm in education. While not stridently political, Noddings' work nevertheless attempts to recast the way we work in schools to emphasize an ethic of care. Her work is thus, to my mind, feminist: a feminist and political critique of administration, teaching, teacher education, and research. I would add that her critique has relevance also to administrator- and teacher-preparation programs. With so much violence in school and society, and with so many children needing care, we can't afford not to place caring above competitive relations in schools. Caring does not mean that standards are lowered, but that the educator acts in the interests of the other, and proceeds based on intuitive, personal ways of knowing, rather than simply on linear, rational ways of knowing (Belenky *et al.* 1986).

> It's a dance, a dance between teacher and student and parent and child and parent and teacher and so on. Knowing when to respond and when to let go and let them find out on their own is a dance, a subtle communication of letting each other know what our needs are and how we can help each other. (Interview, teacher)

As Emihovich and James (1993, 9) suggest, a feminist view of relationships is one in which we offer and give of ourselves in an interactive way rather than simply taking. For instance, relations between parents and educators may be best established through casual and informal means, not through the formalized machinery of "we need two parents on committee x" that is so often used. Authentic casual contact and informal relations between parents and educators may be more important than formalized events.

A declared policy of parent-school collaboration arising from a feminist philosophy, a policy that recognizes the symbiotic relationship between parents and educators, can help set the stage. However, much more than this, the problems and barriers unique to each school that prevent partnership must be recognized, analyzed, and addressed. For example, many parents, particularly working class parents, may be unable to collaborate because of time, money, and work constraints. Ironically, for working-class parents, the new inclusionary schooling may further disadvantage their children. If the only parents who are involved are upper-middle class parents, the educational decision making that occurs with respect to critical issues such as curriculum, personnel, finance, and policy may further alienate working class children. Already, public schools embody a largely middle class culture (Heath 1983), and this may be heightened if those parents are the only ones participating in school decision making. Ways and means have to be found to help balance participation and benefits.

Administrators are served well by getting to know their communities in terms of demographics, particularly in terms of social class. Knowledge of the class make-up of the school and community can help administrators ensure that committees, site-based councils, and other decision making bodies include equal representation by persons from all social classes, instead of being dominated by an elite. It may well be up to the state to provide for work-release for working class parents to allow for school participation, perhaps including free child-minding facilities and taxation benefits. Monetary and time resources are unequally distributed in society; therefore, if we want balanced and representative schools, the state must take responsibility for ensuring that it is possible for all parents to be fully involved in their schools. If the government will not take the responsibility, then private grants can be sought and appeals made to employers to provide for paid time to participate in children's schools. Inequity matters for all children, not only those disadvantaged. If the only parents collaborating with schools are privileged parents, all children are learning that democracy is a sham. Having been historically denied access to the public world and having to continually address injustices, feminists' care ethic and concern for democratic rights is strong.

COLLABORATION AND COMMUNITY BUILDING

Second, *a feminist view of school and community centers on the project of collaboration and community-building*. Working in a school does not mean working in isolation with children or in isolation with administrative tasks, but rather means working with others toward a common project, a project that includes everyone on the team, from classified staff to parents to leaders in the community. In this view, community difference is not a source of negative conflict, but of engagement with one another. There is also less emphasis on competition and more on cooperation and collaboration and community-building, which is thought to lead to increased levels of job satisfaction (Shakeshaft 1993).

Shifting the emphasis from competition to collaboration and community-building means educators and others seek ways to engender a teamwork perspective. For instance, one way to enhance collaboration is to establish smaller units. Size is important in developing personalized communities. Indeed, Fowler and Walberg (1991) argue that school size is the most significant characteristic associated with student achievement levels, after the socioeconomic status of students and schools. And Noddings' work (1988, 225) supports the move to smaller, more cohesive units. In the small private schools I studied (Henry 1993), for instance, strong bonds of collegiality were clearly evident, for parents', teachers', and administrators' lives were inter-related through frequent personal relations and a joint investment in the project of educating children. Large schools allow for economic efficiency and some enhanced curricular and extracurricular offerings, yet they also create distance between clients (parents and students) and service providers (teachers, staff, and administrators). It is more difficult for large schools to find ways to cultivate personal relationships and interactions among participants in school cultures. However, we need to be wary that it is not a false sense of community that is created. Tensions and conflicts and differing views are essential for a healthy relationship, and this also applies to schools. A monolithic one-right-way approach to culture-building is oppressive and undemocratic. The important point is that the focus in the school is on building a school community that is inclusive, and that values the diverse contributions of participants.

Parents will be involved when there's less bureaucracy to intimidate or control them. Teachers and parents can collaborate around real educational issues and build meaningful community. In one school, written about by Scott (1993, 66), the only "office" is a big room—much like a kitchen in a home where people go to converse and share—in which decisions get made "practically, effectively, without a preeminent sense of self-importance on anyone's part. It's because the mental center of gravity is not the institution, bureaucracy, personal position, or territory, but what we all have to do and be for the children."

Creating a responsive school means more than merely instituting programs such as having parents as volunteers, or as low-level administrative assistants, or including parents in the governance of schools. Parent members on school councils, parent volunteers, and other forms of parental assistance may be useful practices, but they do not guarantee a school as an authentic community. Representation of parents may be skewed in favor of one sector of the population, or may be too small to truly give voice to parents' needs and concerns.

A responsive school is instead characterized, to my mind, along the following lines:

A Community of Learners

Teachers and administrators, as well as students, engage in learning and learn from each other; they work together in collaborative relationships centered around students. Diverse voices are heard, and playfulness is likely to be part of the process of working together. In this view, relationships and the playfulness surrounding them allow for new levels of creativity:

> [If we] stop being so serious about getting things "right"—as if there were an objective reality out there—we can engage in life with a different quality, a different level of playfulness . . . Surprised by what nature has revealed, we find that things at first always look startlingly funny. Whenever you can hear laughter . . . and somebody saying, "But that's preposterous!"—you can tell that things are going well and that something probably worth looking at has begun to happen in the lab" (Wheatley 1994, 142 in Judson 1987, 71).

Whether in labs or in schools, we need to be serious about our work, but we also can learn to celebrate our relationships with one another, which will lead to a better process, and ultimately to better outcomes.

Connected School and Community (not bureaucratic enclaves)

Schools are located in a network of relationships among parents, citizens, community groups, social services, universities, and businesses. And those relationships are best built on a collaborative, not competitive basis. The government can also play a key role in helping to establish possibilities for broad-based participation in schools, not in the sense of imposing restrictions, as sometimes happens now, but in reducing bureaucratic restrictions and providing resources for truly local participation in schooling. Some governments have sought in their educational reforms to widen social differences between schools and hence to widen social inequalities (David 1993, 73). For instance, the Reagan administration's *A Nation at Risk* (1983) study shifted the burden for educating young people onto parents, business, and the local community, but it was done in the spirit of *blaming* the community and of widening economic and social differences between schools. Bush's historic education summit in 1989 in Charlottesville, Virginia further established a competitive market economy of schools with a limited federal role in education. By passing the responsibility to the local setting, and ignoring inequities and the needs of disadvantaged districts, the government showed, to my mind, a lack of commitment to public education. Chubb and Moe (1990) call for even more competition and inequality among schools. We have not yet seen a sustained commitment to public education, even from the current Clinton administration. For education, we need a much greater willingness on the part of citizens to invest in the nation's future—commiting their finances and energy for the public good—to provide for the possibility of enabling all parents to participate in schooling and to effect positive changes in schools. If we had many more ethnically and culturally diverse administrators and teachers, and authentic parent-school collaboration, the experiences of those students and their families who are currently alienated from school might be more positive. Reforms are needed that develop opportunities for all children, not just those who have always been served well by schools. And it is worth remembering that those we fail to educate stay with the system a very long time. Can we afford to have a large proportion of disenfranchised and uneducated citizenry?

Inclusive Governance (not hierarchical)

In a feminist, collaborative view of schools, teachers, parents, and administrators are able to make decisions in a shared work environment. Decisions that are related to curricula, staff development, resources, scheduling, student evaluation, and so on, become the domain of many more people, including students, staff, parents, administrators, and community people. Critics charge that such an approach takes more time and is less efficient, but the whole bureaucratic system has been premised on efficiency, and it is not working. I am not convinced that the present system is all that efficient. Moreover, the quickest and shortest way to a goal is not necessarily the best. With ownership of a school taken on by a broader base of people, we can begin to reframe the school as a place where a diverse group of people would be held together by an ethic of care, not by bureaucratic rules; by a spirit of collaboration, not by one of competition; by a commitment to teaching and learning by all, not by a division into management and teachers.

Providing Support for Families

Administrators would also ask how their schools can contribute to the community in terms of economic and social development, community involvement in curriculum, and community service projects.

Schools and community are not isolated units sufficient unto themselves. If the community is hurting, the school will be also. Thus, providing support for families (however configured), working with families, inter-agency collaboration, service-learning and community service for students is part of an approach that values school-community interchange.

> There's so much age isolation in schools. Kids need to interact with old people and the world out there and see how things work. So that they get a sense of themselves. This could be much more than community service as it currently stands. We could do much more through our classes. (Interview, parent)

Awareness of the connections between school and community would be part of administrator and teacher knowledge so that they can better approach the issue of parent-school partnerships. This does not mean educators turn their attention away from the central work of educating children, for that is our primary and most important role. For all students a good education is the best social service available, giving them alternatives and a way out of difficult situations. However, educators and administrators need to make teaching and learning relevant and connected to the needs and interests of students, to be responsive to students' social and emotional needs, and to know how to interface with social agencies. Moreover, inclusive governance means that school decisions and daily practices can be enhanced by the wider interest and investment in the school of parents and community.

A FOCUS ON TEACHING AND LEARNING

Leaders and workers, including parents and community people, act as coworkers, forming lateral relationships and cross-relationships centered around the core technology of teaching and learning. A feminist theory of school organization means that "leaders would be intensely involved in the actual production of units of the organization (teaching and learning) and serve the organizational workers by resolving conflicts and coordinating resources" (Ortiz and Marshall 1988, 138). Teaching children becomes the focus of the school instead of a separation of administration as management or leadership, from teaching as a secondary activity.

In this model, administrators are instructional leaders and professionals within a community, instead of acting like managers or directors of a corporation. The idea of what a professional educator is becomes redefined. Administrators sometimes see their work as shielding classroom teachers from busywork that lies outside the direct work of instruction, such as community relations, personnel, and budget. However, if teachers and administrators are to become an integrated team that includes parents we have to reframe the work of teachers and administrators. For instance, a forum for open discussion could be a means for communication across professional-lay lines.

> We never have a colloquium where we sit down with parents and problem-solve on problems. They need to see us trying to get through to kids instead of doing things to them. We as teachers never get together and talk shop either, let alone with others, the curriculum people or the principal or superintendent. (Interview, teacher)

Similarly, a lateral approach to parent-school partnerships does not start with a top-down approach, but rather would empower parents in the local setting to have their needs met.

> Usually the school tells the parents what to do and they try it and it doesn't work and then they say "You blew it. These people don't know what they're doing." We don't need to tell them how. They're smart. (Interview, teacher)

Giving up control and trusting the process of participatory education, even if it initially requires more time and energy, is necessary for real school reform. It may not be possible for each teacher or administrator to be responsive to each particular parent's agenda, which may be conflicting and not able to be achieved. It *is* possible to bring parents into the conversation, participating with parents as a group to set an educational agenda and to build community.

In this approach, parents would be included as full partners on committees engaging in shared decision making for curriculum development, special education, visioning and strategic planning, levy or bond campaigns, school facilities planning, and multicultural and human relations. And when parents do the work it is not marginalized and treated as "advisory" as sometimes happens. You cannot share power and take it away at the same time. Parents are tired of being given token, advisory roles and then their advice is ignored. I am not arguing that educators do not have important specialized knowledge and skills. They do. Expertise is valuable. The point is that parents also bring different and essential perspectives for a more complete and balanced educational approach. Expertise thus involves knowing how to work with and value the perspectives of others engaged in collaborative work.

Effective educational leaders work together with parents and leaders in the community using an ethic of care and collaborative administrative approaches for the welfare of children. Lip service to collaboration is not enough; there must be authentic collaboration, and if it is not working we need to re-evaluate, be reflective, and ask, Are we going in the right direction? If we start from the premise that parents are to be respected for the knowledge that they have as parents, irrespective of how that differs from the school view of "good parenting," then we are on the right track. As appropriate, parents' needs and concerns can be addressed. Early in the school year, parents can be brought into discussions with educators about how the students will be taught, about school expectations, and about what they can do for children's learning in establishing supportive learning environments. Workshops, videotapes, and computerized phone messages are a few of the means that can be used to establish dialogue around school-home issues of parenting and the child's education. Once again, though, school personnel who put themselves in the position of "expert," transmitting the "one right way" to do things, are unlikely to bring about substantive change.

Listening and dialoguing around the perspectives of parents, teachers, and administrators is necessary. Teachers can suggest to parents how they can best help children from an educator's perspective. We know, for instance, that a way for parents, siblings, relatives, or friends to help children in a non-threatening way is through reading to them. Educators can also learn from the perspectives of parents on how they approach teaching the child in the everyday settings of the home and community. Parents are continually teaching children moral lessons, practical lessons (how to balance a checkbook or change a bike tire), social relationship lessons, and so on. Educators may learn a great deal simply by adopting a position of educational receptivity to parents' educational knowledge and skills.

Parents and educators can also participate together in school in-service programs. As organizer of a leadership conference with a seventy-five-year tradition of serving administrators I was able to experiment with a new concept of leadership: educating "professionals" and "lay" people together. We enlarged the group of educational leaders to include teachers, parents, principals, school board members, and superintendents. A dynamic keynote speaker, who believes strongly in developing a team of all interested participants, was able to inspire a high energy level, spark new ideas, and motivate for change. Establishing a team that works well together and with high levels of trust—a healthy school culture—is more likely if people have the opportunity to do things together, to work on common problems, and to gain mutual understanding. Professional development programs can broaden participation to include parents and school board members, among others. Courses on multicultural education, portfolio assessment, child growth and development, conflict resolution, and leadership would be of interest to many parents. Some of the language of instruction may need to be adjusted or explained, but every educator, including the person doing the in-service, should know how to meet the needs of the students (and in this case, the parents). The benefits may include the building of an ethos of teamwork among parents and educators. Child-minding facilities for parents with young children would need to be provided.

Throughout this book are many more examples of practical strategies for establishing more inclusive school communities. However, the main idea of this book is not to hand people a prescriptive list of parent-school collaborations, but rather to show the social and cultural practices and relations that are causing daily stresses between parents and educators, and to reconceptualize these relations to move toward new possibilities that each school can explore. The key concepts of an ethic of care, collaboration, and community-building, along with a focus on the core technology of teaching and learning, offer a new view of professionalism for educators, one that is in touch with present-day needs.

IMPLICATIONS FOR FURTHER STUDY

We need many more studies of schools and school practices from a feminist standpoint. Historically, male superintendents have dominated the education profession in power and influence, surrounded by their "pedagogical harem" (Tyack and Hansot 1982). Today, we see a similar pattern, with most superintendents being men and the majority of teachers being women. The influential positions in education and in state and federal government are dominated by men. Of course, men can also hold and champion a feminist agenda for change, but given men's different experience of the world, the viewpoint of women is critical. We need studies to critique policy and practice, and to point the way to achievable and tangible changes in schools that allow for opportunities for all children. I believe we already know how to do this, but preservers of the *status quo* have a vested interest in maintaining social inequality.

I have presented many issues and concerns of parents in this book, and have looked at the relationships, interests, and purposes of parents, teachers, and administrators. However, I am an educator and may be blind to how the school appears when one does not have twenty years experience working in schools. The intimacy I have with schools is useful in knowing about processes and relationships; however, we need many more studies, and in particular from vantage points outside the school. Researchers other than educators can bring new conceptual lenses to the study of schools and families and add to our knowledge of schools and families. In my own case, a background in anthropology and experience in various school systems (public and private, urban and rural schools in the United States, Japan, and Australia) helped me to see some of the familiar in schools as strange, and to appreciate the variety of ways that people make sense of the world.

We also need many more studies that focus on how students' educational experiences outside school affect student learning, and how these experiences in the family and community are supportive of learning. Views of the family derived from socioeconomic data tell us nothing about the rich fabric of family life and about how many experiences, including those in low-income families, are educational. We need to examine who does the teaching outside of schools, and how everyday teaching is done out in the wider school community.

Studies are also needed that examine the school from the perspective of the family. As David (1993, 14) and Smith (1987) point out, research on family-school relationships has typically assumed a one-way relationship. Thus, "family practices, organization, and in particular mothering practices are seen as consequential for the child's behavior at school" (Smith 1987, 24). Where are the studies, then, for the impact of the school on home life? For example, homework is organized by the school, and families must then deal with the disruptions to family life and organize responsibility for the supervision of such activities: "Where are the studies telling us anything about the consequences for family organization of societal processes that 'subcontract' educational responsibilities for homework and so forth to the family and in particular to the mother? . . . What are the implications of this role for family relations, particularly relations between mothers and children?" McDermott, Goldman and Varenne (1983) have done some of this work, but we need ongoing research on a variety of home concerns. In addition, I agree with Epstein (1990, 116–117) that there is a lack of studies on the effects on students of family and school programs that provide different experiences for students.

Finally, we also need research on what the educational and social service needs are from the perspectives of different families. Remaley (1995), for instance, examined the implications of domestic violence on the school setting and how what the school does impacts home life, with emphasis on how children negotiate these different settings and the demands made on them. Studies such as this, which recognize the interactive relationship between the home and the school, are important if we are to restructure schooling in meaningful ways. Reforms that do not acknowledge changing family structures and the multiple demands made on mothers in particular (*e.g.*, mandating parent involvement but not providing child-care), further disadvantage working class families and contribute to a widening gap between rich and poor in this country. Those in the advantaged group should also be concerned, for a class of disadvantaged youth becomes the whole society's heritage. I would urge reformers, policy makers, and those implementing reform at the building level, to look carefully at the social fabric of the school community before mandating parent involvement and implementing reforms that could further hurt those who are most in need.

Reforms for parent-school collaboration will only be successful, I believe, if careful consideration is given to the context of the people in the school community, and if financial and other resources are allocated to provide for broad-based community participation. If we are to truly bring parents and the community into the learning circle, then restructuring must occur in the school organization, as well as in day-to-day power relations and in the hearts and intentions of both school people and parents. Historically, teachers, administrators, staff, parents, and community people have had very little power to change the larger organizational structures that shape their work at the school and district levels. The time is right for a shift to organizational structures and leadership that works against racism, sexism and classism, and truly puts students and their needs at the center of the educational conversation. People have a right to be involved in schools, and they also have a responsibility. Opening up the schools to parents and others means that we all have to be prepared to invest more fully in our schools. Schools cannot do it all alone. The future of our children depends on the commitment of society's leaders to educate and bring up young people to be socially responsible. We have to make changes in school policies and practices—to make this possible and to put the *public* into the public schools.

APPENDIX

QUESTIONS TO GUIDE OBSERVATIONS AND INTERVIEWS

1. *What roles do parents typically play in the public schools? Why are parents involved in these particular roles and not in others?*

   In what roles are parents involved in the school? What is the usefulness of these roles? Are there other areas where parents would like to be involved?

   What parent organizations exist in the school (*e.g.*, PTA, PTSA, Athletics Club)? When were they formed and what do they do?

   What does the PTA/PTSA do? How many people attend a typical meeting? What kind of people are involved?

   Does the school have a volunteer program? If so, what do volunteers do in the school? What problems arise with the volunteers? How are the problems resolved? (*e.g.*, Are there any conflicts between the staff and volunteers? What are the conflicts and how are they handled?)

   What is the reputation of the school in the community with regard to school-family involvement?

2. *How is parent participation viewed by parents, teachers, and administrators?*

   How do teachers/administrators/parents describe parents and parent involvement in the school?

   Is there any resistance by the school or by parents to parent involvement? If so, by whom? What reasons are given?

   What do parents, teachers, and administrators complain about with regard to parent involvement? What do they commend?

What avenues do parents have to voice complaints? How are parent complaints handled?

How accessible is the school to parents? What is the school's visiting policy? What rules pertain to visitors? Are visitors commonly seen in the school? Are entrances to the school clearly marked so that new visitors can easily find the office? What messages greet them on entry to the school?

Do parents have a say in the placement of their child in a particular class?

What does the school choose to display and highlight for parents on open days? Is this a realistic representation of what typically goes on in the school? Are parents involved actively in open days or are they just an audience?

What communication occurs between the school and parents? How often does it occur and what is the nature of the communication? How do parents track their child's progress in school (*e.g.*, report cards, conferences, homework, weekly packets)?

What literature is distributed to parents by the school? What is the nature and content of the literature?

How is the physical environment used by parents and the different parent groups when they are in the school? How is space allocated? Do parents have a resource room or other space in the school? Do teachers and parents share a common space? What problems arise and how are they resolved?

What is the nature of student records in the school? Do the records contain a place for parents' grievances? How does this work?

Do parents have ease of access to files containing information about their children? How often do parents exercise those rights?

3. *How are parents involved in financial, curricular, personnel, and other policy decisions, and in the operations of the school?*

What are the major problems the school has faced in the last five years? How are those problems being addressed? How have parents been involved in solving those problems?

How is parent involvement in decision making and policy encouraged? Are parents involved in financial, curricular, and/or personnel decisions and in the general operations of the school? Why/why not?

Do parents want to be involved in important educational decisions, such as finances, personnel, curriculum? Does the school desire parent participation in these matters? Why/why not?

4. *How might parents be more meaningfully included in the process of educating children?*

Are parents consulted in decision making that affects their children? How are they involved and are they satisfied with the level of involvement? How would parents like to be involved?

What is the racial and socioeconomic composition of the school? Does parent participation in the school reflect distinctions such as single- or two-parent families; working or non-working; class, ethnicity, gender, age?

How many families have left the school this past year for reasons of dissatisfaction with the school (*e.g.*, home schoolers)? What are the views of those parents who consider themselves outside/disenfranchised from the school? How might those groups not involved in the school be brought into the school community? What are their needs and how might they be addressed?

Is there less parent involvement at the high school level than at the middle or elementary schools? If so, what reasons are given?

Are there any innovative programs in the school (*e.g.*, parent workshops, school-based child-care programs, home visits with young children, classes for parents, activities for parents and children)? If not, is there a need for any such programs? If there are innovative programs, what are they and how are these received? Who participates in these programs?

5. *How are the reforms for site-based management and participatory governance working? How is the school district implementing shared decision making? Are there any tensions between the reforms and current practices, and if so, how are they resolved?*

What are the reasons given by the school district for the shift to shared governance? How are parents, teachers, and administrators making the shift? Who is resisting and why? What are the problems that people are concerned with? Is power shared equally by all participants? Why/why not? What evidence is there that the structure and organization of schooling has changed with all the talk about shared governance? Is site-based management making a difference in schools? How so?

REFERENCES

Ames, C. 1993. How school-to-home communications influence parent beliefs and perceptions. *Equity and Choice 9* (3): 44–49.

Anderson, J. 1994. School climate for gay and lesbian students and staff members. *Phi Delta Kappan 76* (2): 151–154.

Anderson, J. and G. White. 1986. An empirical investigation of interaction and relationship patterns in functional and dysfunctional nuclear families and stepfamilies. *Family Process 25*: 407–422.

Apple, M. 1985. *Education and power.* Boston: Ark Paperbacks.

Arendt, H. 1972. *Crises of the republic.* New York: Harcourt Brace Jovanovich.

Arnot, M. 1984. A feminist perspective on the relationship between family life and school life. *Journal of Education 166* (1): 5–48.

Ascher, C. 1987. *Improving the school-home connection for poor and minority urban students.* New York: Institute for Urban and Minority Education, Teachers College, Columbia University.

Association of Washington School Principals (AWSP). 1994. *The principal in Olympia.* AWSP Bulletin No. 5. Olympia: Association of Washington School Principles.

Au, K., and C. Jordan. 1981. Teaching reading to Hawaiian children: Finding a culturally appropriate solution. In *Culture and the bilingual classroom*, ed. H. Trueba, G. Guthrie, and K. Au, 139–152. Rowley, MA: Newbury House.

Ayers, W. 1992. Work that is real: Why teachers should be empowered. In *Empowering teachers and parents*, ed. G. Hess, 13–28. Westport: Bergin and Garvey.

Ballantine, J., ed. 1989. *Schools and society: A unified reader.* Mountain View, CA: Mayfield Publishing Company.

Barlett, D., and J. Steel. 1992. *America: What went wrong?* Kansas City: Andrews and McMeel.

Barr, R., and R. Dreeben. 1983. *How schools work.* Chicago: University of Chicago Press.

Barth, R. 1980. *Run, school, run.* Cambridge: Harvard University Press.

———. 1990. *Improving schools from within: Teachers, parents, and principals can make the difference.* San Francisco: Jossey-Bass.

Bateson, G. 1972. *Steps to an ecology of mind.* New York: Ballantine.

Beck, L. 1994. *Reclaiming educational administration as a caring profession.* New York: Teachers College Press.

Becker, H. 1986. *Doing things together.* Evanston, IL: Northwestern University Press.

Belenky, M., B. Clinchy, N. Goldberger, and J. Tarule. 1986. *Women's ways of knowing.* Basic Books.

Bellah, R., R. Madsen, W. Sullivan, A. Swindler, A., and S. Tipton. 1985. *Habits of the heart: Individualism and commitment in American life.* New York: Harper and Row.

Berman, P., and T. Gjelten. 1983. *Improving school improvement: An independent evaluation of the California school improvement program.* Berkeley: Berman, Weiler Associates.

Bhabha, H. 1992. Postcolonial authority and postmodern guilt. In *Cultural studies,* ed. L. Grossberg, C. Nelson, and P. Treichler, 56–68. New York: Routledge.

Bourdieu, P., and J. Passeron. 1977. *Reproduction in Education, Society, and Culture.* Sage: Beverly Hills.

Bowers, C., and D. Flinders. 1990. *Responsive teaching: An ecological approach to classroom patterns of language, culture, and thought.* New York: Teachers College Press.

Bowles, S., and H. Gintis. 1976. *Schooling in capitalist America.* New York: Basic Books.

Boyer, J. 1995. Multicultural curriculum studies, race relations, ethnic relations in the workplace. Presentation to the College of Education, Washington State University, Pullman, WA.

Boykin, A. Wade. 1994. Afrocultural expression and its implications for schooling. In *Teaching Diverse Populations,* ed. E. Hollins, J. King, and W. Hayman, 243–274. Albany: SUNY.

Bray, J., and S. Berger. 1992. Stepfamilies. In *Contemporary Families: A Handbook for School Professionals*, ed. M. Procidano, and C. Fisher, 57–80. New York: Teachers College Press.

Brumback, S. 1992. S.P.I.C.E. (student/parent interactive classroom environment) West Valley parents' timely answer to the challenging concerns of educating our children. *Curriculum in Context 20* (2): 24–25.

Burbules, N. 1989. Issues and trends in the philosophy of education. *Educational Administration Quarterly 25*: 229–252.

Calabrese, R. L. 1990. The public school: A source of alienation for minority parents. *Journal of Negro Education 59* (2): 148–154.

California Department of Education. 1991. Language census reports. California Department of Education.

Capper, C. 1990. Exploring community influences on leadership and reform: A micro-level and macro-level analysis of poverty and culture. Paper presented at annual meeting, American Educational Research Association, Boston.

——— . 1993. Educational administration in a pluralistic society: A multiparadigm approach. In *Educational administration in a puralistic society*, ed. C. Capper, 7–35. Albany: SUNY.

——— . 1993. Administrator practice and preparation for social reconstructionist schooling. In *Educational administration in a puralistic society*, ed. C. Capper, 288–316. Albany: SUNY.

Carlson, C. 1992. Single-parent families. In *Contemporary families: A handbook for professional*, ed. M. Procidano, and C. Fisher, 36–56. New York: Teachers College Press.

Carnegie Task Force on Education of Young Adolescents. 1989. *Turning points: Preparing American youth for the 21st century*. Washington, DC: Carnegie Council on Adolescent Development.

Carnegie Task Force on Teaching as a Profession. 1986. *A nation prepared: Teachers for the 21st century*. New York: Carnegie Forum on Education and the Economy.

Cauce, A., M. Reid, S. Landesman, and N. Gonzalez. 1990. Social support in young children: Measurement, structure, and behavioral impact. In *Social Support: An Interactional View*, ed. B. Sarason, I. Sarason, and G. Pierce, 64–94. New York: Wiley Interscience.

Chavkin, N. F. 1989. Debunking the myth about minority parents and the school. *Educational Horizons 67*: 119–123.

Chavkin, N. F., ed. 1993. *Families and schools in a pluralistic society.* New York: SUNY.

Chubb, J., and T. Moe. 1990. *Politics, markets, and America's schools.* Washington, DC: Brookings Institute.

Cicourel, A., and J. Kitsuse. 1963. *Educational decision makers.* Indianapolis: Bobbs-Merrill.

Clark, R. 1983. *Family life and school achievement: Why poor black children succeed or fail.* Chicago: University of Chicago Press.

Clark, S., and D. Clark. 1994. *Restructuring the middle level school: Implications for school leaders.* Albany: SUNY.

Clifford, J. 1992. Traveling cultures. In *Cultural Studies*, ed. L. Grossberg, C. Nelson, and P. Treichler, 96–116. New York: Routledge.

Coalition of Essential Schools. 1994. The common principles. Providence, RI: Coalition of Essential Schools, Brown University.

Comer, J. 1980. *School power: Implications of an intervention project.* New York: Free Press.

———. 1986. Parent participation in the schools. *Phi Delta Kappan 67* (6): 442–446.

———. 1988. *Maggie's American dream: The life and times of a black family.* New York: New American Library.

———. 1988a. Educating poor minority children. *Scientific American 259* (5): 42–48.

Conant, J. 1959. *The American high school today.* New York: McGraw-Hill.

Connell, R. W., D. J. Ashendon, S. Kessler, and G. Dowsett. 1982. *Making the difference: Schools, families, and social division.* Sydney: George Allen and Unwin.

Crowson, R. 1992. *School-community relations under reform.* Berkeley: McCutchan.

Cuban, L. 1976. *Urban school chiefs under fire.* Chicago: University of Chicago Press.

Dantley, M. 1990. The ineffectiveness of effective schools leadership: An analysis of the effective schools movement from a critical perspective. *Journal of Negro Education 59*: 585–598.

Danzenberger, J., and M. Usdan. 1992. Strengthening a grass roots American institution: The school board. In *School boards: Changing local control*, ed. P. First, and H. Walberg, 91–124. Berkeley: McCutchan Publishing Corporation.

Darling-Hammond, L. 1988. Policy and professionalism. In *Building a professional culture in schools*, ed. A. Lieberman, 55–77. New York: Teachers College Press.

Dauber, S., and J. Epstein. 1993. Parents' attitudes and practices of involvement in inner-city elementary and middle schools. In *Families and schools in a pluralistic society,* ed. N Chavkin, 53–72. New York: SUNY.

David, M. 1993. *Parents, gender, and educational reform.* Oxford: Blackwell publishers.

Davies, B. 1993. *Shards of glass: Children reading and writing beyond gendered identities.* Sydney: Allen and Unwin.

Davies, D. 1988. Benefits and barriers to parent involvement. *Community Education Research Digest 2*: 11–19.

———. 1991. Schools reaching out: Family, school, and community partnership for student success. *Phi Delta Kappan 72* (5): 376–382.

Delpit, L. 1988. Power and pedagogy in educating other people's children. *Harvard Educational Review 58* (3): 280–298.

Desjardins, C. 1995. Women's leadership: A different choice. Paper presented at Leadership Directions and Connections Conference, University of Idaho, Moscow, ID.

Dewey, J. 1938. *Experience and education.* New York: Macmillan.

———. 1956. *The school and society.* Chicago: University of Chicago Press.

Digest of Educational Statistics. 1990. Washington, DC: National Center for Education Statistics, U.S. Department of Education.

Dillon, D. 1989. Showing them that I want them to learn and that I care about who they are: A microethnography of the social organization of a secondary low-track English reading classroom. *American Educational Research Journal 26* (2): 227–259.

Driscoll, M. 1990. The formation of community in public schools: Findings and hypothesis. *Administrator's Notebook 34* (4): 1–4.

Education Week. 1986. Here they come, ready or not. 5 (34): 14–32.

Emihovich, C., and D. James. 1993. Re-Imagining the other: Feminist and critical perspectives in educational research. Paper presented at annual meeting of the American Anthropological Association, Washington, DC.

Epstein, J. 1985. Winter home and school connections in schools of the future: Implications of research on parent involvement. *Peabody Journal of Education 62* (2): 18–41.

———. 1986, January. Parents' reactions to teacher practices of parent involvement. *The Elementary School Journal 86* (3): 277–294.

———. 1987. Parent involvement: What research says to administrators. *Education and Urban Society 19* (2): 119–136.

———. 1988. *Parent Involvement.* Baltimore: Johns Hopkins University, Center for Research on Elementary and Middle Schools.

———. 1990. School and family connections: Theory, research, and implications for integrating sociologies of education and family. *Marriage and family review 15* (1): 99–126.

———. 1991. Paths to partnership: What can we learn from federal, state, district, and school initiatives, *Phi Delta Kappan 72* (5): 344–349.

Erickson, F., and J. Schultz. 1982. *Counselor as gatekeeper: Social interaction in interviews.* New York: Academic Press.

Ernst, G. (N.d.). Beyond language: The many dimensions of an ESL program. *Anthropology and Education Quarterly.* In press.

Etheridge, C., and T. Collins. 1992. Conflict in restructuring the principal-teacher relationship in Memphis. In *Empowering teachers and parents: School restructuring through the eyes of anthropologists*, ed. G. Alfred Hess, Jr., 89–102. Westport, CT: Bergin and Garvey.

Etzioni, A. 1993. *The spirit of community: The reinvention of American society.* New York: Touchstone.

Ferguson, K. 1984. *The feminist case against bureaucracy.* Philadelphia: Temple University Press.

Finch, J. 1984. The deceit of self-help: Preschool playgroups and working class mothers. *Journal of Social Policy 13* (1): 1–21.

Fine, M. 1993. (Ap)parent involvement. *Equity and Choice 9* (3): 4–8.

Finn, C. 1992. Reinventing local control. In *School boards: Changing local control*, ed. P. First, and H. Walberg, 21–26. Berkeley: McCutchan Publishing Corporation.

Fordham, S., and J. Ogbu. 1986. Black students' school success: Coping with the burden of "acting white." *Urban Review 18* (3): 176–206.

Foster, W. 1986. *Paradigms and promises: New approaches in educational administration.* Buffalo, NY: Prometheus.

Fowler, W., and H. Walberg. 1991. School size, characteristics, and outcomes. *Educational evaluation and policy analysis 13* (2): 189–202.

Fry, P., and A. Sher. 1984. The effects of father absence on children's achievement motivation, ego-strength, and locus-of-control orientation: A five-year longitudinal assessment. *British Journal of Developmental Psychology 2*: 167–178.

Fullan, M. 1991. *The new meaning of educational change.* New York: Teachers College Press.

Fuller W. 1982. *The old country school: The story of rural education in the middle west.* Chicago: University of Chicago Press.

Garlington, J. 1991. *Helping dreams survive: The story of a project involving African-American families and the education of their children.* Washington, DC: National Committee for Citizens in Education.

———. 1993. Helping dreams survive. *Equity and choice IX* (3): 9–21.

Geer, B. 1969. First days in the field. In *Issues in participant observation: A text and reader*, ed. G. McCall, and J. Simmons, 144–162. Reading, MA: Addison-Wesley Publishing Company.

Gibson, M. 1987. Playing by the rules. In *Interpretive ethnography of education: At home and abroad*, ed. G. and L. Spindler, 274–282. New Jersey: Lawrence Erlbaum Association.

Gilligan, C. 1982. *In a different voice: Psychological theory and women's development.* Cambridge, Massachusetts: Harvard University Press.

Glaser, B., and A. Strauss. 1967. *The discovery of grounded theory.* Chicago: Aldine.

———. 1971. *Status passages.* Chicago: Aldine.

Goldman, S., and R. McDermott. 1987. The culture of competition in American schools. In *Education and cultural process: Anthropological approaches.* 2d ed., ed. G. Spindler, 282–300. Prospect Heights, IL: Waveland Press.

Goodlad, J. 1984. *A place called school.* New York: McGraw-Hill.

Grant, C. 1988. *The world we created at Hamilton high.* Cambridge: Harvard University Press.

Grant, C., and C. Sleeter. 1986. *After the school bell rings.* Philadelphia: The Falmer Press.

Greene, M. 1973. *Teacher as stranger: Educational philosophy for the modern age.* Belmont, CA: Wordsworth Publishing Co.

———. 1988. *The Dialectic of Freedom.* New York: Teachers College Press.

Greenfield, W. 1986. The decline and fall of science in educational administration. *Interchange 17:* 57–80.

———. 1988. Moral imagination, interpersonal competence, and the work of school administrators. In *Leaders for America's schools,* ed. D. Griffiths, R. Stout, and P. Forsyth, 207–233. Berkeley: McCutchan Publishing Corporation.

Grogan, M. 1994. Aspiring to the superintendency in U.S. public school systems. Ph.D. diss., Washington State University, Pullman.

Guidabaldi, J., J. Perry, and H. Cleminshaw. 1984. The legacy of parental divorce: A nationwide study of family status and selected mediating variables on children's academic social competencies. In *Advances in clinical child psychology 7,* ed. B. Lahey, and A. Kazdin, 109–151. New York: Plenum.

Haraway, D. 1992. The promises of monsters: A regenerative politics for inappropriate/d others. In *Cultural studies,* ed. L. Grossberg, C. Nelson, and P. Treichler, 295–337. New York: Routledge.

Harding, S. 1993. Gender, method, and knowledge: New issues. Paper presented at Annual Meeting of the American Eductional Research Association, Atlanta, GA.

Harrington, D., and P. Cookson. 1992. School reform in East Harlem: Alternative schools vs. "schools of choice." In *Empowering teachers and parents: School restructuring through the eyes of anthropologists,* ed. G. Hess, 177–186. Westport, Connecticut: Bergin and Garvey.

Harris, L., et al. 1987. *The Metropolitan Life survey of the American teacher in 1987—Strengthening links between home and school.* New York: Author.

Havighurst, R., P. Bowman, G. Liddle, C. Matthews, and J. Pierce. 1962. *Growing up in River City.* New York: John Wiley and Sons.

Heath, S. 1983. *Ways with words: Language, life, and work in communities and classrooms.* New York: Cambridge University Press.

Heck, S., and R. Williams. 1984. *The complex roles of the teacher.* New York: Teachers College Press.

Heckscher, C., and A. Donnellon, eds. 1994. *The post-bureaucratic organization: New perspectives on organizational change.* Thousand Oaks, CA: Sage Publications.

Henderson, A. 1987. *The evidence continues to grow: Parents involvement improves student achievement.* Columbia, MD: National Committee for Citizens in Education.

Hendrick, I. 1992. New designs in schooling. *Fiat Lux* (November): 49–51.

Henry, M. 1993. *School cultures: Universes of meaning in private schools.* Ablex Publishing Corporation: New Jersey.

———. 1993a. Parents, the forgotten educators: An analysis of parent involvement in a public high school. Paper presented at annual meeting of the American Educational Research Association, Atlanta, GA.

———. 1994. Parent-school partnerships: Problem-solving the professional-lay distinction. Paper presented at annual meeting of the American Educational Research Association, New Orleans.

———. 1995. Putting the public back into public schools: Relationships between parents and educators. Paper presented at annual meeting of the American Educational Research Association, San Francisco.

Hess, G. 1991. *Chicago school reform: What it is and how it came to be.* Chicago: Chicago Panel on Public School Policy and Finance.

Hess, G., and J. Easton. 1992. Who's making what decisions: Monitoring authority shifts in Chicago school reform. In *Empowering teachers and parents: School restructuring through the eyes of anthropologists,* ed. G. Hess, 157–176. Westport, Connecticut: Bergin and Garvey.

Hirsch, E. 1987. *Cultural literacy: What every American needs to know.* Boston: Houghton Mifflin.

Hodgkinson, H. 1985. All one system: Demographics of education, kindergarten through graduate school. Washington, DC: Institute for Educational Leadership.

———. 1987. Changing society: Unchanging curriculum. *National Forum 67* (3): 8–11.

Holmes Group. 1986. *Tomorrow's teachers: A report of the Holmes Group.* East Lansing, Mich: The Holmes Group.

Jackson, P. 1968. *Life in classrooms.* New York: Holt, Rinehart and Winston.

Johnson, V. R. 1993. *Parent/family centers: Dimensions of functioning in 28 schools in 14 states.* Report No. 20. Baltimore, MD: Center on Families, Communities, Schools, and Children's Learning.

———. 1994. Parent/family centers: Linking families, schools, and communities. AERA Families as Educators SIG newsletter. Winter.

———. 1994a. *Parent centers in urban schools: Four case studies.* Baltimore, MD: Center on Families, Communities, Schools, and Children's Learning.

Johnson, S. 1989. Schoolwork and its reform. In *The politics of reforming school administration*, ed. J. Hannaway, and R. Crowson, 95–112. New York: Falmer Press.

Jones, B., and R. Maloy. 1988. *Partnerships for improving schools.* New York: Greenwood Press.

Jones, E., and X. Montenegro. 1990. *Women and minorities in school administration: Facts and figures, 1989–1990.* Washington, DC: American Association of School Administrators, Office of Minority Affairs.

Kaestle, C. 1983. *Pillars of the republic: Common schools and American society 1780–1860.* New York: Hill and Wang.

Kanter, R. 1983. *Men and women of the corporation.* New York: Basic Books.

Katz, M., ed. 1971. *School reform: Past and present.* Boston: Little, Brown and Company.

Katz, M. 1975. *Class, bureaucracy, and schools: The illusion of educational change in America*, expanded edition. New York: Praeger Publishers.

Keller, E. 1985. *Reflections on gender and science.* New Haven, CT: Yale University Press.

Kerr, N. 1964. The school board as an agency of legitimation. *Sociology of Education 38*: 34–59.

King, J. 1994. The purpose of schooling for African American children: Including cultural knowledge. In *Teaching diverse populations*, eds. E. Hollins, J. King, and W. Hayman, 25–60. Albany: SUNY.

Kohlberg, L. 1976. *Collected papers on moral development and moral education.* Cambridge, MA: Center for Moral Education.

Koza, M., and W. Levy. 1977–1978. School organization and community participation. *Administrator's Notebook 26* (9): 1–4.

Lareau, A. 1989. *Home advantage: Social class and parental intervention in elementary education.* London: Falmer Press.

———. 1989a. Social class differences in family-school relationships: The importance of cultural capital. *Sociology of Education 60*: 73–85.

———. 1989b. Family-school relationships: A view from the classroom. *Educational Policy 3* (2): 245–259.

Lareau, A., and C. Benson. 1984. The economics of home/school relationships: A cautionary note. *Phi Delta Kappan 65* (6): 401–404.

Lasch, C. 1980. *The culture of narcissism.* London: Abacus Books.

LeCompte, M., and J. Goetz, eds. 1992. *Handbook of Qualitative Research in Education.* San Diego: Academic Press.

Levering, M. 1993. *The 100 best companies to work for in America.* New York: Currency/Doubleday.

Lightfoot, S. 1978. *Worlds apart: Relationships between families and schools.* New York: Basic Books.

Lightfoot, S. 1983. *The good high school: Portraits of character and culture.* New York: Basic Books.

Lincoln, Y., and E. Guba. 1985. *Naturalistic inquiry.* Beverly Hills, Ca: Sage Publications.

Lyons, N. 1983. Two perspectives: On self, relationships, and morality. *Harvard Educational Review 53* (2): 125–145.

Lytle, J. 1990. Reforming urban education: A review of recent reports and legislation. *Urban Review 22*: 199–220.

Malen, B., R. Ogawa, and J. Kranz. 1990. What do we know about school-based management? A case study of the literature—a call for research. In *Choice and control in American education*, ed. W. Clune, and J. White, 289–342. New York: Falmer Press.

Mann, D. 1976. *The Politics of Administrative Representation*. Lexington, Mass: Lexington Books.

Mannan, G., and J. Blackwell. 1992. Parent involvement: Barriers and opportunities. *Urban Review 24* (3): 219–226.

Marburger, C. L. 1990. The school site level: Involving parents in reform. In *Educational reform: Making sense of it all*, ed. S. Bacharach. Boston, Mass: Allyn and Bacon.

Marshall, C. 1992. *The assistant principal*. Corwin Press: Newbury Park.

————. 1992a. School administrators' values: A focus on atypicals. *Educational Administration Quarterly 28* (3): 368–386.

Martin, B. 1993. Who owns the problem? *Equity and Choice 9* (3): 55–56.

Martin, E. 1992. Body narratives, body boundaries. In *Cultural studies*, ed. L. Grossberg, C. Nelson, and P. Treichler, 409–423. New York: Routledge.

McCaleb, S. 1994. *Building communities of learners: A collaboration among teachers, students, families, and community*. New York: St Martin's Press.

McCarthy Brown, K. 1992. Writing about the other: New approaches to fieldwork can end the colonial mindset of anthropological research. *The Chronicle of Higher Education*, vol. 38, A56.

McDermott, R. 1989. The family as educator. Course syllabus, University of Virginia, Charlottesville, VA. Xerox.

McDermott, R., Goldman, S., and H. Varenne. 1983. When school goes home: Some problems in the organization of homework. *Teachers College Record 85* (3): 391–410.

McLaughlin, M. W., and P. M. Shields. 1987. Involving low-income parents in the schools: A role for policy? *Phi Delta Kappan 69* (2): 156–160.

Mearig, J. 1992. Families with learning-disabled children. In *Contemporary families: A handbook for school professionals*, ed. M. Procidano, and C. Fisher, 209–233. New York: Teachers College Press.

Meier, D. 1991. Choice can save public education. *Nation*: (March 4) 266–271.

Merz, C. 1994. Sociological frameworks for educational reform. New Orleans: Division A, American Educational Research Association.

Moore, H. 1988. *Feminism and anthropology*. Cambridge, UK: Polity Press.

Moore, D. 1992. The case for parent and community involvement. In *Empowering teachers and parents: School restructuring through the eyes of anthropologists*, ed. G. Alfred Hess, 131–156. Westport, Connecticut: Bergin and Garvey.

Morris, V., R. Crowson, C. Porter-Gehrie, and E. Hurwitz. 1984. *Principals in action: The reality of managing schools*. Columbus, Ohio: Charles E. Merrill.

Mulhern, M. 1994. Webs of meaning: The literate lives of three Mexican-American kindergartners. Ph.D. diss. University of Illinois at Chicago.

Murray, C. 1990. *The emerging British underclass*. London: IEA Health and Welfare Unit.

NASSP Council on Middle Level Education. 1985. *An agenda for excellence at the middle level*. Reston, VA: National Association of Secondary School Principals.

National Commission on Excellence in Education. 1983. *A Nation at Risk*. Washington, DC: National Commission on Excellence in Education.

Nemzoff, R. 1993. Sex bias in individual education plans. *Equity and Choice 9* (3): 61–62.

Nicklos, L., and W. Brown. 1989. Recruiting minorities into the teaching profession: An educational imperative. *Educational Horizons 67*: 145–149.

Nieto, S. 1992. *Affirming diversity: The socio-political context of multicultural education*. New York: Longman.

Noddings, N. 1984. *Caring: A feminine approach to ethics and moral education*. Berkeley: University of California Press.

———. 1986. Fidelity in teaching, teacher education, and research for teaching. *Harvard Educational Review 56*: 496–510.

———. 1988. An ethic of care and its implications for instructional arrangements. *American Journal of Education 96* (2): 215–230.

———. 1989. *Women and evil*. Berkeley: University of California Press.

————. 1991/1992. The gender issue. *Educational Leadership* (December/ January) 49 (4): 65–70.

————. 1992. *The challenge to care in schools: An alternative approach to education.* New York: Teachers College Press.

Norton A., and J. Moorman. 1992. Marriage and divorce patterns of U.S. women. *Journal of Marriage and the Family 49*: 3–14.

Ogbu, J. 1974. *The next generation: An ehnography of education in an urban neighborhood.* New York: Academic Press.

————. 1978. Minority education and caste: The American system in cross-cultural perspective. New York: Academic Press.

————. 1987. Variability in minority school performance: A problem in search of an explanation. *Anthropology and Education Quarterly 18*: 312–334.

————. 1988. Diversity and equity in public education: Community forces and minority school adjustment and performance. In *Policies for America's public schools: Teachers, equity, and indications*, ed. R. Haskins, and D. MacRae, 127–170. Norwood, New Jersey: Ablex Publishing Company.

Ogletree, E., and L. Schmidt. 1989. Faculty involvement in administration of schools. *Illinois Schools Journal,* Focus issue: 40–45.

Oliver, B., and B. Sibley-Chears. 1994. "It takes the whole village": Research on culturally relevant contexts and pedagogy in African American education from students to administrators. Discussants for Symposium. Papers presented at annual meeting of the American Educational Research Association, Houston.

Ooka Pang, V. 1988. Ethnic prejudice: Still alive and hurtful. *Harvard Educational Review 58*: 375–379.

Ortiz, F., and C. Marshall. 1988. Women in educational administration. In *Handbook of research on educational administration*, ed. N. Boyan, 123–141. New York: Longman.

Page, R. 1990. Cultures and curricula: Differences between and within schools. *Educational Foundations 4* (1): 49–76.

Palmer, P. 1987. Community, conflict, and ways of knowing. *Change 19* (5): 20–25.

Parker, L., and J. Shapiro. 1993. The context of educational administration and social class. In *Educational administration in a pluralistic society*, ed. C. Capper, 36–65. Albany: SUNY.

Patterson, R. 1993. School-based management and/or decision making and the law: Legal authority and concerns and/or impediments under existing Washington state law. State of Washington: School Law Academy.

Peshkin, A. 1978. *Growing up American: Schooling and the survival of community.* Chicago: University of Chicago Press.

———. 1986. *God's choice: The total world of a fundamentalist Christian school.* Chicago: University of Chicago Press.

———. 1988. In search of subjectivity—one's own. *Educational Researcher 17* (7): 17–21.

Peters, T., and R. Waterman. 1982. *In search of excellence: Lessons from America's best run corporations.* New York: Harper and Row.

Philips, S. 1972. Participation structures and communicative competence: Warm Springs children in community and classroom. In *Functions of language in the classroom,* ed. C. Cazden, V. P. John, and D. Hymes, 370–394. New York: Teachers College Press.

Pierce, A. 1992. Will I have a friend? A qualitative study of the transition of new students into the school. Ph.D. diss., Washington State University, Pullman.

Plath, D. 1980. *Long engagements.* Stanford: Stanford University Press.

Poster, M. 1986. *Critical theory of the family.* New York: The Seabury Press.

Poston, W. 1994. Introduction. In *Effective school board governance,* ed. W. Poston, i–iv. Bloomington, IN: Phi Delta Kappa Center for Evaluation, Development, Research.

Powell, A., E. Farrar, and D. Cohen. 1985. *The shopping mall high school: Winners and losers in the educational marketplace.* Boston: Houghton Mifflin.

Prillaman, A., D. Eaker, and D. Kendrick, eds. 1994. *The tapestry of caring: Education as nurturance.* New Jersey: Ablex.

Raywid, M. 1990. Rethinking school governance. In *Restructuring schools: The next generation of educational reform,* ed. R. Elmore, 152–205. San Francisco: Jossey-Bass.

Reed, D., and D. Mitchell. 1975. The structure of citizen participation: Public decisions for public schools. In *Public testimony on public schools,* ed. S. Weinstein, and D. Mitchell, 183–217. Berkeley: McCutchan.

Remaley, A. 1995. The effects of family violence on children in school: Implications for educators. Unpublished doctoral diss. College of Education, Washington State University, Pullman.

Reyes, P., W. Velez, and R. Pena. 1993. School reform: Introducing race, culture, and ethnicity into the discourse. In *Educational Administration in a pluralistic society*, ed. C. Capper, 66–85. SUNY: Albany.

Richard Day Associates. 1990. *A survey of members of Chicago local school councils for leadership for quality education*. Chicago: Leadership for Quality Education.

Rist, R. 1970. Student social class and teacher expectations: The self-fulfilling prophecy in ghetto education. *Harvard Educational Review 40*: 411–451.

Ritter, P. L., R. Mont-Reynaud, and S. M. Dornbusch. 1993. Minority parents and their youth: Concern, encouragement, and support for school achievement. In *Families and schools in a pluralistic society*, ed. N. F. Chavkin, 107–120. Albany, NY: SUNY Press.

Rivera, R. 1987. Legal issues in gay and lesbian parenting. In *Gay and lesbian parents*, ed. R. Bozett, 199–227. Westport, Conn: Praeger.

Rockhill, K. 1987. Gender, language, and the politics of literacy. *British Journal of Sociology of Education 8* (2): 153–169.

———. 1987b. Literacy as a threat/desire: Longing to be SOMEBODY. In *Women and education: A Canadian perspective*, ed. J. S. Gaskell, and A. T. McLaren. Calgary: Detselig.

Rofes, E. 1989. *Socrates, Plato, and guys like me: Confessions of a gay schoolteacher*. Boston: Alyson.

Roman, L. 1992. The political significance of other ways of narrating ethnography: A feminist materialist approach. In *The handbook of qualitative research in education*, Ed. M. LeCompte, W. Millroy, and J. Preissle, 555–591. San Diego, CA: Academic Press.

Roman, L., and M. Apple. 1990. Is naturalism a move away from positivism? Materialist and feminist approaches to subjectivity in ethnographic research. In *Qualitative inquiry in education: The continuing debate*, ed. E. Eisner, and A. Peshkin, 38–73. New York: Teachers College Press.

Rosenfeld, G. 1971. *Shut those thick lips! A study of slum school failure*. Prospect Heights, IL: Waveland Press.

Sacken, D. May, 1994. No more principals! *Phi Delta Kappan 75* (9): 664–670.

Sarason, S. 1990. *The predictable failure of educational reform: Can we change course before it's too late?* San Francisco: Jossey-Bass.

Scheurich, J., and M. Imber. 1991. Educational reforms can reproduce social inequities: A case study. *Educational Administration Quarterly 27*: 297–320.

Schrage, M. 1990. *Shared minds: The new technologies of collaboration.* New York: Random House.

Scott, B. 1993. Toward the survivability of vision. *Equity and Choice 9* (3): 63–66.

Scott-Jones, D. 1993. Families as educators in a pluralistic society. In *Families and Schools in a Pluralistic Society*, ed. N. Chavkin, 245–254. SUNY: Albany.

Sears, J. 1992. Reproducing the body politic: Dilemmas and possibilities in sexuality education. In *Sexuality and the curriculum*, ed. J. Sears, 19–50. New York: Teachers College Press.

———. 1993. Responding to the sexual diversity of faculty and students: Sexual praxis and the critically reflective administrator. In *Educational administration in a pluralistic society*, ed. C. Capper, 110–172. Albany, NY: SUNY.

Seeley, D. 1989. A new paradigm of parent involvement. *Educational Leadership 47* (2): 47–48.

Shakeshaft, C. 1987. *Women in educational administration.* Newbury Park, CA: Sage Publications.

———. 1993. Gender equity in schools. In *Educational administration in a pluralistic society*, ed. C. Capper, 86–109. Albany: SUNY.

Sharratt, G., and M. Derrington. 1993. Female superintendents: Attributes that attract and barriers that discourage their successful applications. *Management Information* (Fall) 6–10.

Shinn, M. 1978. Father absence and children's cognitive development. *Psychological Bulletin 85* (2): 295–324.

Simoni J., and H. Adelman. 1993. School-based mutual support groups for low-income parents. *The Urban Review 25* (4): 335–350.

Simpson, J. 1994. *The politics of school administration: Focus on the superintendency.* Presentation at final administrative internship meeting, Washington State University, Vancouver.

————. 1994b. *On power*. Presentation to the final administrative internship meeting, Washington State University, Vancouver, WA, April 22.

Smith, D. 1987. *The everyday world as problematic: A feminist sociology.* Boston: Northwestern University Press.

Smith, J. 1988. The evaluator/researcher as person vs. the person as evaluator/researcher. *Educational Researcher 17* (2): 18–23.

Smylie, M. 1994. Redesigning teachers' work: Connections to the classroom. *Review of research in education 20*: 129–177.

Snyder, D. 1991. Learning for life in revolutionary times: A strategic briefing for special education administrators. Paper presented at Missouri Special Education Administration Conference. Lake Ozark.

Spindler, G., ed. 1987. *Education and cultural process: Anthropological approaches.* 2d ed. Prospect Heights, IL: Waveland.

Spring, J. 1986. *The American school, 1642–1985.* New York: Longman.

Stacey, J. 1988. Can there be a feminist ethnography? *Women's Studies International Forum 11* (1): 21–27.

Stevenson, D., and D. Baker. 1987. The family-school relation and the child's school performance. *Child Development 58*: 1348.

Strathern, M. 1987. An awkward relationship: The case of feminism and anthropology. *Signs: Journal of Women in Culture and Society 12* (2): 276–293.

————. 1991. *Partial connections.* Lanham, Md: Rowman and Littlefield.

Strauss, A. 1987. *Qualitative analysis for social scientists.* New York: Cambridge University Press.

Streshly, W., and L. Frase. 1992. *Avoiding legal hassles: What school administrators really need to know.* Newbury Park, CA: Corwin Press.

Talmage, C. 1994. The politics of school administration: Focus on the principalship. Presentation by the Executive Director of the Association for Washington School Principals (AWSP), Washington State University, Vancouver, WA.

Tanizaki, J. 1982. *The key.* New York: Perigree.

Tannen, D. 1990. *You just don't understand: Women and men in conversation.* New York: William Morrow and Company.

Thayer, F. 1981. *An end to hierarchy and competition: Administration in the post-affluent world.* New York: New viewpoints.

Tonnies, F. 1957. *Community and society.* Translated and edited by C. Loomis. East Lansing: Michigan State University Press.

Topping, K. 1986. *Parents as educators.* London: Croom Helm.

Treiman, J. 1994. A conflict of character: A study of elementary teachers' role stress in authentic assessment reform, Division A, American Educational Research Association, New Orleans.

Tronto, J. 1987. Beyond gender difference to a theory of care. *Signs: Journal of Women in Culture and Society 12* (4): 644–663.

Trubowitz, S., J. Duncan, W. Fibkins, P. Longo, and S. Sarason. 1984. *When a college works with a public school: A case study of school-college collaboration.* Boston: Institute for Responsive Education.

Trudel, T., and C. Fisher. 1992. Dual-wage families. In *Contemporary families: A handbook for school professionals*, ed. M. Procidano, and C. Fisher, 17–35. New York: Teachers College Press.

Twain, M. [1885[1981. *The adventures of Huckelberry Finn.* New York: Bantam.

Tyack, D. 1981. Governance and goals: Historical perspectives on public education. In *Communities and their schools*, ed. D. Davies, 11–31). New York: McGraw-Hill Book Co.

Tyack, D., and E. Hansot. 1982. *Managers of virtue: Public school leadership in America, 1820–1980.* New York: Basic Books.

Ulich, K. 1989. Parents and students: The impact of the school on education in the family. *Zeitschrift fur socialisations forschung und erzietungssoci-ologie 9* (3): 179–184.

United States Census Bureau. 1988. *Current populations reports.* Washington, DC: U.S. Government Printing Office.

U.S. Department of Education. 1988. *Youth indicators 1988.* Washington, DC: U. S. Government Printing Office.

Valente, W. 1987. *Law in the school.* 2d ed. Columbus, Ohio: Merrill.

Van Galen, J. 1987. Maintaining control: The structuring of parent involvement. In *Schooling in social context: Qualitative studies*, ed. G. Noblit, and W. Pink, 78–90. Norwood, New Jersey: Ablex.

Wadsworth, M., and M. Maclearn. 1986. Parental divorce and children's life chances. *Children and Youth Services Review 8*: 145–161.

Walberg, H. 1984. Families as partners in educational productivity. *Phi Delta Kappan*, 397–400.

———. 1984a. Improving the productivity of America's schools. *Educational Leadership 41* (8): 19–27.

Walberg, H., and R. Niemiec. 1994. Is Chicago school reform working? *Phi Delta Kappan 75* (9): 713–715.

Waller, W. 1932. *Sociology of Teaching*. New York: John Wiley and Sons.

Weiss, R. 1979. Growing up a little faster: The experience of growing up in a single-parent household. *Journal of Social Issues 35* (4): 97–111.

Welch, S. 1991. An ethic of solidarity and difference. In *Postmodernism, feminism, and cultural politics*, ed. H. Giroux, 83–99. Albany, NY: SUNY.

West, C. 1987. Race and social theory: Towards a genealogical materialist analysis. In *The year left*, ed. M. Davis, F. Pfeil, and M. Sprinker, 75–90. London: Verso.

Wheatley, M. 1994. *Leadership and the new science: Learning about organization from an orderly universe.* San Francisco: Berrett-Koehler.

Whitehead, T., and M. Conaway. 1986. Self, sex, and gender in cross-cultural fieldwork. Urbana: University of Illinois Press.

Winters, W. 1993. *African American mothers and urban schools: The power of participation.* New York: Lexington Books.

Wolcott, H. 1987. The teacher as an enemy. In *Education and cultural process: Anthropological approaches.* 2d ed., ed. G. Spindler, 136–150. Prospect Heights, IL: Waveland Press.

———. 1973. *The man in the principal's offfce: An ethnography.* Holt, Rinehart and Winston: New York.

Wolfendale, S. 1992. *Primary schools and special needs: Policy, planning, and provision.* 2d ed. London: Cassell.

Woods, P. 1988. A strategic view of parent participation. *Journal of Educational Policy 3*: 323–334.

Wyner, N., ed. 1991. *Current perspectives on the culture of schools.* Cambridge, Mass.: Brookline Books.

Yates, J., and F. Ortiz. 1991. Professional development needs of teachers who serve exceptional language minorities in today's schools. *Teacher Education and Special Education 4*: 11–18.

Ziegler, L., H. Tucker, and L. Wilson. 1977. Communication and decision making in American public education: A longitudinal and comparative study. In *The politics of education*, ed. J. Scribner, 218–254. Chicago: University of Chicago Press.

INDEX

Abuse, 45; monitoring, 46

Accelerated Schools Project, 168

Administrators: autonomy issues, 7; as business leaders, 20, 65, 137–138, 181*tab*; collaborative stances by, 56; control of classroom activities, 66; control of planning by, 80; decision-making issues, 7; feminist, 139; gender issues, 13, 73–74, 76–77, 155, 178–179; guarding of control, 55; hiring by parents, 56; as instructional leaders, 66; loyalty issues, 60–61; management approach, 56; need for diversity among, 186; professionalization of, 26; relations with school boards, 10, 57–60; retention of traditional practices, 12; vulnerability to parents, 82

Advocacy, 10, 16, 100, 117–118

Advocates for Children of New York, 8

Affirmative action, 110

Alienation, 40, 70, 84, 117, 133; of parents, 21; and socioeconomic status, 94

Atomism, 133

Autonomy, 62; and parent involvement, 7; student, 88; teacher concerns with, 48–50, 95–96

Bateson, Gregory, 36

Bateson, Mary Catherine, 75–76

Board of Education, 30, 37; composition, 10–11; control of policy, 72; as legitimators of school decisions, 57–60; motives for participating on, 59; power on, 10; representativeness of, 57–60; responsibilities of, 58, 72

Boundaries, 40–41, 63; organizational, 181*tab*

Bureaucracy: as barrier to change, 67; changes in, 17; competition in, 37, 65–84; culture of, 39, 67; dominance of, 37; in education, 13; and efficiency, 67; and intimidation, 184; in schools, 5, 23*n2*; sidestepping, 78, 156; structure of, 37

Care, ethic of, xi, 19, 107–129, 154; authenticity in, 127–128; and collaboration, 154–176; cultural knowledge in, 127–128; and diversity, 123–128; in education, 178–193; establishing links in, 125–126; need for, 38; power-sharing in, 126; universal nature of, 20

Carnegie Task Force, 14, 104*n1*

Child-care, 69, 77, 121, 183, 191